What Is Justification About?

What Is Justification About?

Reformed Contributions to an Ecumenical Theme

Edited by

Michael Weinrich *&* John P. Burgess

William B. Eerdmans Publishing Company

Grand Rapids, Michigan / Cambridge, U.K.

Published 2009 by
Wm. B. Eerdmans Publishing Co.
2140 Oak Industrial Drive N.E., Grand Rapids, Michigan 49505 /
P.O. Box 163, Cambridge CB3 9PU U.K.

Printed in the United States of America

14 13 12 11 10 09   7 6 5 4 3 2 1

Library of Congress Cataloging-in-Publication Data

What is justification about? : Reformed contributions to an ecumenical theme /
edited by Michael Weinrich & John P. Burgess.
    p.   cm.
Includes bibliographical references and index.
ISBN 978-0-8028-6249-5 (pbk.: alk. paper)
   1. Justification (Christian theology) 2. Reformed Church — Doctrines.
I. Weinrich, Michael.   II. Burgess, John P., 1954-

BT764.3.W43 2009
234′.7 — dc22

                  2008051813

www.eerdmans.com

CONTENTS

Justification: An Ongoing Ecumenical Debate

What is justification about? It may seem peculiar to pose a question of this sort when we are talking about a fundamental article of faith. The Reformers were unanimous in their emphasis that it is God alone who justifies the sinner without any merit on the latter's part. Justification is only through Christ *(solus Christus)*, only through his grace *(sola gratia)*, and therefore only through faith *(sola fide)*. There are, undoubtedly, many areas of theology with unanswered questions and even unanswerable questions. But when the issue is the center of faith itself, we expect lucidity about fundamental definitions. The reality is otherwise. The fundamental questions of faith are and must continue to be the subject of much wrestling.

As clear as it may be *where* the fundamental questions lie (although this is not always obvious either), just *how* to go about addressing them is also a matter of dispute. This is precisely the case with the issue of justification. Justification is taken up and discussed controversially not only within interconfessional ecumenical dialogues[1] but also within the circle of those churches stemming from the Reformation.[2] Today a key issue in these dis-

---

1. See Martien Brinkman, "Justification in Ecumenical Dialogue: Central Aspects of Christian Soteriology," in *Debate* (IIMO Research Publication 45) (Zoetermeer: Meinema, 1996).

2. See Michael Beintker, *Rechtfertigung in der neuzeitlichen Lebenswelt* (Tübingen: J. C. B. Mohr, 1998); Eberhard Jüngel, *Justification: The Heart of the Christian Faith* (Edinburgh: T. & T. Clark, 2001); Dieter Schellong, "Verlegenheiten um die Rechtfertigungslehre," in *Die Gemeinde als Ort von Theologie: Festschrift für Jürgen Seim zum 70. Geburtstag,* ed. Katja Kriener et al. (Bonn: Dr. Rudolf Habelt Verlag, 2002), pp. 423-39; "Zur Rechtferti-

cussions is whether the doctrine of justification is truly the center of the Christian faith still. It seems to be the case that during the long period from the Reformation until now, other questions have forced themselves into the center of theological reflection, such as theodicy or of the meaning of life.[3]

Perhaps it is time to rethink what we mean by justification, recognizing that theological statements always have a historical dimension and must be reformulated in light of historical changes. In the course of history, both the key theological questions and their answers change. Those who hope to preserve a doctrine by stubbornly adhering to it will eventually have to concede defeat. Theology is continually changing, precisely because it wants to be true to those divine realities upon which it reflects, and to give account of them as faithfully and persuasively as possible. So, just what is justification about *today?*

A high point, or at least a milestone, in the discussion of the doctrine of justification was undoubtedly the signing of the *Joint Declaration on the Doctrine of Justification* by the Lutheran World Federation (Bishop Christian Krause) and the Pontifical Council for Promoting Christian Unity (Cardinal Edward Cassidy) on October 31, 1999, in Augsburg, Germany.[4] During a lengthy bilateral dialogue, the signatory churches formulated, despite their historical condemnations on the subject, the most far-reaching consensus possible. Although not all differences could be overcome, the two churches did take visible steps toward each other.

One can certainly dispute the meaningfulness of such consensus documents and what reception they will receive in the larger church, for they can be read very differently and always suggest more agreement than is really the case. But at the same time we must appreciate every effort to remedy confessional difference and schism. For that reason, we must also take seriously the commitment expressed in the *Declaration* to continue work on this topic, in particular with respect to its contemporary relevance.

---

gungslehre," Beiheft (Supplement) Nr. 10, *Zeitschrift für Theologie und Kirche* (Tübingen: Mohr Siebeck, 1998).

3. See Michael Weinrich, "On the Way into Psychology: On a Modern Change in the Understanding of Justification," in *Contextuality in Reformed Europe* (Currents of Encounter 23), ed. Christine Lienemann-Perrin et al. (Amsterdam and New York: Rodopi, 2004), pp. 225-40. This volume is the product of the Theological Subcommittee of the European Area Committee of WARC.

4. The Lutheran World Federation and the Roman Catholic Church, *Joint Declaration on the Doctrine of Justification* (Grand Rapids and Cambridge: Eerdmans, 2000).

Here, however, a question arises: How do the churches that did not participate in the preparation of the Augsburg *Declaration* relate to the "differentiated consensus" reached between the Roman Catholic Church and the Lutheran World Federation? Further discussion of the doctrine of justification must be broadened ecumenically.

Such considerations were the genesis of this book. The *Joint Declaration on the Doctrine of Justification* was the product of a bilateral dialogue. But its subject has considerable, even central significance for the self-understanding of other churches. In the fall of 2001 the signatories of *The Joint Declaration* invited the World Methodist Council and the World Alliance of Reformed Churches, along with observers from the World Council of Churches (Faith and Order) and the Anglican Church, to a theological consultation in Columbus, Ohio. The goals of this consultation consisted in, first, an assessment of the *Declaration* by churches that had not been involved in formulating it, and, second, ways to involve these churches in continuing discussion of the topic. While the delegates of the World Methodist Council had little problem with the content of the *Declaration* — and in July 2006 the Council confirmed the *Declaration* at its world conference in Seoul (in the presence of Ishmael Noko of the Lutheran World Federation and Cardinal Walter Kasper) — the situation proved to be quite different for the Reformed delegates.[5]

One of the fundamental concerns of the Reformed churches, also widely appreciated in the Lutheran tradition, is the distinction between the *message* of justification and the *doctrine* of justification. Here one should keep in mind that our understanding of doctrine is different from the Reformers', for whom doctrine was first of all the doctrine of Scripture, and thus divine doctrine, and therefore closer to what we today understand by the word message.[6] We, however, can understand the distinction as follows: the message is the irreplaceable and primary focus of the church and theology, whereas doctrine is secondary and derived, and in turn needs to be grounded again and again in the message. While neither can be separated from the other, we can make a distinction between the

---

5. See the document *Unity in Faith* (Geneva: Lutheran World Federation, Office for Ecumenical Affairs, 2002); and *Reformed World* 52, no. 1 (2002), with contributions by Russel Botman, Pierre Bühler, Anna Case-Winters, Gabriel Fackre, Allan Falconer, and Michael Weinrich.

6. See Karl Gerhard Steck, *Lehre und Kirche bei Luther* (Munich: Chr. Kaiser, 1963).

grounds for speaking of justification and its articulation theologically in a particular time and place.

If we can acknowledge that different *doctrines* of justification have their common ground in the *message* of justification, which is not the property of any particular church, we will be able to discuss the *doctrine* of justification without suggesting that the whole of theological doctrine is open to debate.[7] We will know the importance of doctrine, yet also, precisely in the ecumenical context, its essential limitedness. The basic message that has been entrusted to us is superior to any of its doctrinal variations. The distinction between message and doctrine — if approached in a systematically consistent way — holds forth the promise (as yet unfulfilled) of liberation of ecumenical discussion from its fixation on traditional theological formulations.[8]

In addition to this distinction between message and doctrine, Reformed response to the *Declaration* has sought to clarify the specific respects in which the doctrine of justification *functions* differently in Reformed thought from other theological traditions. One cannot say that the Reformed have defined justification differently from the Lutherans. Nevertheless, it is clear that in the Reformed tradition the doctrine of justification — in spite of all formal agreement with Lutheran thinking — has been integrated into the larger theological system rather differently. For the Reformed, the doctrine of justification has been an *integrative* theological principle. It has acquired a special importance in the *whole* of theology — a point that can be most easily illustrated by the centrality of covenant in Reformed theology. This Reformed insight deserves additional attention and development.

Out of the experiences in Columbus, the Theological Subcommittee of the European Area Committee of the World Alliance of Reformed Churches decided to take up the theme of the doctrine of justification.[9]

---

7. See Michael Weinrich, "Die Ökumene in der Rechtfertigungslehre in evangelisch-reformierter Perspektive," in *Von Gott angenommen — in Christus verwandelt: Die Rechtfertigungslehre im multilateralen ökumenischen Dialog* (Beiheft zur Ökumenischen Rundschau Nr. 78), ed. Uwe Swarat et al. (Frankfurt am Main: Otto Lembeck, 2006), pp. 125-54.

8. See, among others, Dietrich Ritschl, *Theorie und Konkretion in der Ökumenischen Theologie* (Münster: Lit Verlag, 2005).

9. See Michael Weinrich, "Bekenntnis als dynamischer Prozess: Calvinisten kritisieren, wie Katholiken und Lutheraner sich über die Rechtfertigung verständigt haben," *Zeitzeichen* 3 (2002): 14-16.

Under the chairmanship of Michael Weinrich, the Subcommittee identified an extensive range of theological issues in Reformed thought in which justification plays a prominent role, and which, conversely, distinctively shape a Reformed understanding of justification. These issues have also shaped the structure of this book: the Reformed understanding of doctrine, the indissoluble connection between justification and sanctification (justification as an aspect of reconciliation), the meaning of the justice of God, the connection of justification with the doctrine of election, the sensitive question of how to treat the sacrifice of Christ, the ecclesiological consequences of justification, eschatological implications, the question of human justice and its correspondence to divine justice, the connection between justification and historical, interhuman reconciliation (such as the healing of memory), and the integration of covenant theology into the whole of theology. In addition, the issue of the influence of post-Enlightenment secularization on the doctrine of justification has merited special consideration: Is it possible today simply to take over, without change, the fundamental Reformed convictions of the sixteenth century? Or have there been shifts in theological understanding that require us to revise our understanding of justification?[10]

Given the genesis of this project, it has come to have two principal goals. First, it should help to clarify the *Reformed* understanding of the doctrine of justification for the Reformed churches themselves. This clarification is not simply a matter of delineating the historical development of the doctrine, but also and more importantly of thematizing its contemporary significance. Second, the book should contribute to current *ecumenical* discussion of the issue of justification. It demonstrates the implications of the doctrine of justification not just for Reformed theology but for all efforts to think systematically about the Christian faith. Here, we believe, is an instance in which confessional concentration and ecumenical openness do not stand in opposition to each other but condition each other mutually all for the better.

The Western context of this volume is apparent in the nationalities of its contributors (Germany, the Netherlands, Hungary, Australia, South Africa, and the United States). It does not pretend to represent the whole spectrum of the worldwide Reformed community; indeed, any such at-

---

10. See n. 3 above. Also, see Martien Brinkman and Michael Weinrich, "Justification as Reconciliation," *Reformed World* 54 (2004): 69-75.

tempt would only divert discussion from the full theological implications of the topic of justification, and shift it instead to questions of common or diverse cultural perspectives. This does not, however, mean that the contributors are in any way indifferent to the challenges of the theologies of the south or reject them. On the contrary, they believe that their resistance to privileging the context of theology can ultimately support the concerns of liberation theology, especially in cultural contexts not stamped by that particular theology. The point is not to set a context-specific theology of the north over against a context-specific theology of the south but rather to turn together to the liberating Word of justification to which the Scriptures testify, and which should underlie and challenge every theology in every social context.

The contributions here are best understood as a call from a limited Reformed perspective for the catholicity that is confessed in the Apostles' Creed. We believe that this catholicity will enable all of us better to assess the full significance of the growing number of theological statements that are being issued by ecumenical commissions. Such statements often depend on ambiguous language that unless clarified will inevitably lead to mistrust and even rejection of these statements and similar ecumenical efforts. A healthy catholicity will see these statements as a beginning point for theological work, not a conclusion. In addition, the catholicity for which we are calling will enable Christians to assess each other's differing socio-political and ethical positions on the basis of a deeper mutual trust than is presently the case. Only a deep theology deeply shared can bring us to real progress in Christian efforts to speak to the world and its needs. We recognize that our words here about ecumenical theological and ethical statements imply a certain assessment of present ecumenical work. Nevertheless, they are in no way meant to discourage this work but rather to emphasize the need for a workable catholicity and for the real advancement of lived community among the different Christian churches.

The European Area Committee of the World Alliance of Reformed Churches not only followed the development of this book with great interest but also contributed to it financially by funding an authors' conference in Amsterdam in June 2005. Discussion of the various contributions enabled authors to sharpen their work and to become aware of each other's concerns, thus strengthening the overall coherence of the book. In addition, the Committee funded necessary translations into the English language. We therefore hope that this volume will be especially useful to the continuing work of the World Alliance of Reformed Churches, even as it seeks to attain to a catholicity of the church beyond the borders of the Reformed churches and to influence concrete ecumenical debates relating to the contemporary significance of the message of justification.

Justification in a Reformed Perspective: Key Theses

Michael Weinrich and John P. Burgess

A basic insight of this volume is that for Reformation Protestants the doctrine of justification is the right way into the other parts of a systematic theology — i.e., a comprehensive explication of what we believe as Christians and why. While this volume does not undertake to develop a systematic theology, it does propose to demonstrate the promise of such an approach. Each chapter carefully explores the relation of the doctrine of justification to other key theological doctrines and issues. In each case, the doctrine of justification helps to frame and clarify what is at stake as Christians speak about the entirety of their faith.

Nevertheless, as we shall see, the doctrine of justification does not stand alone as a key that unlocks the door of the theological system. Rather, it is built into the theological building itself; it is more like a door than a key. The architecture and construction of the theological system — both of each individual part and of the whole — affect the way in which we see and use the door that lets us in. There is a dynamic interaction between the doctrine of justification and the other theological doctrines and issues to which it is related.

Our understanding of justification is shaped first of all by the *biblical* materials, which bear witness to the God of Israel and the church. This God is a God of relationality and relationship both within his own triune being and with the world that he has created. Scriptural notions of covenant are especially important here. The Bible testifies again and again to the God who reaches into history and calls forth relationship with a people. Second, these notions of relationality and relationship can be developed in a more explicitly *theological* manner, such as occurred already early in the church's history in its formulation of the doctrine of the Trinity. Together, covenant and Trinity underlie the doctrine of justification and help to account for its critical place in the overall theological, confessional system.

A hallmark of a Reformed theology of justification has been not only this concern with biblical foundations of covenant and theological foundations of Trinity, but also — and of equal importance — with the implications of the doctrine of justification for the *practice* of Christian life and faith. For Reformed Christians, theology is not first of all a speculative intellectual discipline but rather a practical, existential way of thinking that invites us into ever-deeper appropriation of the benefits of Christ "for us and our salvation." Rightly understood, the doctrine of justification inevitably frames how we think about the way we will live as Christians, the way we will shape life together in the church, the way we will minister to the world, and the way we will seek justice. Indeed, as several of the essays in this volume will make clear, the doctrine of justification in its most dynamic form does not simply inform us about God and what he has done "once upon a time," but rather invites us to encounter the living God here and now even as he continues to effect our justification and the world's. The doctrine of justification has the amazing potential ever again to confront us with the good news of the risen Jesus Christ, and to be transformed by God's mighty promise of reconciliation with a world that has rejected him and yet remains blessedly his and under his claim.

The doctrine of justification thus has pastoral, ecclesiastical, and ethical implications. It so shapes our understanding of such matters as election, sanctification, eschatology, and justice that we grow into greater capacity for relationality and relationship with God and with each other. By the power of the Holy Spirit, we ourselves can become more deeply committed to reflecting in our own words and deeds the ways of a God who makes all things right. The justifying God is the self-giving God, who in Jesus Christ empties himself, takes on the form of a servant, and dies on a cross, so that we might take on a self-giving, thanks-giving love that is patient and faithful unto death and a life yet to come.

Justified by grace alone through faith — this great watchword of the Reformation seems self-evidently true to many Protestant churches, and yet they are words that easily devolve into an empty formula, a rote recitation. They can quickly be distorted into the cheap grace that Dietrich Bonhoeffer criticized — or, as Luther warned against again and again, into new forms of works-righteousness in which grace becomes something that we choose to acknowledge and appropriate: thus, more our achievement than the occasion of our repentance and regeneration. "What is justification about *today?*" is therefore a question that we must pose ever again, if we are to hear the liberating news of the gospel rightly — and to live by the renewing power of the Holy Spirit.

Each of the approaches to justification in the essays in this volume bears the imprint of its particular author. Each has points of both tension and complementarity with the others. As editors and contributors, we have not attempted to compare and contrast these different lines of thought, but rather have conceived of this particular assembly of saints as partners in a conversation to which we now invite others: Protestants, Catholics, and Orthodox; theologians, pastors, and church leaders; participants in ecumenical dialogues; and ordinary members of congregations, who offer extraordinary testimony to God's justifying activity in their personal and corporate lives of faith.

As a roadmap to those who would join us in this conversation, we offer these preliminary, summative theses — landmarks along the way that the essays in this volume will take us:

1. The meaning of a particular theological doctrine depends on how it is related to other theological doctrines. The doctrine of justification is no different. It can be approached from different theological angles, each of which yields different nuances of meaning relating to the doctrine of justification.

2. The doctrine of justification never stands in isolation from other doctrines but rather is an essential aspect of every effort to think comprehensively about the Christian faith. It is arguably the interpretive key to all other doctrines, even as it is conditioned by each of them.

3. Nevertheless, the doctrine of justification must not be elevated to the position of a super-doctrine that determines the meaning of all other doctrines. That would only be a form of theological idolatry. Rather, we must attend to how justification and other doctrines of the faith mutually implicate and condition each other. In this way, reflection on the doctrine of justification becomes nothing less than an opportunity to reflect systematically on the Christian faith as a whole.

4. A proper understanding of justification will always remain anchored in the biblical witness to God. The doctrine of justification can serve

to illuminate questions of soteriology and anthropology only when it first shapes determinatively our understanding of God and God's self-revelation. Scripture testifies again and again that God's very character is to justify — to make relationship right with human beings and indeed with the whole of creation, despite every force of sin and evil. Any understanding of God that neglects God's justifying character is deficient and even distorted. Justification is not an isolated work or special effect of God — rather, it goes to the very heart of who God is, both in himself and for us.

5. Scripture teaches that the will of God is inseparable from the act of God. What God intends, God effects. The doctrine of justification is therefore essentially interrelated with the doctrine of election. God's justification is not merely a wish for right relationship with humans, but rather its realization. An understanding of justification that fails to acknowledge the merciful power of God to make things right quickly deteriorates into pious moralisms in which God is understood merely to make an offer that humans can choose to accept or not.

6. When we consider the significance of the doctrine of election for the doctrine of justification, we immediately confront the question of the freedom of the human will. To be sure, there is little ecumenical debate about this issue today, and no one wishes for it to become a source of theological conflict (even though it was once so vehemently debated). Nevertheless, Lutheran as well as Reformed churches should be clear that their profile as *Reformation* churches is at stake exactly at this point. To put it starkly, the freedom that the Reformers understood to be grounded in justification absolutely dispels any notion of human cooperation, even in relation to human *acknowledgment* of divine justification. Only when Protestantism succeeds again in clarifying the relation of *Christian* freedom to the enslaved will, will we be able to have productive ecumenical discussion of the matter.

7. God's character as an electing God is closely related to God's character as a self-giving, self-sacrificing God. The connection between election and self-giving reveals the nature of God's sovereignty as it comes to appearance in his justifying work. Even though the significance of this connection has been lost to a great deal of contemporary theological thinking and seems strange to many contemporary people, it nevertheless promises us immense comfort. Humans will ever again be in the position of needing this divine promise.

8. The doctrine of justification has legal connotations that require careful clarification. In particular, we must always guard against the temptation to impose human understandings of justice or law on God. It is all the more important to investigate the specific contours of justice and law associated with the biblical testimony to God and how God's justice and law make concrete human living conditions right — right for a good life before God.

9. The question of how we understand justice and law reminds us that discussion of the doctrine of justification always takes place in particular social contexts. The fact of historical change poses the question of how the categories and language by which we understand and evaluate reality may change, sometimes fundamentally. To be sure, theology can never simply adopt the changing semantics of an ever-restless world, but neither can it ignore changes in how people think about life. Theology must remain true to its task to give account of the Christian faith in present circumstances. The doctrine of justification was never simply an answer to a general human question; rather, it has always been a way of interpreting the human condition. Christian theology therefore still faces the challenge of how to communicate the critical meaning of justification to people, such that they can hear it and understand it today. We cannot simply hold on to traditional historical language if we are to set forth the meaning of justification. The best way to proceed is to return to the biblical narratives and themes themselves. If we allow ourselves to be oriented by them, we will find that they can also help to frame and deepen *ecumenical* discussion of God's justifying work.

10. The biblical witness itself, more than the specific contours that it receives in the federal theology of the Reformed tradition, relates God's will to be righteous to his will to make covenant. The New Testament message of justification is grounded in this biblical covenant theology. The covenant in all its biblical manifestations powerfully expresses God's merciful attention to his human partner. The trustworthiness of the covenant is rooted in the fact that God in his mercy elevates humans to partnership with him, thus making mutual relationship and interaction possible. God endows humans with the dignity of being covenant partners with him. Moreover, God's promise to make relationship possible and *right* is the pledge of his faithfulness. When Scripture speaks of Christ as the fulfillment of the covenant, it has pre-

cisely this relationship between God's righteousness and faithfulness in mind.

11. In the Reformed tradition, the doctrine of justification is, on the one hand, an essential element of the doctrine of reconciliation, i.e., the soteriological dimension of Christology. This theological linkage guards against isolating the doctrine of justification and treating it in abstraction. On the other hand, the doctrine of justification is not complete without an account of sanctification and the nature of the Christian life, both understood as the work of God. Together, these different doctrines help to explicate the meaning of the "communion of saints" as it is grounded in God's merciful will.

12. Because the doctrine of justification finds its rightful place in the context of the doctrine of reconciliation, any discussion of justification will inevitably raise a variety of questions related to how Christians should shape their lives individually as well as communally. On one side arises the question of how Christians should deal responsibly with the freedom that is theirs in Christ; from another side comes the question of how in orienting the Christian life, biblical law and instruction can be understood as forms of the gospel. Theological reflection on justification will remain incomplete until we have explored the full range of such practical issues, especially in relation to the concrete life of the church. At the same time, we must never lose sight of catholicity as an essential dimension of the church.

13. The distinction between the proclamation of justification and the doctrine of justification is of fundamental importance for ecumenical conversation. The doctrine of justification as shaped by the Reformation is by no means the only way by which Christians can articulate the biblical proclamation of justification. In addition, we must reckon with the fact that different Christian confessions locate the center of the gospel proclamation in vastly different places. Justification is only one possibility among several. Only deep and sustained theological conversation can determine, for example, where the Orthodox doctrine of deification (theosis) does or does not correspond to the proclamation of the justification of humanity by grace alone.

14. The eschatological dimensions of the doctrine of justification relieve it from having to carry the full weight of questions relating to human salvation and the righteousness of God. Contemporary ecumenical concerns about how to articulate a common understanding of the

gospel can be helpfully addressed only with reference to the eschatological horizon of the gospel. This relativization of the doctrine of justification in no way diminishes its critical significance. On the contrary, the doctrine of justification is of fundamental importance for how we think about eschatology, even while the latter picks up and goes beyond the concerns of the former. Only when we are clear about the theological limits of the doctrine of justification will we be able to preserve — or, as the case may be, win back — its rich, deep power for the life of the church and individual believers today.

In the end, we hope that these key theses, as developed in the essays that follow, will stimulate not only responsible theological reflection on the doctrine of justification but also the church's worship of the triune God. We believe that when the church grasps the full meaning of justification, it understands that justification is ultimately not a doctrine but the very presupposition of all theology and so draws us into contemplating the character of the living God. A renewed, Reformed understanding of justification can therefore contribute to the life of the church catholic as it seeks to be more faithful to proclamation, sacraments, and mission in the world today.

1 Justified for Covenant Fellowship:
A Key Biblical Theme for the Whole of Theology

Michael Weinrich

There is a kind of overestimation of the doctrine of justification, especially in the Lutheran tradition. But there is also, especially in the Reformed tradition, an underestimation of it by concentrating predominately on the meaning of the law for the justified. Both views are problematic and miss the decisive discovery of the Reformers. They emphasized, on the one hand, the foundational significance of God's prior grace as the center of the gospel and drew — partly different — conclusions from this basic insight for all areas of church life and theology, on the other. The conclusions were probably more controversial than the content of the doctrine itself, which is actually quite simple and commonly accepted. It is essentially because of its far-reaching consequences that Protestant theologians view justification as more than one topic among many others.

In this sense, justification is not a doctrine that can be clearly separated from others. It has often been stated that the understanding of the doctrine of justification is crucial for the existence of the church: *articulus stantis et cadentis ecclesiae.*[1] As Luther said, "The church stands, if this article stands, and the church falls, if it falls."[2] Luther's words, we should note, appeared not in the context of Christology but in relation to Psalm 130:4: "But there is forgiveness with you, so that you may be revered." This is the epitome of Christian doctrine and the "sun which illuminates God's holy

---

1. This phrase is first mentioned by Valentin Ernst Löscher in 1712; see Friedrich Loofs, "Der articulus stantis et cadentis ecclesiae," *Theologische Studien und Kritiken* 90 (1917): 323-420.

2. WA 40/III, p. 352.

church." Luther called the doctrine of justification the "sole solid rock"[3] on which the whole church is based. He believed that if one is right on this point, one will also be right on all other theological questions.[4] In the Schmalkald Articles, which now belong to the binding confessions of the Lutheran Church, he emphasized that no one should deviate from this article or relent even if heaven or earth were to collapse.[5] In the Reformers' context, "articles" *(articuli)* are principles of faith that shape the church's profession of faith.[6] Philipp Melanchthon, author of the Augsburg Confession of 1530, therefore defended the chapter on justification as key to understanding Holy Scripture in its entirety.[7] Similarly, Calvin, who signed the Augsburg Confession in 1539, called the question of justification "the most important pillar of our reverence of God."[8]

If we are to consider the Reformed contribution to ecumenical discussion of justification and the range of its meaning, the far-reaching theological convergence with Luther should be emphasized first. Apart from all differences in detail, the Reformers were substantially in agreement on the importance and the central content of the doctrine of justification.[9] Calvin was convinced that his understanding of justification was completely the same as Luther's, even if they developed its implications differently.

3. WA 40/I, p. 33.

4. See WA 40/I, p. 441.

5. Martin Luther, "Schmalkaldische Artikel (1537)," part 2, art. 1, in *Die Bekenntnisschriften der evangelisch-lutherischen Kirche*, 6th ed. (Göttingen: Vandenhoeck & Ruprecht, 1967), p. 415.

6. See Gerhard Sauter, "Zur Einführung," in *Rechtfertigung* (Theologische Bücherei 78), ed. Gerhard Sauter (Munich: Chr. Kaiser, 1989), p. 11.

7. Philipp Melanchthon, "Apologia der Confession," in *Bekenntnisschriften*, p. 159.

8. *Institutio* III.11.1 (author's translation). The McNeill edition of the *Institutes* speaks of justification as "the main hinge on which religion turns." See John Calvin, *Institutes of the Christian Religion*, ed. John T. McNeill (Philadelphia: Westminster Press, 1960), 3.11.1, p. 726.

9. After hinting at all the differences, Alasdair I. C. Heron emphasizes "a core of unity in the assertion over against the semi-Pelagian tendencies of late medieval theology and piety that the justification of the ungodly — i.e., of sinners — is a divine work, founded alone in God's free will and gracious goodwill and apprehended and appropriated solely by faith, which is not in any sense a 'work' or achievement, but itself the gift of God. On this point . . . there was no confessional dispute between the Lutheran and the Reformed traditions." See Heron, "Justification and Sanctification in the Reformed Tradition," in *Justification and Sanctification in the Traditions of the Reformation* (Studies from the World Alliance of Reformed Churches 42), ed. Milan Opočenský and Páraic Réamonn (Geneva: World Alliance of Reformed Churches, 1999), p. 113.

Actually, the divergences between Lutherans and Reformed are taken much more seriously today than they were taken by the Reformers themselves.

And important too is this: it was clear to all of the Reformers that the doctrine of justification has revolutionary impact on the whole of theology. Virtually every theological question is affected and changed by it. At stake is the catholicity of the church and thus the church as such. Justification is not one isolated article among others of equal importance — which is what the *Joint Declaration on the Doctrine of Justification* would have us believe[10] — but is rather a kind of theological yeast that has the power to make a consistent and stable whole from the entire range of theological ingredients. This means that the exclusiveness of the doctrine of justification must be understood in terms of its substantial theological inclusiveness.

We must nevertheless remember that every theological key or guideline — and thus also justification — remains relative to the main goal of theology: to support our human worship (in a broad sense) in response to God's affection for us. Not we and our religious needs stand at the center of our theological efforts but God and God's glory.[11] We do not believe in dogmas but in the triune God. "Soli Deo Gloria!" has to remain the decisive horizon of all theological considerations, whatever they are. The doctrine of justification too has to be clearly related to Soli Deo Gloria. In the case of justification, the doctrine's relative significance is clearly related to its special emphasis.

Beyond this fundamental differentiation, we should also distinguish other ways justification can be understood. On the one hand, focus can fall on the juridical dimension of God's soteriological act in Christ's crucifixion and resurrection, the high point of God's intercession for sinful humanity. On the other hand, this particular divine act places all of God's acts in a special light. Nowhere are we allowed to disregard this high point as it is mirrored in the history of God with humankind. If the cross and resurrection are characteristic for God and God's attitude to humans, we meet this same God beyond the cross and resurrection in all divine acts to which the Bible witnesses. We would otherwise have to speak of different gods. In this view, justification may be envisaged as a key theme in the Bi-

10. The Lutheran World Federation and the Roman Catholic Church, *Joint Declaration on the Doctrine of Justification* (Grand Rapids and Cambridge: Eerdmans, 2000); also, see Michael Weinrich, "The Reformed Reception of the Joint Declaration," *Reformed World* 52 (2002): 18-26.

11. See the article by John Webster in this volume.

ble as a whole, even where the Bible does not speak explicitly about justification and the juridical side of God's justice. There is a non-juridical use of justification that functions as the yeast in the whole of God's history with Israel and all humanity. This is what this chapter is about: God's particular act in Christ is reflected in the whole of his intentions and in all realizations of his will.[12] For this reason, we will draw on the terminology of justification wherever it helps us to understand God's faithfulness, both to us and to himself.[13]

To put it more in terms of content: it is critical for a proper understanding of justification that the biblical message not be measured simply by ordinary understandings of law or justice. In common usage, law does not apply just to judgments made by particular people — rather, justitia is a blindfolded woman with a pair of scales in her hands. We should not neglect the deep meaning of this image for human law and its implementation in societal life. Nevertheless, the theological meaning of justification goes far beyond human law. We face God's law, and this means that all legal terms also have a theological dimension. If we speak about God's law, we must never abstract our insights from the will of God as creator, reconciler, and redeemer. Rather, we have to be aware that an appropriate understanding of justification depends on a proper consciousness of the whole reality of God as we know it in creation and in his special relationship to Israel and the whole of humankind. Wherever God acts, God is righteous; God gives his justification to what he created, and in the end God justifies himself — "so that God may be all in all" (1 Cor. 15:28). Justification, broadly speaking, is a key theme of God's history throughout the biblical canon. Even where no legal terms as such appear, wherever God is saying or doing something we are confronted with God's righteousness, which always implies justification. To a certain extent, one may say that justification is the means by which human beings become aware of God and God's will — wherever we face the distinction between righteousness and unrighteousness, we inevitably touch on the question of the specific charac-

---

12. In regard to these themes, see also Otfried Hofius, "'Rechtfertigung des Gottlosen' als Thema biblischer Theologie," in *Paulusstudien* (WUNT 51) (Tübingen: J. C. B. Mohr [Paul Siebeck], 1989), pp. 121-47. Hofius provides an exegetical study in which the doctrine of justification is regarded as the chief theme of the entire Bible.

13. My intention in no way contradicts John Webster's (see Chapter 2 of this volume) with regard to content. Our perspectives should be distinguished clearly from one another, but they do not exclude each other.

ter of God's justice. The divine justice determines what will and will not be justified by God.

My considerations will proceed along five steps. First, I will emphasize the special character of the theological understanding of justice. Justice is not simply justice; it always needs an interpretive framework. The theological use of justice stands in the framework of God's relation to humankind as his creatures. The theological concept of reality is rooted in the vitality of this relationship. Second, I will show that the meaning of this relationship is based on justification. If we want to focus on reality from the perspective of the biblical witness, we have to look at relationships. Third, we have to consider how humanity rejects God's justifying inclusiveness and instead tries to develop a consciousness of itself based on itself. Humans exclude God in order to try to realize themselves. The fourth point will consider God as the covenanting God who wants to bring humans back into the reality of relationship. God justifies Israel and humankind by making them covenant partners. The plurality of biblical covenants reflects God's will to be the covenanting God in particular contexts. The seriousness of God's will is related to God's faithfulness, which lies at the heart of justification. And finally, fifth, I will sum up the results by underlining the indissoluble relation between God's loving justice and the human being's liberating justification as the core of the biblical witness in its entirety.

I. The Different Justice *(iustitia aliena)*

To get some idea of the range of the meaning of justification, we have to reconstruct the question that best fits the doctrine of justification as its answer. What are the theological prerequisites for a proper understanding of justification? These prerequisites concern God's justice, but God's justice has to be understood on the basis of its divine character. We cannot draw conclusions from our common understandings of justice to God and his justice. What are we saying about God's relationship to humankind when we claim that he is a just God? What kind of justice do we envisage when we understand God's relation to his creation as just? What are the implications if we concede that God is righteous? This issue concerns not the notion that God is righteous *per definitionem* but rather the special character of his justice and the righteousness in which he acts and is revealed to us.

Justice is not justice as such but rather only in reference to the reality from which it gains its importance. This leads immediately to the question of what reality is, because reality also is not self-evident but rather a question of interpretation and the criteria of its interpretation.[14] Different people encounter the same event yet experience it differently because of their different interpretations of what happened. The same event means something different to each of them. What strikes fear in one person may create hope in another. It depends on one's personal hermeneutics as to whether something is important or not. On what do we rely, and what gives us the courage to trust in anything at all? We are prepared to justify something as long as it fits our understanding of reality. Whatever contradicts or confuses our understanding of reality, we refuse to acknowledge and accept. Instead, we become critical. The measure of what we call right or wrong depends on our specific understanding of reality. For theologians, the proper thing to do is to consult the biblical witness.

The first time the Bible speaks about humankind, it says that God will create humankind in his own image: "Let us make humankind in our image, according to our likeness" (Gen. 1:26). And so it happens: "God created humankind in his image, in the image of God he created them; male and female he created them" (Gen. 1:27). God creates humankind (singular) by creating two. Right from the beginning humankind exists in the plural and with a degree of dissimilarity: male and female. We can understand this literally as well as symbolically: every human is as different from another as man and woman are different. According to the biblical witness, God too is a kind of plural, and the human plural emerges in analogy to God's plural. The image of God is not one human but at least two humans — the one humankind is differentiated just as the oneness of God can be differentiated. That means that the image of God exists only in the relationship of human to human on the one hand and of humans to God on the other. In the biblical understanding, a single human would be an abstraction from the image of God which exists in that twofold relationship and as such "was very good" (Gen. 1:31). Here God explicitly justifies what he created.

Within this framework, justification is something the creator does and not the creature. This is important, as we will note later. A creature is unable to justify itself. Its justification as the creator's creature comes from

---

14. See Michael Weinrich, *Theologie und Biographie: Zum Verhältnis von Leben und Lehre* (Wuppertal: Foedus, 1999), pp. 63-79.

outside itself and is not something that it can achieve on its own. The creature has an honor of its own in its limited existence as a creature, but it is an honor provided by the creator's acceptance of the creature — so to speak by God's justification.[15]

If we speak of humankind as the image of God, we have to understand the plurality on both sides.[16] The "Godlikeness" of humankind is expressed more in this plurality than in the imagery of any particular capacity of a single human being. The plural is not just the prerequisite for biological reproduction but also the basis for relationship and partnership ("a helper as his partner" [Gen. 2:18]). The similarity lies in the understanding that to be is not to be alone. The decisive act of God's free love in eternity is to elect humankind as his partner. God decided to be God in relationship to humankind. The divine self-determination is directed toward covenant, and for there to be the covenant, God created humankind as a partner who is able to respond as a subject. That God created humankind in his own image means that he created humans as beings capable of answering when they are addressed by God. It is their privilege to have access to God through their free ability to interact with God, whereas all other beings are completely dependent on God's access to them. This and nothing else is the distinct nobility of humankind — that they have the possibility of a reciprocal relationship to God and to their fellow humans.[17]

This implies that humankind cannot realize itself unless it makes use of this distinctive ability. Self-knowledge, if it involves looking only at the self, does not hold much promise; we have to go beyond ourselves to get at the reality of humankind. Humans have to look at their relationships if

---

15. See Karl Barth, *Church Dogmatics* III/4, ed. G. W. Bromiley and T. F. Torrance (Edinburgh: T. & T. Clark, 1961), §56, pp. 565-685.

16. There are many good reasons for Christian theology to appeal immediately to Christology and the doctrine of the triune God. This theme of relationality is also evident in the Old Testament without the explicit Christological criterion. Gary Deddo has shown how key the concept of relationality is in Barth's theology: "The Grammar of Barth's Theology of Personal Relations," *Scottish Journal of Theology* 47 (1994): 183-222. In some ways, Barth's Christological perspective is more a matter of methodology than of content. It integrates his decisive insights. But even in regards to content, Barth's observations are more powerful than those of most other theologies.

17. See Michael Weinrich, "Wir sind aber Menschen: Von der möglichen Unmöglichkeit, von Gott zu reden," in *Gretchenfrage: Von Gott reden — aber wie?*, vol. 1 (Jabboq 2), ed. Jürgen Ebach et al. (Gütersloh: Chr. Kaiser/Gütersloher Verlagshaus, 2002), pp. 36-98, esp. 68-72.

they want to get an idea of who they are. Let us recall an insight from the modern human sciences: there is no self-knowledge without an awareness of one's social context — no identity that does not take into account the relationships that make us what we are.[18] An individual's true self is to be found only in relation to another's.[19] This may be said on a general level as well as on a theological level. In the words of Karl Barth, "Human life participates in the freedom of all God's creatures to the extent that it does not have its aim in itself and cannot therefore be lived in self-concentration and self-centeredness, but only in a relationship which moves outwards and upwards to another."[20] God provides space and time for the distinctive creature that he wishes to be a partner for his covenant.[21] In theological perspective the creation is the prerequisite for God's covenant, that is, for the realization of God's will to live in relationship to humankind.[22]

In this framework life is not just action but rather interaction. Life is the circumstance of being addressed and having the opportunity to answer. We are not challenged first and foremost by objects and facts. Life is challenged by life — by the living God and the living next-door neighbor. In the words of Gary Deddo, "life-giving relations consist in engaging in a history of interactions, of encounters with others in a way which tells the other the truth about themselves as God has determined them to be."[23] Reality is not a situation that is merely given and, as such, silent; rather, it is more of an event. Reality is not real as long as nothing happens.

Modern times would have us believe that human life is meant to exist in a permanent competition of everybody against everybody. The principle of modern economics has simply been transferred into anthropology: one exists if one competes. One proves oneself to be a subject by competing with others. And in this competition the subjectivity of the other is a

---

18. See the controversial debate in Harriet A. Harris, "Should We Say That Personhood Is Relational?," *Scottish Journal of Theology* 51 (1998): 214-34.

19. See Barth, *CD* III/4, p. 473.

20. See Barth, *CD* III/4, p. 477f.

21. This is exactly why Karl Barth speaks about creation as the external reason for the covenant (*CD* III/1, §41,2) and the covenant as the internal reason for the creation (*CD* III/1, §41,3).

22. This anthropocentric view of creation implies no disparagement of non-human creation, intended as the good living space for humankind and not as a resource for unlimited exploitation.

23. Deddo, "The Grammar of Barth's Theology of Personal Relations," p. 194.

natural threat to one's own subjectivity. Human reality is shaped by a permanent rivalry resulting in painful sacrifices. This is exactly the counter-image to that of biblical anthropology, which sees the individual's subjectivity as not threatened or limited by the subjectivity of others but as stirred to life by it: life is one subject being inspired by the other. Real life can only be found in the mutuality of subject and subject. It is life that encourages life — in contradiction to Thomas Hobbes, who asserted that success is the basis of human subjectivity and happiness.[24] Not the lonely thinking subject and its fundamental skepticism, à la René Descartes, is the result of God's creative act but rather social subjects who enjoy the ability to communicate and interact. Again in Barth's words, "the humanity of each and every man . . . consists in the determination of man's being as a being with others, or rather with the other man. It is not as he is for himself but with others, not in loneliness but in fellowship, that he is genuinely human, that he achieves true humanity, that he corresponds to his determination to be God's covenant-partner."[25] This points in the direction of the biblical words shalom and *tzedakah*. Human community is the place where life may flourish in shalom and *tzedakah*.

We have been so deeply socialized by the modern idea of the human self-centered subject that whatever is done for its justification can expect to win our approval. This is why the biblical idea of the social subject and an inter-subjective understanding of life look so strange to us. Our distance from the theological understanding of justification is rooted in our fundamental estrangement from the biblical view of humankind as a social being. It is through relationships that a person is justified or not justified. There is no justification simply for itself. Moreover, it is through relationship to God that we are justified or not justified. And finally, it is humanity that is justified or not and not an abstract single subject that claims to remain a subject even when it retreats into itself.

It is a mistake to expect the question of justification to be a common question to contemporary people. It never was a common question. It has always been something with which humans have to be confronted, because justification by God is alien *(iustitia aliena)* to people, who are always used

24. "Felicity, therefore (by which we mean continual delight), consisteth not in having prospered but in prospering." Thomas Hobbes, *The Elements of Law, Natural and Politic*, 2nd ed., ed. Ferdinand Tönnies (London: Frank Cass & Co., Ltd., 1969), p. 30.

25. Barth, *CD* III/2, ed. G. W. Bromiley and T. F. Torrance (Edinburgh: T. & T. Clark, 1960), p. 243.

to justifying themselves. People may ask about the meaning of life, but this question is quite different from that of justification.[26] Luther was convinced that the doctrine of justification is not a matter for apologetics, for justification is about yielding to God and not about giving free rein to one's own possibilities.

In a fundamental sense, the question answered by the doctrine of justification concerns the relation between God as the creator and humankind as God's creature. What brings humanity into the position to accept itself as creature? — only God's revelation of himself as the creator, because the notion that God could actually will relationship with us is inaccessible to us. Justification never rests on a human decision but only on God's. Reconciliation in a theological sense means that the godless, who claimed to be their own creators (with the result that the whole world has been damaged), are restored to their rightful status as creatures who realize the grace of living in relationship to their creator and to each other.

II. Created for Freedom in Relationship

In theological perspective, the realization that we are justified depends not on a law, a quality, or a kind of moral value but rather on the existential awareness of not being alone. We are called to interaction — to listen and to react to what is said to us. This is also the way to understand the word *responsibility* in its fullest sense. Justification points to a dimension of life that no one can achieve alone. It is this reality of relationship that delivers humans from the loneliness of having to justify themselves.

The recognition of being justified is linked fundamentally to a special kind of freedom. Freedom in this respect is not so much an ontological or metaphysical term attesting that humans have the opportunity to begin anew without being forced to do so by external or internal reasons. It is an ethical term. It was Immanuel Kant who rejected an empirical approach to freedom,[27] envisaging the need for freedom in the social sphere of eth-

26. See Michael Weinrich, "On the Way into Psychology: On a Modern Change in the Understanding of Justification," in *Contextuality in Reformed Europe: The Mission of the Church in the Transformation of European Culture* (Currents of Encounter, vol. 23), ed. Christine Lienemann-Perrin, Hendrik M. Vroom, and Michael Weinrich (Amsterdam and New York: Rodopi, 2004), pp. 225-40. Also see Vroom's contribution in the present volume.

27. See Immanuel Kant, *Kritik der reinen Vernunft.*

ics.[28] If we reflect on the sociality of life, said Kant, it is not enough to realize that the limit of one's freedom is the freedom of the other. Rather, freedom is needed as a constructive possibility for a reasonable ethics. Kant saw no possibility of pointing to freedom in itself, but because of the needs of human beings living together, he postulated freedom as the human capacity to decide for reasons of duty to make life worthwhile. According to Kant, life becomes worthwhile with respect to its social dimensions only when they are regulated by ethical decisions, and these decisions can be ethical only if they are made in freedom.

In this view, freedom is defined by its limits and determined by duty. It is quite clear to Kant that the dignity of humankind is rooted in its selfless responsibility for the sociality of life. Freedom has to be postulated solely for the sake of recognizing the ethical destiny of human life. The background of this perspective is that fellow humans turn out to be limitations to my own freedom. And this is the reason why this concept remains problematic. As long as I view my fellow humans as competitors or limiters of my opportunities to develop, freedom will be debased to nothing more than a duty of reason. In the perspective of theological anthropology, fellow humans are not primarily limitations but the basis of life's fullness. The fellow human is not a challenge or an opportunity to prove my ethical ability and dignity but rather a gift that makes life lively and rich. Barth says, "This is not a collapse of one into another, but the recognition that the law of my own being is fulfilled in being so completely with the other. In this correspondence there is the sense of an unimpeachable appropriateness and freedom and so joy."[29]

In its first sense, freedom is not probation. It means rather to make something possible. Freedom in its deep sense is not only the possibility to act but also the already mentioned space for interaction.[30] It is not so much a demand as, rather, the existential realization of life's reality. It is not the necessity of struggling for life by using and exploiting everything, i.e., by ruling all objects for one's own benefit (which too often has meant that fellow humans are also used as objects). The specific freedom of human beings is stimulated at its best in the encounter of subject and subject. Existing in fellowship constitutes the specific space for human freedom in

---

28. See Immanuel Kant, *Kritik der praktischen Vernunft*.
29. Barth, *CD* III/2, p. 267.
30. See Weinrich, "Wir sind aber Menschen," pp. 73-77.

which real life can emerge. Human subjectivity is meant to be inclusive and not usurpatory. Freedom does not mean human power to make one's own decisions but rather interactive aliveness. It is not so much an authorization as an aptitude. God's own inclusiveness has its image in his creation: in this alignment of life for life, humankind is the image of God.

Creation of humankind means: God provides space for this lively freedom for a life in covenant fellowship. We miss the purpose and the reality of creation if we do not recognize this interactive freedom.[31] The dignity of the particular human creature lies in the fact that it has the possibility to respond to the relationship that God has opened to it. That God is the creator means that he wants to be the God of his creation. As God wants to relate to humankind, humans are also intended to relate to their neighbors. The meaning of creation is deeply undervalued if we just state that God is the first or final cause of everything. Creation means qualifying things more than it does creating them.[32] As God qualifies himself in his creation as the creator, he also qualifies his image as his particular creation. He himself will be measured by his creation in this specific sense. In his freedom, God submits himself to a certain extent to the question of justification.

The biblical caution regarding the human "I" is not a criticism of human subjectivity but of its self-centeredness. The modern idea of competition as the natural reality of humankind is more an ideology than a description of human nature. Being an "I" includes being a person to others in mutuality. "I am as I am in relationship."[33] Being human includes being open to fellow humans. If the "I" is abstracted from its social basis, it loses its reality.[34] Only within its sociality can the subjectivity of the "I" realize its destiny and justification.

---

31. "This is the meaning and purpose of creation, to find its being in fellowship with another." See Deddo, "The Grammar of Barth's Theology of Personal Relations," p. 218.

32. The core of Barth's theology of creation is: from chaos God separates a space for created life to live in; he provides reasonable conditions and an order for a worthwhile life — this is the meaning of creation out of nothing. Chaos is nothing, but after giving living things the sense that there is something one can rely on, there is creation.

33. Barth, *CD* III/2, p. 246.

34. "Do I see what is really at stake? It is really a matter of myself. I cannot be without accepting this claim of the other, without letting him come to me, and therefore without hearing him. . . . I am affected myself if I do not hear him, and do so in all seriousness." Barth, *CD* III/2, pp. 258-59. We cannot understand subjectivity as the monarchical perspective of the "I" if we look at nature as God's creation. "As I myself am, and posit myself, I confront the other no less than he does me with his being and positing. He is my Thou, he is

Sociality does not limit particular opportunities of individual development. Rather, it makes subjectivity possible in a proper sense. Encounter with the other enlarges and enriches one's own life.[35] Fellowship is the fertile soil in which humans can cultivate their creational subjectivity, which is based and will reach its perfection in reverence toward God. Within this framework, it is unthinkable that people could worship God without being related to other people. We would misjudge the goodness of creation if we did not realize that the richness of interhuman relations is the root of life. This insight is decisive for the question of justification and its proper understanding. In the first and fundamental sense, being justified is more a matter of trust in the intention of the creator than a legal question.

III. The Exclusiveness of Self-Centered Consciousness

The question posed by contemporary people is not that of justification. If there is any question at all, it probably concerns the problem of the meaning of life. The answer to this question does not necessarily depend on a human or divine counterpart. In the modern period, the world has become more and more mono-polar, concentrated in the self-centered human subject. Modern people do not accept the idea of being dependent on a justification from outside of themselves. Of course they have many interpersonal relationships and perhaps even networks of relationships, but in most cases these relationships are based merely on what benefits oneself. This precisely mirrors the philosophy of not only the predominant economic system but also all major social institutions and organizations, i.e., the ideology that society will flourish best if everyone looks after his or her own interests alone.

Self-reliance seems to be a kind of magic formula that is supposed to solve every problem and threat. And this mentality also shapes people's concept of life, their hopes and fears for the future, and the guidelines by which they live in the present. The world is becoming smaller and smaller, but no rules are globally accepted, and if one is skillful enough, one can get

---

reached and affected by me no less than I am by him." Barth, *CD* III/2, p. 247. Barth refers in his description of the interhuman reality to Martin Buber's concept of "I and Thou" as a concept of anthropological reality. See Michael Weinrich, *Grenzgänger: Martin Bubers Anstöße zum Weitergehen* (Munich: Chr. Kaiser, 1987).

35. See Deddo, "The Grammar of Barth's Theology of Personal Relations," p. 204.

almost whatever one wants. The individual alone is responsible for his or her success. Success becomes an instrument for self-acceptance. We engage in a kind of self-justification. And if success eludes one, one feels lost to society and to oneself. Without success, it is impossible to justify oneself. In a self-centered world, one cannot justify oneself unless one has something to show for one's efforts. Whatever is missing in the individual's life has to be provided by the individual himself. It is therefore not surprising that people today have quit asking the question of justification, because there can be no real answer to this question as long as the world is centered in the human subject. A question for which no one expects an answer makes no sense.

The quest for the meaning of life reflects this situation in which we are not supposed to expect any answers for life beyond ourselves. The quest for meaning is a sign that meaning is absent, and the question arises because there is no answer. Insofar as this question clearly confirms the nonexistence of what it calls for, it is its own answer.

If the world is merely centered on the human subject, we cannot expect to encounter concepts of life that emphasize response. The German psychologist Horst Eberhard Richter speaks of a God complex that emerges in a Cartesian world.[36] Humankind gradually became subject to the delusion that it was omnipotent. In modern times, the self-centered consciousness has made people individualistic but also lonely. Humans claim to be the center of reality, especially of history. According to Friedrich Nietzsche, they killed God, and so they had to do everything that God did for them before. This was (and still is) the prominent expression of self-justification. Humans have not claimed to be God but have taken over God's role in nearly all areas of life. They may continue to speak about God and to participate in religious services, but their deeds reveal their true attitudes, i.e., that they do not truly take God in account as they live their lives.

According to Ludwig Feuerbach, God is simply a relic of the past that still preoccupies many people. He is no more than a "ghost in their heads."[37] This "ghost," however, prevents people from discovering their fellow humans. It was this God who shaped relationship more and more as

---

36. Horst Eberhard Richter, *Der Gotteskomplex: Die Geburt und die Krise des Glaubens an die Allmacht des Menschen* (Reinbeck: Rowohlt, 1979).

37. Ludwig Feuerbach, *Das Wesen des Christentums* [1841] (Stuttgart: Reclam, 1994), p. 10.

self-relationship. Even interhuman relations have lost their human counterparts. Other people merely serve as objects whereby I ensure the righteousness of myself as the predominant "I."

Theologically, we are confronted here with the second side of biblical anthropology. We spoke first about the anthropological perspective of human beings as the image of God. This remains fundamental but has to be supplemented by a second equally fundamental aspect: from the very beginning of human history humans have had to face the inexplicable fact that they constantly appear to be sinners. They have never truly been ready to respond to the trust that God placed in them. According to the wisdom of the Bible, human history always took place east of Eden. The story of the so-called fall in Genesis is not an explanation but rather a narrative of what is actually the case, or to echo the philosopher Ludwig Wittgenstein, the story is about "was der Fall ist" — the German language uses the same word, "fall," in the sense of sin and in the sense of what is in fact "the case." For the moment, let us focus on the meaning of sin.

The account in Genesis 3 does not relate a single incident but rather "what never happened but always is."[38] And this applies to the whole Urgeschichte in Genesis 1–11. As such, this Urgeschichte can tell us what history is about. We are looking at humans who are easily persuaded to act against God's explicit will, who want to be like God and forget that the creature cannot be the creator. We are looking at humans who kill their brothers out of uncontrolled jealousy. We are looking at human beings who choose evil and reject good. Thus, it is easy to understand God's wrath toward them. And, finally, we are looking at people filled with hubris who imagine themselves to be almighty and then build a tower "with its top in the heavens" (Gen. 11:4), without any fear that they could fail. We are looking into a huge mirror in which we see the actual condition of humanity as it is today and as it has obviously been throughout history. This story tells us that there was no need for any of this to have happened, because it all began in the Garden of Eden.

We call it paradise because it provided all of life's necessities. Nobody needs more than everything, and for someone who already has everything, it is not reasonable to want more. To expect more than everything can only mean to have something less. It is mistrust of the creator's assurance that

---

38. Erich Zenger, "Das Blut deines Bruders schreit zu mir," in *Kain und Abel*, ed. D. Bader (Regensburg: Schnell & Steiner, 1983), pp. 9-28, esp. 11.

everything is already provided, insinuating that God as the creator is imperfect. As soon as someone claims to have a better solution, he or she is claiming to be a better creator, whether this is even possible or not. Indeed, this is the story about humans in the Garden of Eden.

God did not create people with mistrust as part of their condition. The story speaks of a serpent that leads these two people into temptation. But the serpent simply stands for the powerless evil that needs to find a subject in order to become powerful. Evil needs a helper — an assistant or abettor — to become real. By itself it is too weak to do anything against God's will. Only humans can be such helpers and supporters, for they are created as subjects free to give their own answer when God addresses them. This ability is not the possibility to refuse to answer God. Nor is it the possibility of submitting to the appeals of evil. Nevertheless, it does not exclude these possibilities, however unforeseen (and impossible) they seem.[39] And this is exactly the weak point that the serpent uncovers. Indeed, it must have been "more crafty than any other wild animal that the LORD God had made" (Gen. 3:1). Evil had to look for subjects who were able to transform it into reality. Humans exercise power beyond all possibilities for one particular impossible possibility — namely, the impossible possibility of a creature becoming a creator.

Since God had already completed his creation, there was nothing to add to it. If everything is created, the creation needs no further creator. If one, however, wants to be a creator, he or she has only one possibility: to create something that God did not want in his creation. There was only the possibility of calling something into existence that God wanted to keep in "non-existence." This is the only possibility left to humans by God, and this is precisely where the serpent strikes.

Humans tried to make themselves the free interpreters of God's will, and they used the space opened up by the subjunctive of the serpent's question ("did God say — i.e., *would* God say?" [see Gen. 3:1]). They wanted their action to appear as something that happened according to God's will. They claimed to have a higher way of understanding God's commandment, not as stated literally but in its intentions. By assuming that God always wants the best for humankind, they felt free to decide for themselves what was best for them and did not shrink from violating the only explicit prohibition given to them.

39. Barth spoke of sin as the impossible possibility.

What exactly is sin in this case — violation of God's prohibition or human selfishness? In the nineteenth century the fall was celebrated as the happiest event in humans' history: *felix culpa!* Friedrich Schiller and Georg Friedrich Hegel called the fall a stroke of luck, because it indicated that humans had come of age and had become responsible and free citizens.[40] According to Schiller, "The human fall away from instinct . . . is without question the happiest and greatest event in human history. From this moment on, his freedom is authorized, and the first piece of his moral foundation is laid."[41] From this optimistic perspective, historical development is continuous progress toward humanity's final determination and perfection. The worst place for humans would be the Garden of Eden, where God provides everything and humans simply rely on him. Without a well-measured dose of healthy selfishness, humanity would never have developed and progressed.

This view belongs to a variety of ideas in the modern period that minimize the meaning of sin. The question is whether they are on the mark, and here there may be some doubt. The biblical perspective always harks back to one crucial insight: it is not so much human selfishness but the shameful human's mistrust of God's intentions and reliability that offends God. Once more, the story does not tell us that the mistrust originated within humans themselves. It was inaugurated, rather, by the serpent with the simple but subtle question: "Did God say, 'You shall not eat from any tree in the garden?'" (Gen. 3:1). Apparently, the serpent knows about God's commandment and uses this knowledge to sow uncertainty about the clarity and resoluteness of God's will. In this way, the serpent opens the door to the possibility of doubt. Upon hearing the serpent's question, Adam and Eve could immediately sense the doubt in the air. But they did not reject

---

40. See Christine Axt-Piscalar, "Sünde VII. Reformationszeit und Neuzeit," in *Theologische Realenzyklopädie,* vol. 32 (Berlin and New York: Walter de Gruyter, 2001), pp. 400-436; Wolfgang Trillhaas, "Felix culpa: Zur Deutung der Geschichte vom Sündenfall bei Hegel," in *Probleme biblischer Hermeneutik: Festschrift für Gerhard von Rad,* ed. Hans Walter Wolff (Munich: Chr. Kaiser, 1971), pp. 589-602.

41. "Dieser Abfall des Menschen vom Instinkte . . . ist ohne Widerspruch die glücklichste und größte Begebenheit in der Menschheitsgeschichte, von diesem Augenblick her schreibt sich seine Freiheit, hier wurde zu seiner Moralität der erste entfernte Grundstein gelegt." See Friedrich Schiller, "Etwas über die erste Menschengesellschaft nach dem Leitfaden der mosaischen Urkunde," in *Sämtliche Werke,* vol. 4, ed. G. Fricke and H. G. Göpfert (Munich: Hanser, 1958), p. 769 (author's translation).

the question and its powerful implications;[42] instead, they entered into a debate that they were bound to lose. And so they did. They accepted the serpent's teaching about God, the doubt by which the serpent interprets God, i.e., evil's interpretation of God.

If human knowledge about God has vanished or at least become cloudy, knowledge about fellow humans will inevitably be blurred too. One's relationship to fellow humans changes from a necessary and essential relationship of one's existence into an arbitrary one. And fellow humans, who are their own subjects in reciprocal relationship to us, become objects of our desires and fears. There is a close link between respect for God and respect for one's neighbor. As Barth notes, misapprehension of God culminates in misapprehension of people:

> . . . man, who in virtue of . . . his foolish attempt to equate God with himself and himself with God, does not know God . . . does not know his fellow man either. His ignorance of God culminates and manifests itself in his ignorance of his fellow man. He regards him as an object to whom he as subject may or may not be in relation according to his own free choice and disposal, whom he may pass by as he does so many other objects, or with whom, if this is out of the question, he may have dealings as it suits himself within the limits of what is possible for him. He does not know him as a fellow subject whom God has set unavoidably beside him, to whom he is unavoidably linked in his relation to God, so that apart from him he cannot himself be a subject, a person. He is not for him an indispensable, but in certain cases a dispensable, companion, associate, and fellow — not to mention brother. He can get along just as well without him as with him. By chance or caprice or free judgment he can just as well be to him a tyrant or slave as a free supporter, just as well a hater as an admirer, a foe as a friend, a corrupter as a helper. . . . In relationship to his fellow man, also, he exists in total ambivalence. . . . [T]here is no necessary and solid relationship between man and man but only incidental, arbitrary, and temporary connections.[43]

---

42. On the manipulative power and suggestiveness of questions, see the psychologist Aron R. Bodenheimer, *Warum? Von der Obszönität des Fragens,* 5th ed. (Stuttgart: Reclam, 1999); and Weinrich, "Wir sind aber Menschen," pp. 57-67.

43. Karl Barth, *The Christian Life: Church Dogmatics IV/4, Lecture Fragments,* trans. Geoffrey W. Bromiley (Grand Rapids: Eerdmans, 1981), pp. 131-32.

Barth draws a strict parallel between recognition of God and treatment of fellow humans. In his view, interhuman relationships depend on how well humans respect God and his will to create human beings in his image. This is the reason why the biblical witness focuses in the first place on the relationship of humans to God.

The biblical option is resolute. If trust in God is damaged, the relationship to God is fundamentally flawed. God may still be present in a human's life, but he is marginalized. God is no longer the counterpart in a relationship in which humankind discovers its justification. Even after they noticed their nakedness in paradise, *nota bene,* God himself made them "garments of skins . . . and clothed them" (Gen. 3:21). But things had changed so fundamentally that they could not stay in the Garden of Eden. To a certain extent God accepted their self-reliance — as he had done before — and sent them to a place where they could demonstrate it in the distance from God that they had claimed for themselves. Paradise was already lost before history began, but we are told about it so that we will be aware that God's goal for humanity was different from that chosen by humans.

Human reservation over against God implies a separation. Humankind attacks the core of God's confidence in his creation, while at the same time provoking God by behaving as though it were its own creator. Nothing is the same as before, or — to put it more precisely — nothing in the human sphere is as God intended it any longer. Separation from God leads inevitably to self-enslavement. This is the unavoidable result of the essential exclusiveness of human self-centeredness. Mistrust causes loneliness, and loneliness estranges us from God. Reliance on mere self-confidence leads to inevitable separation from God. So the circle is closed. Humankind chose the impossible possibility of competing with God and has run from failure to failure and from misery to misery. Now it seems as if God is dependent on humanity to justify itself. We do not adequately grasp the situation unless we recognize the deep violation done to God and understand God's wrath to be thoroughly justified.

IV. The Covenanting God: God's Inclusive Faithfulness

We will stay with Genesis 1–11. This time we will look not at the shape of humanity that becomes visible in these chapters but at God's response, his way of punishing people, and his search for new ways into the future. Usually, we focus on God's harsh reactions, the punishments that show the severe character of God's justice. It is not necessary to go so far as to say that God's wrath shows his love for the law more than for humanity. We need not be friends of Marcion, yet may nevertheless emphasize that God demonstrates his sovereignty especially in the Urgeschichte by being the almighty Lord of the cosmos and history. In this regard, the Flood seems to function as the outstanding example of God's character. The only criterion for what happens seems to be God's unshakable will to pursue his objectives.

There may be reasons for such a view, but the overwhelming majority of God's acts point in another direction and place his severity in a different light. In no case do we find severity without mercy. God's severity always leads to new arrangements to benefit life. In my understanding, the Urgeschichte better reveals the far-reaching challenges with which God is confronted in his affection for his creatures than it does the harshness of his rule. Every punitive measure has protective aspects. Indeed, I would express this more pointedly: whatever God does, he does for the sake of his mercy. As long as God's mercy is not immediately visible, we have to open our eyes and ears to discover it, because otherwise we will miss the decisive point.

When God drove Adam and Eve from the Garden of Eden, he kept them from touching the other tree — the "tree of life." The "tree of life" promised eternal life, and God obviously cannot agree that a life based on mistrust should become eternal. This would have destroyed the whole project of creation as it aimed at the covenant. Because God allowed his creature to do almost everything, he originally had the confidence that it would respect his only prohibition for its own sake. But after the experience regarding the "tree of the knowledge of good and evil," God interferes before the enterprise collapses by itself. Outside the Garden of Eden conditions become harder, but life no longer exists in the danger that one deed could threaten everything. God protected Adam and Eve from being able to destroy themselves as God's creatures, i.e., God defended them by banishing them from the Garden of Eden.

If we look at Cain, we note that his deed left its marks on his life. But we also see that the special mark upon him is God's, "so that no one who came upon him would kill him" (Gen. 4:15). God marked Cain not to minimize Cain's deed — he had to suffer the consequences — but rather to stop evil, to interrupt the self-nurturing process of violence. The mark was intended both to stigmatize him as a murderer and to protect him. Although God could not prevent Cain's deed, he could prevent the consequences of the deed from prevailing in later history.

It is especially difficult to see God's mercy and grace in connection with the Flood. God himself decided, "I will blot out from the earth the human beings I have created" (Gen. 6:7). God repented of creation (Gen. 6:6), or to be more exact, not of the whole of creation but of the creation of human beings. They are at the heart of creation, and if this heart is evil the whole becomes rotten. God is not just disappointed. Human beings put God's confidence in them into question, and so they questioned God as such. The relationship for which the whole enterprise was set up has been destroyed, and that means that the whole enterprise of God's generosity has failed. So God wanted to put an end to everything — there was no reason to continue — but with one exception. God protected Noah and his family, and only then let the Flood take its course.

One may get the impression that God changed his mind about humanity because of the pleasing fragrance of Noah's offer after the Flood.[44] Yet, nothing has really changed: "the inclination of the human heart is evil from youth" (Gen. 8:21). The only thing that has changed is that God now makes the rule out of what had been the exception. Here for the first time the biblical witness speaks of a covenant: "I am establishing my covenant with you and your descendants after you" (Gen. 9:9). It is not just any covenant but expressly God's covenant ("my covenant"). It is decisive for the understanding of the whole Bible that this covenant is mentioned already in the Urgeschichte. The aim of the Flood narrative is this covenant. This story establishes that God's covenant precedes the history that follows.[45] Although "the inclination of the human heart is evil from youth," God establishes his covenant, and — as the biblical witness testifies — he will reconfirm his intentions many times. These may appear to be different covenants, but they are all expressions of the oneness of God's covenanting will. That is why the covenant had to be included in the Urgeschichte. We cannot properly recognize God until we realize that God establishes his covenant not only for pious people but for all human beings as they are. We cannot be closer to the issue of justification than here. The

---

44. Jürgen Ebach, *Noah: Die Geschichte eines Überlebenden* (Leipzig: Evangelische Verlagsanstalt, 2001), p. 119. Ebach speaks of God's double repentance.

45. It may be that the plot of the Flood narrative was already given and was inserted into the Urgeschichte.

Urgeschichte establishes that justification is key for the whole of the biblical witness and thus for the whole of theology.[46]

Unconditional covenantal love is the center of God's self-revelation. In Barth's words,

> God is He who seeks and creates fellowship with us, and who (because His revelation is also His self-revelation) does this in himself and in His eternal essence. . . . He wills to be ours, and he wills that we should be His. He wills to belong to us and He wills that we should belong to Him. He does not will to be without us, and He does not will that we should be without Him. . . . That He is God — the Godhead of God — consists in the fact that He loves, and it is the expression of His loving that He seeks and creates fellowship with us.[47]

The covenant — as Gary Deddo summarizes it — "is not a kind of contractual agreement between two parties on the basis of mutually agreed terms which if violated annuls the contract. It is a commitment to the benefit of the other by doing whatever is lovingly necessary to include them in fellowship originally active in the Triune life."[48] This means in anthropological terms that the determination of humanity culminates in its determination as the covenant partner of God.

The last scene of the Urgeschichte is the Tower of Babel. This story is perhaps not primarily about justification, but it is nevertheless a wonderful story about God's protective grace, the result of which always means justification. God does not wait — as he could have done — until the gigantic tower caves in by itself, which clearly would have occurred if the master builder had built it "with its top in the heavens" (Gen. 11:4). The aim to reach the heavens reveals the hubris of the builders and the self-destructive character of the project. The longer people worked on it, the greater was the threat that it would collapse and kill everyone involved.

If human beings are determined to enter "the heavens" or to "make a name for themselves," nobody will be able to stop them. Even God needed a special trick to convince them that they should give up this project before

---

46. Calvin and Barth especially emphasized the centrality of covenant. This may be a special Reformed accent, but it is also one of the main threads of the biblical witness.

47. Barth, *CD* II/1, ed. G. W. Bromiley and T. F. Torrance (Edinburgh: T. & T. Clark, 1957), pp. 274-75.

48. Deddo, "The Grammar of Barth's Theology of Personal Relations," p. 202.

it collapsed of itself. The grace of the confusion of language is that they had to halt their efforts at building and had to invest instead in learning to communicate with each other.[49] The end of the towering project saved their lives. There is something protective about the need for communication. Unless we pay attention to communication, our relationships fall apart. It is a great but also a wonderful challenge to learn to understand one another — this is what should be at the top of our agenda and not towers stretching into the heavens. The need to communicate helps prevent such gigantically tragic projects. Here again, God stopped the enterprise before it destroyed itself. God saves people from self-destruction. In this case, it was not a Flood sent from God but rather humankind's own ambitions that threatened — and still threaten — the existence of human life.

The Urgeschichte provides vivid images of the fundamental tension between God's determination of and care for his creature on the one hand and the creature's mistrust and ungrateful selfishness on the other. Like a magnifying glass, the Urgeschichte concentrates our attention on the immense disproportion between God's genuine, concerned relatedness to humanity and the latter's unconcerned and aggressive attempt to prove its ability to live independently. God's trust is answered by mistrust. From the very beginning there is a fundamental discrepancy between the creation as justified by God and justice as defined by humans. Instead of living the justification granted by God, humans ask God to justify himself.

This is the breakthrough achieved by the serpent and its question: "Did God [truly] say?" (Gen. 3:1). The amazing thing in the Urgeschichte is that God does not give up but does everything to find a way to humanity in spite of the destroyed relationship. God again and again looks for a way to justify his disobedient creature. The wonder of the justification of the creation is surpassed by the wonder of justification through the covenant established for fallen humanity. The Urgeschichte gives us a condensed characterization of the relationship between God and human beings. God is revealed in his unconditional and faithful option for the established covenant and for human beings, despite their self-aggrandizing confidence in their own possibilities for building up the world in virtually open competition with God. As God is introduced to us in the Urgeschichte, we are

---

49. Even if I, a German, suffered and felt handicapped by being forced to write this contribution in English!

also introduced to ourselves — perhaps in a surprising manner but nevertheless a much less surprising manner than the introduction of God to us. The biblical understanding of God is impossible without the accompanying understanding of human beings. There is no doctrine of God without anthropology and no anthropology without a proper understanding of God. That is something everyone knows but always forgets.

Instead of the Urgeschichte we could have looked at the history that begins with Abraham and ends with the later epistles of the New Testament. Perhaps the picture would be much more complex, as not everything fits without difficulty into the framework outlined by the Urgeschichte.[50] We would have realized that there are always unexpected solutions, unexpected promises, and also unexpected letdowns. Biblical history is not just a story about victories and triumphs. And so it is necessary to tell the whole history, with both its high points and its low points. From the very beginning, we are a part of it. All the strange twists and turns are related to us to reveal to us our place in this story, which is not everywhere but somewhere. The story is complicated because everything we can learn from it confirms the unintended and not easily accepted lesson that even if we are very pious and upright, we are at best comparable to Peter — who denied the Lord. And again, the only thing we can do is to rely on the promise that this (pious) denier is — as the story relates — nevertheless a beloved disciple of Jesus. This is how biblical realism treats human beings — their doubts, unfaithfulness, and wickedness, even in their piety.

V. God's Loving Justice: Humanity's Liberating Justification

We have to come back to the role of justification as the leaven of the whole of theology. The pivotal point is the mutual connection between love and justice. It is not enough to say that God loves justice or that God is the loving God also in his justice. Rather, God's justice is the expression of his love, just as his love always expresses itself in acts of justice and justification.

---

50. Generally speaking, it is not a question of which part of the Bible we are dealing with, but of the hermeneutical approach to scripture as Holy Scripture. On this important issue, see John Burgess, *Why Scripture Matters* (Louisville: Westminster John Knox Press, 1998); and John Webster, *Holy Scripture: A Dogmatic Sketch* (Cambridge: Cambridge University Press, 2003).

The most concrete expression of this connection is God's faithfulness to the covenant that he initiated with Noah and reconfirmed many times throughout history, ultimately in Jesus Christ (Luke 22:20; 1 Cor. 11:25). Because this covenant had to be adjusted several times, its earlier forms may now appear outdated and even obsolete (the harshest judgments in this direction can be found in Heb. 8:13 and 9:15[51]), but in all of these covenants, the will of God remains the same: to promote the justification of individual humans, the people of Israel, or the whole of humanity as partners in a reciprocal relationship to the living God. We may choose to distinguish different covenants, but God's intention does not change. The form of the covenant may differ from one situation to another, but each reflects the justice of God's love — his loving justice in which our justification is entirely his achievement again and again.

God is still the God of Israel, and we too rely on his faithfulness to his covenant with Israel. God never cancelled his covenant with Israel (Rom. 11:1), and Christians would not have reason to trust in God's faithfulness to them if they felt that God had ceased to be faithful to Israel. The reason for God's faithfulness is not the church's behavior in the world; nor is it Israel's history that convinces God to stand by Israel. Rather, it is simply God's own loving justice, through which he sticks to his covenant and the promise of its final fulfillment.[52]

This is exactly what the Reformers rediscovered — that it is God alone who establishes, nurtures, and fulfills his relationship to humanity, while human beings do everything they can to mistrust and marginalize God. At best, human beings employ a kind of calculable justice: they hope to gain access to God by doing this or that. They are not free to revere God for his own sake. We creatures fail to thank the creator for ourselves. We do not view God as being righteous, even though he views us as righteous. We do not respond to God's trust in us with a comparable trust in him. It remains an asymmetrical situation in which we completely depend on God's faithfulness to the covenant that he established east of Eden in a world already branded by sin rooted in the apparently irresistible temptation of mistrust.

---

51. For a proper understanding of these points, see Knut Backhaus, *Der neue Bund und das Werden der Kirche: Die Diatheke-Bedeutung des Hebräerbriefs im Rahmen der frühchristlichen Theologiegeschichte* (Münster: Aschendorff, 1996).

52. See Michael Weinrich, "Die Kirche als Volk Gottes an der Seite Israels," in *Kirche glauben: Evangelische Annäherungen an eine ökumenische Ekklesiologie*, ed. Michael Weinrich (Wuppertal: Foedus, 1998), pp. 190-223.

The poison of mistrust destroys human relationship with God, and no one is able to heal the breach.

This is not simply a question of good or bad will. Rather, the reality based on the reciprocal relationship of God and human beings has been destroyed. God does everything to protect humanity from self-destruction. God establishes his merciful covenant and even justifies sinful people as his partners, but on the human side mistrust and unfaithfulness remain. Even human piety becomes an expression of mistrust, because it becomes mere obedience to God's commandments for the sake of personal salvation. God justifies the godless, but they still live in alienation from God. There seems to be no way out of the reality of destroyed relationship, and even God's hands seem to be tied as long as he wants to be faithful to his creature as its own subject. In his free love, God as creator makes himself dependent on the human answer. God justifies human beings as his creation but has to wait for the creature's trust in its creator. God seems to be the prisoner of his own generous election of human beings to relationship.

Here we face age-old questions of Christology. In the words of Anselm of Canterbury, "Cur deus homo?"[53] I will touch on this matter, but only briefly; other chapters in this volume address it more fully. God needs a human being to reestablish the destroyed reality of relationship. But no one emerges. The only possibility is for he himself to act. It is his Word which "became flesh and lived among us, and we have seen his glory, the glory as of a father's only son, full of grace and truth" (John 1:14). God's Word becomes incarnate in Jesus Christ, who was the true human being, living in relationship with God and fulfilling God's intentions for all humanity. Christ gives the necessary human answer. In him the covenant was not only reconfirmed but fulfilled, i.e., it arrived at its destination. Christ is the real and true human being, the representative of all humanity, and his cross illumines our situation in relation to loving justice. As the accused, he becomes the accuser, just as the accusers become the accused. Our recognition of justification is linked to our recognition of sin. They belong together, but in this order.

Here we face the core of Christological dogma. But the focus of this chapter is in a different direction. On the one hand, we want to state that Christology is the decisive key for the understanding of faith; on the other,

---

53. See Stephen R. Holmes, "The Upholding of Beauty: A Reading of Anselm's Cur Deus Homo," *Scottish Journal of Theology* 54 (2001): 189-203.

Christology tells us nothing that we could not learn from other parts of the Bible. Or to put it in another way, Christology teaches us to recognize the same God throughout the Bible, just as the whole Bible enriches our understanding of Christ. Scripture is not just disconnected bits and pieces of literature. Rather, it has continuous lines that hold the plurality and variety of its content together. In my view, it is very significant that Karl Barth begins his explanation of justification and reconciliation as the center of the Christian message by referring to the prophet Isaiah and his use of the name Immanuel, "God with us," which is then cited in Matthew 1:23.[54] What happens in Christ is not an isolated event but rather the goal of all divine deeds: as Barth says, ". . . the eternal activity in which He is both in Himself and in the history of His acts in the world created by Him. It is of this that the 'God with us' speaks."[55] God's faithfulness in Christ allows us to recognize God's justifying attitude throughout the whole of history.

I will not try to sum up my reflections. Theological doctrines are always abstractions and conclusions of things that the biblical witness tells us in a great variety of narratives. Proper theological insight can never be more than an aid to entering into the spirit and mind of the biblical witness and its views of the relationship between God and human beings. We always have to touch ground with the biblical narratives, even though they may complicate our doctrinal conclusions. In the end, the important thing is not how to safeguard the doctrinal insights that have been passed on to us but to be reminded of the vivid divine and human reality of God's merciful covenant that justifies us in order to arouse our weak and sleepy faith.

54. Barth, *CD* IV/1, ed. G. W. Bromiley and T. F. Torrance (Edinburgh: T. & T. Clark, 1956), §57, pp. 3-154.
55. Barth, *CD* IV/1, §57, p. 8.

2 *Rector et iudex super omnia genera doctrinarum?*
The Place of the Doctrine of Justification

John Webster

I

The ruler and judge over all other Christian doctrines is the doctrine of the Holy Trinity. The doctrine of the Trinity is not one doctrine among others; it is both foundational and pervasive. To expound any Christian doctrine is to expound with varying degrees of directness the doctrine of the Trinity; to expound the doctrine of the Trinity in its full scope is to expound the entirety of Christian dogmatics.

This is a formal assertion about the structure of Christian doctrine. But it is also, more significantly, a material claim. Indeed, its legitimacy as a directive about the organization of Christian dogmatics depends upon its coherence with the substance of the Christian confession of God. In its praise, testimony, and action, the church confesses: God is. It makes that confession in response to God's self-expressive form — his "revelation" — which shapes the specific content of what the church confesses. That content may be spelled out in summary form as follows: The statement "God is" is not a closed statement but an open and inclusive one. Because and only because it is a statement about this one, who is who he is and who demonstrates himself to be such in his self-communication, it is also a statement about the ways of God with creatures. This is why the doctrine of the Trinity comprehends within itself all further teaching about creatures, their natures and ends. Further, this is why theological talk about creatures — including talk about the justification of creatures before God — does not require us to move away from talk about the triune God, but simply to follow the direction and content of the divine self-exposition.

Because — and, once again, only because — there is this God, there are other realities of which Christian doctrine is obligated to speak. By way of a more extended account of this, we may reflect on the statement: God — Father, Son, and Holy Spirit — is life in himself. This can be expanded in two ways.

First: God is life in himself. God's being is the wholly original, uncaused, and glorious fullness of life of the three-in-one. God is in and from himself, *in se* and *a se*. This aseity of the triune God is primarily not a negative characterization, differentiating God from created being by denying that his being originates from or is in any way causally dependent upon another. God's aseity is most properly defined (defined, that is, in trinitarian fashion) as inseity; God is not merely the unconditioned, but is within himself an unrestricted fullness of personal relations. Aseity is life: God's life in and from himself, in the relations of Father, Son, and Spirit. The self-existence of the triune God is his existence in the *opera Dei personalia ad intra,* the personal internal works of God. These inner-divine acts are the personal relations which are God's being, the modes of subsistence in which each particular person of the Trinity is identified in terms of relations to the other two persons. God's life is thus his perfect life in the eternal relations of paternity, filiation, and spiration, the inner processions of the Godhead in which God's self-existence consists. Aseity is therefore the eternal lively plenitude of the Father who begets, the Son who is begotten, and the Spirit who proceeds from both. Further, this fullness of life in relation is the order or righteousness of God's being. God's righteousness in himself, his *iustitia interna,* is his perfect correspondence with the law of his being, the integrity of his will, and his existence. It is the perfect order of his self-relation, which is the perfect fulfillment of his self-determination.

Second: God is the giver of life. God wills both his own life and the life of creatures. As the one who is antecedently and eternally life in himself, God directs himself to that which is not himself. What God intends, according to the Christian confession, is not only his own perfection and plenitude in the *opera Dei ad intra* but also a corresponding creaturely perfection and plenitude. The *consilium Dei* includes an intentional act, namely the *decretum Dei* in which he actively, immediately, and eternally wills that there should be a domain of life other than his own. This domain is wholly dependent upon him, not *a se* but *ab alio;* yet it is given the gift of life. God's life therefore includes a movement of life-giving, in the *opera Dei exeuntia* in which he directs himself toward creatures. This purposive turning of the life of God is the utterly spontaneous and unconditioned bestowal of being, as a result of which alongside the creator there is also creaturely being, life, and history, willed and affirmed by him. God's intending of creatures is thus an act of *love.*

The love of God, made known in his works *ad extra,* is entirely a matter of God's free self-determination. God does not lose himself in this intention; the destiny of the creature is not bought at the price of some diminishing of the divine being. Of his own will, God designs that his life should execute this further movement. Its necessity is therefore solely a *necessitas naturae,* arising from the divine nature in its free self-enactment. But what God freely wills is, precisely, that in his perfection he should stretch forth to creatures as life-giver. God wills that the fellowship of his wholly self-realized life should be repeated in his fellowship with creatures. To the divine processions there correspond the divine missions, so that the righteous order of the being of God should find a creaturely echo. God "accomplishes all things according to the counsel of his will" (Eph. 1:11); and the things that he accomplishes are, first, his entire perfection as Father, Son, and Spirit, and, second, the appointment of creatures to live for the praise of his glory.

What are the consequences of this for the way in which Christian doctrine is structured? First, there are two constituent parts of Christian doctrine: God and the works of God. The content of the first part is the doctrine of the triune life *ad intra;* that of the second is the doctrine of God's life *ad extra,* and thus the doctrines of creation, providence, salvation, the church, and the consummation. In one sense, there is only one Christian doctrine, the doctrine of the triune God, because in following that doctrine to its end theology will treat all the topics customarily brought together in a systematic theology. But to state the matter in such terms might attract the charge of theomonism, however unjust. A rather happier way of putting the matter would be to say that the content of Christian dogmatics is the double theme of God and his works.

Second, both parts of this double theme are integral to any adequate theological account of the Christian confession, and neither may be considered in isolation from the other. A theology of the life of God *a se* and *in se* that failed to depict the *opera Dei exeuntia* would not simply be a severely diminished account; it would fail precisely as an account of God's life in himself. Conversely, a theology of God as life-giver detached from the exposition of God as life in himself would be wholly inadequate as an account of the works of God *ad extra,* precisely because the *opera Dei* are the opera *Dei.*

Third, there is a specific order proper to this double theme. The topic of God is materially (and so logically) prior to the topic of God's works, because these works are grounded in God's being in and for himself. This order should not be taken to imply that the second element is merely accidental. The works of God are not contingently related to God's being in and for himself, because God's determination to be the life-giver is eternal, "before the foundation of the world" (Eph. 1:4). Nor should we conclude from the order that in turning to the second theme we leave the first behind as just so much ballast. (Attempts to do this have been strangely persistent in Protestant theology after Kant.) The material order is irreversible. Nevertheless, the material order is not necessarily the order of exposition, and it would be quite possible to begin an account of Christian doctrine at any point, provided that proper attention is paid to systematic scope in order to prevent the hypertrophy of one article at the price of the atrophy of another.

In sum: the only Christian doctrine that may legitimately claim to exercise a magisterial and judicial role in the corpus of Christian teaching is the doctrine of the Trinity, since in that doctrine alone all other doctrines have their ultimate basis. Other topics of Christian teaching may from time to time become particularly acute points of theological conscience, in which the fidelity of church and theology to the gospel is at stake. Among such topics, teachings about the person and work of Christ have in the course of Christian history had a high profile. But they have played that role, not because they are in and of themselves the sole bearers of Christian truth or because they comprehend all teaching within themselves, but because in them is made especially visible the fact that the triune God is in himself the first and the last.

II

The setting of Christian soteriology, and therefore of Christian teaching about justification, is in a comprehensive account of the works of God, which is in its turn grounded in a theology of the *opera Dei immanentia.*

Theologies in the Reformation tradition have sometimes been tempted to make soteriology into the material center of a systematic account of the Christian faith. This has taken a particular form in the wake of Kant, where the severe restrictions placed upon the reach of the mind encouraged some theologians to divert toward "promeity," thus generating expositions of the Christian faith that make extensive use of a moral or existential idiom of salvation as human reality. Such expositions could appeal — selectively — to elements in the work of the magisterial Reformers. Most of all, appeal could be made to the Reformers' perception that inflation of the intermediary role of church office and sacramental action threatened the unique, non-transferable character of Jesus Christ's office as mediator, a threat that could be countered by insisting on a certain theology of the immediacy of access to saving grace as fundamental to the gospel. Yet, detached from the trinitarian and incarnational metaphysics presupposed by the Reformers, this soteriological accent can distort, most obviously in the direction of a theology of salvation that is little more than lightly revised anthropology. When that happens, soteriology becomes a theology of Christian existence, around which the objectivities of the Christian confession are ranged as so much raw material for appropriation. When this distortion presents itself, it needs to be countered by a twofold relativization of soteriology.

First, the setting of a Christian theology of salvation is not in anthropology, but in the works of God *ad extra;* those works, in turn, have their setting in and refer back to the *opera Dei immanentia* as their condition and ground. "Salvation" as a determination of Christian existence is a function of the divine work; the divine work is the work of the one who is perfect in himself. The recital in which God's work of salvation has its place does not begin with the moment of his redemptive dealings with sinful creatures, but with the infinite peace and glory of the Father, Son, and Holy Spirit. Why is this — perhaps counterintuitive — move of such dogmatic consequence?

It is vital to articulating the sheer gratuity of God's work of salvation. The origins of the saving act of God lie wholly within the being of God. Whatever necessity the work of salvation has is a necessity internal to God's own being, not a necessity laid upon God from outside. Salvation is grace: spontaneous, uncaused, rooted in the eternal sufficiency of God. Accordingly, soteriology has to be grounded upon a doctrine of the Trinity in order to ensure the ontological depth of what theology has to say about salvation. The history in which the salvation of the world is achieved is not simply a set of contingent or accidental transactions. It takes place, rather, at the frontier or intersection point of the eternal and the temporal. Its course is not that of a self-enclosed "natural" history, for it is a sequence of events open to the divine reality upon which it is founded and from which alone it draws its substance. The condition for there being a history of salvation is that these events are the temporal outworking of God's self-consistency. In them is made actual the eternal divine decree to be and therefore to act thus. Without this reference backward to the divine intention, there is only a temporal surface, and so no prospect of the creature's redemption. Consequently, the grounding of the theology of salvation in the doctrine of the immanent Trinity is necessary to avoid what has been a persistent problem in modern Christian theology, namely a certain Christological and soteriological nominalism. This is the assumption that the person and mission of Jesus are intelligible per se, without immediate reference to the Christian doctrine of God or to such Christological teaching as the pre-existence of Christ or the theology of the *regnum Christi.* This is, of course, an aspect of the larger problem already identified: the insertion of a gap between the works of God and the being of God, which allows the former to be expounded in relative isolation from the latter. When the works of God are isolated from the being of God, the *pro nobis* character of God's external works is understood in a different way. It is no longer a trinitarian and Christological affirmation of God's eternal love for creatures, but rather a condition for true theological discourse, providing it with existential warrants and applicability. Thereby the objective is subordinated to the subjective, and the immanent life of God ceases to play any perceptible role in an account of salvation.

All this suggests that, far from being a mere background idea without any directly operative consequences for soteriology, the doctrine of the Trinity is in fact critical in ensuring the correct placement and proportions of the Christian doctrine of salvation. Accordingly, a Christian theology of salvation has to be undergirded by a double theological principle: (1) God's saving history with creatures is to be conceived as the outworking of the divine missions in which the sending of the Son and the Spirit is the bodying forth of the Father's eternal divine counsel, and not simply as an intra-historical reality; (2) description of God's saving history through a theology of divine missions must rest upon a theology of the divine processions, in accordance with the principle *missiones sequuntur processiones.* The saving roles of Son and Spirit are grounded upon their processional roles in the inner life of the Godhead.

A second relativization of soteriology follows from this. If the first relativization sets soteriology in relation to the doctrine of the Trinity as its foundation, the second sets soteriology in relation to the other topics that make up the corpus of Christian teaching about God's external works. This sets soteriology in a horizontal axis, corresponding to the vertical axis that has been discussed so far.

The scope of the *opera Dei exeuntia* is wider than that of the single theme of salvation, however widely ramified that theme may be. A theological account of the works of God has the task of tracing the entire history of God with creatures as it is announced in the canonical witnesses and confessed in the church. In attempting to give such an account, dogmatics (at least in the form which it received at the hands of the seventeenth-century practitioners and which remains the shape of most sophisticated accounts of the material) arranges its presentation both narratively and topically. The "plot" of a systematic theology tends to be roughly historical — God and then God's works treated in what is basically the order of canonical salvation history, particular stages in the history of salvation providing the opportunity for discussion of associated topics. Further, an overall account of the works of God will be shaped by an overall construal of their theme or matter. If such a construal is not to prove reductive, it must be able to demonstrate that it emerges in a natural, unforced way from the canonical materials, and that it is sufficiently spacious to do justice to the range of the canon.

Broadly described, the matter of the *opera Dei exeuntia* is the fellowship of life between God and God's creatures. The form of this fellowship is the history in which God who is life in himself gives life to creatures, defends them against the mortal enemy of sin, and brings them to fullness of life in the kingdom of God. This history can be set forth as a series as "moments" (both temporal and topical): election, creation, providence; the history of the covenant people; the sending of the Son and his life, passion, and glorification; the bestowal of the Holy Spirit; the time of the church; and the consummation of all things. Taken together, these moments are the enactment of the fellowship in which creatures have their being at the hands of this God. No one moment of the history can bear the weight of the whole; none can be isolated from the others. Even that moment which of all others has a special claim to supremacy — the incarnation of the divine Word — is only the center of this history because around it other moments are ranged. And so the moment of the Son's saving work cannot be secluded from what encompasses it. God's act of salvation is his intervention in the history of creation to ensure that the creature with whom he purposes fellowship (election) and to whom he gives life (creation) will finally attain perfection in the coming kingdom (consummation). Soteriology is not an erratic doctrine, and cannot of itself constitute the heart of the system of Christian truth.

To speak in such terms is not to rob soteriology of its proper significance, but simply to indicate what soteriology is about. The subject matter of the theology of salvation is how the triune God acts with the sovereign competence and authority of his love to establish the perfection of the creature. Creaturely being is life in fellowship with the creator. By dealing a death-blow to the creature's resistance to its own well-being, contending with and overcoming the creature's futile contention with God, God gives the creature a new and further gift of life. God alone is able to give this gift because God alone has life in himself. "God is said to have life in himself," Calvin writes, "not only because he alone lives by his own inherent power, but because he contains the fullness of life in himself and quickens all things."[1] Soteriology is a particular intensification of this double theme — the life of God in himself and his quickening power as the one who has the fullness of life. And to say this is to say that the setting of soteriology is the theology of the being and works of the triune God.

III

The dogmatic location of justification is a comprehensive trinitarian soteriology.[2]

1. John Calvin, *The Gospel according to St. John 1–10* (Edinburgh: St. Andrew Press, 1959), p. 131.

2. This matter remains seriously underexplored. The most stimulating current account is Robert Jenson, "Justification as Triune Event," *Modern Theology* 11 (1995): 421-27, slightly modified in his *Systematic Theology,* vol. 2 (Oxford: Oxford University Press, 1999), pp. 290-301. On Jenson, see Tuomo Mannermaa, "Doctrine of Justification and Trinitarian Ontology," in *Trinity, Time and Church: A Response to the Theology of Robert W. Jenson,* ed. Colin E. Gunton (Grand Rapids: Eerdmans, 2000), pp. 139-45. More generally here, see Paul Molnar, "The Doctrine of Justification in Dogmatic Context," in *Justification,* ed. Mark Husbands and Daniel Treier (Downers Grove, IL: Apollos, 2004), pp. 225-48. Attention should also be drawn to the important recent study by Robert J. Sherman, *King, Priest and Prophet: A Trinitarian Theology of Atonement* (London: T. & T. Clark, 2004), which weaves together the three

At this point we move to reflect directly on claims that the doctrine of justification by faith is the *articulus stantis et cadentis ecclesiae*. It is important at the outset to note the diversity of claims that cluster around this slogan, concerning such matters as: the prevenient character of sovereign grace in human salvation; the sole sufficiency and effectiveness of the work of Christ; resistance against moralizing or sacramentalizing construals of Christian faith, or against self-realization as a motif in anthropology; the properly forensic character of God's dealings with creatures; and the definitive significance of the Word of God for the life of the church. Here we are not concerned with these particular issues or with the appropriateness of deploying the doctrine of justification to sound an alarm signal, but rather with the need to place the theology of justification within a larger trinitarian structure.

We may orient ourselves from one of the most penetrating recent defenses of the centrality of justification for the entire corpus of Christian teaching, Eberhard Jüngel's *Justification*,[3] arguably the most impressive presentation of justification as the *evangelische Grundartikel* since Kähler.[4] Says Jüngel, "At the heart of the Christian faith lies a declared belief in Jesus Christ. This confession, however, also has a centre, a living focal point, which turns the confession of Christ into something that vitally concerns my own existence. Thus the heart of the heart of the Christian faith is the belief in the justification of the sinner through the one 'who was handed over to death for our sins and was raised for our justification.'"[5]

The metaphors by which Jüngel describes the place of justification within the Christian confession — "centre," "focal point," "the heart of the

---

persons of the Trinity, the three offices of Christ, and three major soteriological motifs (victory, sacrifice, and instruction). Sherman does not treat justification directly, but his account is compatible with what is proposed here, although I am less concerned to appropriate specific aspects of salvation to specific trinitarian persons, and have a heavier investment in the doctrine of the immanent Trinity.

3. Eberhard Jüngel, *Justification: The Heart of the Christian Faith* (Edinburgh: T. & T. Clark, 2001).

4. Martin Kähler, *Die Wissenschaft der christlichen Lehre von dem evangelischen Grundartikel aus im Abrisse dargestellt* [1905] (Neukirchen: Neukirchener Verlag, 1966), pp. 67-79. For an important note about historical context here, see Eckhard Lessing, "Der evangelische Grundartikel in theologiegeschichtlicher Perspektive: Die Rechtfertigungslehre zwischen Ritschl und Holl," in *Rechtfertigung und Erfahrung: Für Gerhard Sauter zum 60. Geburtstag*, ed. Michael Beintker et al. (Gütersloh: Gütersloher Verlagshaus, 1995), pp. 59-76.

5. Jüngel, *Justification*, p. 15.

heart" — are double-edged. On the one hand, part of their intention is to ensure that justification is not isolated from other tracts of Christian teaching, and so to resist the charge of one-sided Paulinism. Indeed, Jüngel starts his analysis by relating justification to some primary topics in Christian teaching: the nature of life with God, what it means to be a human person, the identity of God, and God's relation to creatures through the death and resurrection of Jesus Christ.[6] On the other hand, Jüngel is insistent that what Christian faith has to say about these topics acquires full definition only through the doctrine of justification:

> [I]n the justification article all these statements come to a head. The decision is made here first of all as to who this God is, and what it really means to be creatively active. Next, it says what it means to die for others and to bring forth new life in the midst of death: a life that imparts itself through the power of the Spirit to our passing world in such a way that a new community arises — the Christian church. The justification article brings out emphatically the truth of the relationship between God and people and in so doing the correct understanding of God's divinity and our humanity. And since the Christian church draws its life from the relationship between God and people, and only from that relationship, the justification article is the one article by which the church stands and without which it falls. So every other truth of the faith must be weighed and judged by that article.[7]

Here we may already be able to sense a certain constriction: justification is moving from being a potent soteriological article that connects across the corpus of doctrines, and is beginning to adopt the role of norm for all other areas of teaching. Following a suggestion from Gloege, Jüngel proposes that "the best way to express the central function of justification is to highlight its hermeneutical significance for the whole of theological knowledge and . . . to see it accordingly as *the* 'hermeneutical category' of theology."[8] He explains: "By using the doctrine of justification, all theological statements gain their distinctive image, focus and character. . . . The

---

6. Jüngel, *Justification*, pp. 3-5.

7. Jüngel, *Justification*, p. 16.

8. Jüngel, *Justification*, p. 47; see also Gerhard Gloege, "Die Rechtfertigungslehre als hermeneutische Kategorie," in *Gnade für die Welt: Kritik und Krise des Luthertums* (Göttingen: Vandenhoeck & Ruprecht, 1964), pp. 34-54.

doctrine of justification has this strength of a hermeneutical category because it brings all of theology into the dimension of a legal dispute: that is,
the legal dispute of God about his honor, which is at the same time a legal
dispute about the worth of human beings."[9]

Two comments are in order here. The first concerns the systematic
range of a theological account of the Christian faith. The proposal that "all
of theology" is determined by the forensic idiom of a legal dispute about
divine honor and human worth risks not only narrowing the scope of the
divine economy but also isolating the forensic from the context of election,
covenant, and eschatology within which it has to be understood. Like
other soteriological metaphors such as sacrifice or ransom, that of a legal
dispute acquires its force from a broader conception of the nature and
purposes of God, and of his relations to creatures, in which the identities
of the "disputants" are set forth.

The second comment is more material. The emphasis upon the centrality of justification gives high profile to the soteriological *pro me.*
Thus, for example, responding to Barth's prioritizing of Christology over
justification, Jüngel argues that it is "precisely the function of the doctrine of justification . . . to convey the being and work of Jesus Christ for
us, to us and with us. It is only when explained by means of that doctrine
that Christology becomes appropriate [*sachgemäß*] Christology at all. It
is *appropriate* Christology when it is the doctrine of justification."[10] Behind that "only" lies a long history of post-Ritschlian Lutheran theology,
and in particular its unease about the way in which the metaphysics of
substance may push theology into abstraction or objectification. According to Jüngel, "The doctrine of justification goes beyond the 'fact' of the
personal unity of Godhead and humanity in the person of Jesus Christ to
make clear the soteriological effectiveness of that unity, an effectiveness
which belongs to the *being* of the God-man."[11] From his early attempts
to make sense of the double legacy of Bultmann and Barth,[12] Jüngel is
undoubtedly alert to the perils that afflict theology when the soteriological *pro me* is expounded primarily as a qualification of Christian existence and only derivatively as a determination of the divine being; this

---

9. Jüngel, *Justification*, p. 48.

10. Jüngel, *Justification*, pp. 28f. (author's italics).

11. Jüngel, *Justification*, p. 30.

12. Notably, of course, in *God's Being Is in Becoming: The Trinitarian Being of God in the
Theology of Karl Barth* (Edinburgh: T. & T. Clark, 2001).

is why he roots soteriological effectiveness in "the *being* of the God-man." He is aware, too, that spelling this out requires trinitarian language: God's righteous relations to creatures in justifying sinners are grounded "in his relation to himself" as Father, Son, and Spirit.[13] Yet the trinitarian theology remains largely economic,[14] and when combined with an inflamed doctrine of justification and a gravitational pull toward anthropology, the effect is some loss of dogmatic proportion in presenting the *mysterium salutis.*

For salvation, and therefore justification, is *mystery.* It can be conceived in its fullness only in relation to its deep ground in the eternal divine counsel, "the mystery of God's will" (Eph. 1:9), which is inseparable from the eternal divine being. This mystery is of course "revealed," that is, enacted and made known in Christ and the Spirit. But its revelation derives its force from the perfection of the being and will of God, which turns to us in self-communicative love and mercy. Soteriology cannot be therefore the *principium* of Christian doctrine. The saving work of God, including his work as the one who justifies sinners, is a central episode in the gospel. The theme of the gospel, however, is the eternal glory of the triune God, a glory that includes (though infinitely exceeds) the glorification of God's creatures. Soteriology may be the leading edge of a theological account of the gospel; but the order of knowing may not so shape the order of being that God's immanent life and glory are relegated to mere background.

From the vantage point of soteriology we are afforded a particular view of the entire range of God's ways with creatures in the history of fellowship. The canonical witnesses articulate this history of fellowship, and above all its central temporal episode in the person and work of the Word made flesh, in varying ways: as the giving of life, as the bearing of punishment, as substitutionary and representative action, as revelation or sacrifice or ransom or liberation, as victory and rule. Among these different articulations of God's saving work, the idiom of justification has an indispensable place for at least four reasons. First, justification is a primary theme in some of the key texts of one of the major New Testament wit-

---

13. Jüngel, *Justification*, p. 82.

14. The differentiation of Father and Son, for example, is expounded in terms of incarnation without reference to paternity and filiation: "The heavenly Father is the Other to the Son who became man, in that he, the eternal Source and Creator of life, sends the Son into the world of sinners" (Jüngel, *Justification*, p. 83).

nesses; an "apostolic" soteriology loses its claim to the title if it diminishes the importance of *dikaiosunē theou*.[15] Second, justification is inseparable from many other themes in the economy of salvation (covenant, sin, law, the death and resurrection of the Son, and God's holiness and the sanctification of the people of God) and so has greater scope than more narrowly focused concepts such as ransom or penal substitution. Third, the idiom of justification lays particular emphasis upon salvation as historical encounter, what Dantine called "die Gott-Mensch Konfrontation."[16] Fourth, justification — especially a radical notion of *iustitia imputata* — is especially suited to convey the anthropological entailments of the sheer gratuity of God's work. Again, as Jüngel puts it, "The *articulus iustificationis* reminds us that God's grace is the fundamental and all-determining dimension of human life."[17]

Yet none of this entails that justification is the *articulus stantis et cadentis ecclesiae*. Confessional polemic — however necessary for the maintenance of the church's fidelity to the gospel — should not be allowed to distort exegetical or dogmatic proportion. Indeed, one of the primary functions of a system of Christian doctrine is to restrain the capacity of a confessional focus upon one particular aspect of Christian teaching from deforming or reducing the scope of the church's apprehension of the gospel as a whole. In the case of the *locus de iustificatione,* this means that dogmatics, as the servant of exegesis, must seek to ensure that this element of soteriological teaching does not either atrophy or grow beyond its limits, but undertakes its task in an orderly account of the mystery of God's sav-

15. Equally, of course, the apostolic gospel is not to be restricted to the Pauline gospel: Johannine themes such as life and light are no less significant in the presentation of the nature of salvation.

16. Wilhelm Dantine, "Krise und Verheissung der Lehre von der Rechtfertigung," in *Recht und Rechtfertigung: Ausgewählte rechtstheologische und kirchenrechtliche Aufsätze* (Tübingen: Mohr, 1982), p. 4; whether Dantine is correct to see this as in competition with "Augustinian ontologism" is an open question.

17. Michael Beintker, "Einleitung: Zugänge zur Rechtfertigungsbotschaft in der heutigen Lebenswelt," in *Rechtfertigung in der neuzeitlichen Lebenswelt: Theologische Erkundungen* (Tübingen: Mohr Siebeck, 1998), p. 4; the rest of Beintker's book examines some primary anthropological themes, such as guilt, freedom, and meaning, in this light. See also Jüngel, *Justification,* pp. 261-77; Wilfried Härle, *Dogmatik* (Berlin: De Gruyter, 1995), pp. 505-10; Oswald Bayer, *Living by Faith: Justification and Sanctification* (Grand Rapids: Eerdmans, 2003); and Oswald Bayer, "The Doctrine of Justification and Ontology," *Neue Zeitschrift für Systematische Theologie und Religionsphilosophie* 43 (2001): 44-53.

ing work. As Barth says, "The problem of justification does not need artificially to be absolutized and given a monopoly."[18]

Consider such statements as the following:

(1) All theological frameworks are subordinate to the doctrine of justification. . . . The doctrine of justification is the basis for theology, since it directs theology's task as giving Jesus Christ as *sacramentum* to those oppressed by the law, living under the divine wrath or being made uncertain by the hidden God. . . . It is the *boundary* of theology in that it sets limits to all attempts to subordinate this activity to any other comprehensive task.[19]

(2) Justification is not to be seen as the foundation for the structure of one's theology. Rather, it is the *discrimen* by which all theological loci are to be evaluated.[20]

(3) In the doctrine of justification there is not handed over to us one doctrine alongside others; rather, there is entrusted to us the "category" which determines all our thought, speech, and action "before God."[21]

(4) Whatever is asserted about God, his essence, his truth, his attributes, his providence, his actions, and his will, must be done in such a way that he appears as the God who summons man to the bar of his court.[22]

(5) Justification "should, like a mathematical term, stand in front of a parenthesis, within which the individual dogmatic *loci* are lined up."[23]

Claims such as these — they are ubiquitous in the literature — accord a transcendental status to the doctrine of justification. Justification is not so much a locus as the *discrimen,* a kind of first theology. (Dantine suggests that its treatment should precede all special theological topics.) What makes them problematic, however, is not the formal place accorded to the

18. Karl Barth, *Church Dogmatics* IV/1, trans. G. W. Bromiley (Edinburgh: T. & T. Clark, 1956), p. 528.

19. Mark C. Mattes, *The Role of Justification in Contemporary Theology* (Grand Rapids: Eerdmans, 2004), p. 5.

20. Mattes, *Role of Justification,* p. 15.

21. Gloege, "Gnade für die Welt," in *Gnade für die Welt,* p. 26.

22. Wilhelm Dantine, *Justification of the Ungodly,* trans. Eric W. Gritsch and Ruth C. Gritsch (St. Louis: Concordia, 1968), p. 130.

23. Dantine, *Justification of the Ungodly,* p. 131.

doctrine of justification but rather its material superordination to all other doctrines, which situates justification in a position that it is not suited to occupy and places upon it demands that it cannot be expected to meet.

The matter can be approached by observing that claims for the transcendental or foundational status of the doctrine of justification commonly make the concession that justification is inseparable from Christology. Gloege, for example, having emphasized the hermeneutical function of justification goes on somewhat bizarrely to admit that, because Jesus Christ is the "Person-Mitte" of Holy Scripture, then "in view of the exclusive place which from the beginning Jesus Christ has within Christianity, the doctrine of justification has no special privilege"; indeed, that doctrine has what he calls "enclitic significance."[24] In effect, therefore, because of the identity between "the message of justification" and "Jesus Christ," the article on justification is a function of the person and work of Christ which is its content. Or again, Beintker's presentation of the doctrine of justification as *casus regens* or matrix of all other teaching is, in fact, a commendation of the status of "Jesus Christ as the event of the love of God made man."[25] "Since in a comprehensive way the theme of the message of justification is the relation of God and humankind, obliging us to see this relation out of the Christ event, the doctrine which interprets the message of justification is not one doctrine *alongside* other doctrines of the Christian faith, but . . . the description of the Archimedean point from which *all* themes of theology and proclamation must be thought";[26] but this is to say that the person of Christ (to which justification points) is *rector et iudex,* not justification itself.

These concessions indicate the impossibility of arranging all Christian teaching around the doctrine of justification. It is simply not possible to maintain the unqualified claim that of itself justification suffices to answer the questions: "Who or what is a really divine God? Who or what is a really human human being?"[27] Such questions can only receive a full theological answer in the course of a trinitarian dogmatics in which the drama of God's fellowship with his creatures is allowed to unfold itself as a matter for thought and praise. In drastically simplified form, a dogmatic treatment of the matter would include the following elements:

---

24. Gloege, "Die Rechtfertigungslehre als hermeneutische Kategorie," p. 42.
25. Beintker, *Rechtfertigung in der neuzeitlichen Lebenswelt*, p. 2.
26. Beintker, *Rechtfertigung in der neuzeitlichen Lebenswelt*, p. 15.
27. Jüngel, *Justification*, p. 3.

(1) The triune God is in himself righteous. His righteousness is, as we have already noted, the peace and order of his perfect self-relation as Father, Son, and Spirit. In this perfect communion God corresponds with himself, that is, perfectly fulfills his own will to be the one he is, and so perfectly enacts the law of his being. His righteousness is the unbroken and fully realized harmony of God's life and his will, in the eternal moments of paternity, filiation, and spiration that constitute his being.

(2) The triune God is righteous in his relations with creatures, willing, establishing, and perfecting righteous fellowship. His perfectly righteous self-relation which stands in need of no repetition or completion but is antecedently full, extends itself as God purposes and calls into being a reality that is an object of his love other than his own being. God wills this object and bestows life upon it. This life is truly given, that is, given in such a way that the creature does indeed have a proper substance and is not merely an extension of or emanation from the being of the creator. The relation of God to the living creature is thus wholly different from the relation of the living God to himself, for the creature is not integral to God's own life, but a recipient, a *made* reality. The creature "has" life, but its life is not *in se* but "in" the divine gift. It is characterized, therefore, by that peculiar condition of creaturely being, namely being in the event of dependent relation, having no being as a term apart from the relation to it of the other term. This does not mean the creature's instability; rather, it is a characterization of the kind of stability that is proper to the creature, that which is had in the course of the creature's relation to God the Father who purposes life, God the Son who enacts and protects the Father's will, and God the Holy Spirit who perfects it as the lordly life-giver. Creaturely life is life in this "order" of being which is the fulfillment of the righteous divine will. That is, creaturely life is not indeterminate or unformed, a kind of raw material handed over to the creature for projects of the creature's devising. It is life in relation, life whose content is fellowship with the righteous God. To be a creature is to have one's being in the divine gift; it is therefore to stand beneath the divine requirement. To live before the righteous God is to be summoned to life in righteous fellowship.

(3) The shape of this righteous fellowship is life under the law or declared will of the triune God. Law is not arbitrary command, but the imperative presence of God, quickening creatures to responsible life in accordance with the nature given to them by the creator; law is not simply statute, but the form of fellowship. The internal righteousness of God is

manifest in his external righteousness *(iustitia externa)*. This external righteousness, grounded in God's nature and in his eternal will to be the one he is, characterizes the dealings that the triune God has with creatures, giving shape to the life that creatures have from, with, and for God. It may be conceptualized as legislative righteousness (righteousness as acts of commanding, *iustitia legislativa*) and judicial righteousness (righteousness as acts of judging, *iustitia iudicalis*). God gives life; but he does not give it away, casting it from himself to take any form that it may choose. God stands in permanent relation to the life he gives; he is not simply its origin but the one who maintains it for the end he establishes for it. This he does as legislator and judge. Of course, these terms quickly run away from us, and we need to be on our guard to ensure that we do not allow even a hair's breadth of distance between them and the identity of the one who here acts as legislator and judge, namely the triune God in his directedness to creatures. Righteousness, command, law, and judgment only make Christian theological sense in direct and immediate relation to this God and the history of fellowship between him and those whom he calls into life. Put formally: *iustitia interna* and *iustitia externa* are both iustitia *Dei;* and the *deus* in question is not mere transcendent cause or magistrate, but the Father, the Son, and the Spirit who are righteous and give and sustain righteous life.

(4) Sin is law-breaking, and so unrighteousness. Law-breaking is a repudiation of the righteous order of fellowship in which alone the creature has life. It is a refusal of the summons of God to fellowship. It is the perversity in which the creature considers it possible to be a creature in a way other than that established by the will of the creator. The one who breaks the law believes himself capable of transcending the law, somehow able to occupy a position outside the order of creaturely being. Law-breaking treats that order as contingent rather than as something given to the creature with absolute authority. But in rejecting the law, the law-breaker rejects God whose righteousness is manifest in his righteous will. Again, in formal scholastic terms: sin rejects the *lex ectypa,* the law that God promulgates as his will for creatures and as the shape for creaturely existence. But thereby sin rejects the *lex archetypa,* God's inner righteousness which is the ground of his dealings with creatures. To reject the law of God is to reject God. To reject God is to destroy life in righteous fellowship with God.

As law-breaking, sin draws punishment on the sinner, exposing him to the punitive righteousness of God in which God asserts the authority and right of his holy purpose. God is the moral governor of those with whom he enters into the fellowship of life. That "moral government" is not remote, merely the application of an abstract standard or distribution of reward or punishment after the manner of an official. God's moral government is the maintenance of his will to fellowship, eradicating unrighteousness so that the creature may indeed have life. God's work as moral governor is an integral part of his purposive work as creator, savior, and consummator, that is, part of the full scope of his covenant acts.

(5) How does God help and guard the creature in the situation of absolute jeopardy that is brought about by spurning the law of life? In what way does God act to restore the creature's righteousness and so reconcile the creature to fellowship with himself? The righteous triune God interposes himself between the creature and its unrighteousness, thereby arresting its self-eradication. This means, first, that the will of the Father before the foundation of the world, the will to righteous fellowship, prevails against the unrighteousness of the creature. The Father's purpose cannot be overthrown by the creature's fall into sin; his will is wholly superior and resistant to any creaturely onslaught. In the matter of the overthrow of unrighteousness, the Father is once again he "who accomplishes all things according to the counsel of his will" (Eph. 1:11). In purposing righteous fellowship with his creature the Father also purposes reconciliation; this purpose is the deep ground of justification.

Second, the creature's restoration to fellowship rests upon the perfect filial relation of the Son to the Father. The eternal relation of Father and Son, in which the Father begets and the Son is eternally generated, is soteriologically indispensable. This is because the divine procession is the inner-divine potency of the Son's temporal mission in which he comes to creatures to restore fellowship and reestablish righteousness. The Son's mission is savingly effective only because its depth is his eternal sonship. Only because the Son is God himself, within the divine *iustitia interna*, is he empowered and authorized to restore the creature to righteousness.

Third, creatures become righteous because the Holy Spirit, who seals their fellowship with the righteous God, is himself Lord. Only because the Spirit, too, shares in the eternal divine righteousness is he able to reincorporate creatures into communion with the Father through the Son. In sum: the justification of creatures, as part of their reconciliation to God, rests upon the entire and equal deity of Father, Son, and Spirit.

(6) The end of the Son's temporal mission is to restore righteous fellowship between God and lost creatures. Reconciliation is effected and righteous relations are restored in his person and work, that is, in what he does as the one he is. The Word became flesh. He took to himself ruined human nature, making its unrighteousness his own, though it was not his own and though it was utterly hostile to him and an object of his abhorrence. He took upon himself the situation of the transgressors, the breakers of the law. In this is his righteousness: that he, the righteous one, sharing in the inner-divine righteousness and administering the divine law and its just commands, takes upon himself the guilt and alienation of the unrighteous creature. His divine righteousness is not in opposition to this assumption of the creature's burden; he does not have to lay aside or negate the *iustitia Dei interna* to come to our aid. Quite the opposite: his taking the part of the unrighteous is the enactment of his righteousness, precisely because in so doing he recreates righteous fellowship. As with God's holiness, so with his righteousness: God's holiness *in se* is made known *ad extra* not in the destruction of creatures but in the fulfillment of his purpose in election by purging the creature of sin and so perfecting a people for himself. God's righteousness *in se* is made known *ad extra* not in delivering the creature over to the penalty of the law but in the supreme act of fellowship, in which he takes the creature's penalty upon himself. In making the creature's just condemnation his own in the person of the Son, he arrests the creature's plunge into nothingness, holding creaturely being in relation to himself. Without ceasing to be the divine Word, without renouncing his deity and so ceasing to be capable of acting as savior, the Son continues the Father's purpose of righteous fellowship, entering into the creature's unrighteous state and appropriating it to himself. The Son's work in this matter is his suffering of the Father's judgment upon sin, in passive obedience. In our place and for our sakes, the righteous judge submits to God's judicial righteousness. He does not do so helplessly, abandoning himself to the Father's judgment as its victim. He does so, rather, as the eternal Son who actively fulfills the Father's will, in relation to which he is not mere object but also subject. In our place and for our sakes, submitting to the Father's will, he affirms and establishes from the creaturely side the righteous order of life. He enacts the relation that creatures are to have to God who gives life and therefore gives the law. In him, therefore, creatures are accounted righteous — that is, the good order of creaturely being in fellowship with God is restored by a person and an action not the creature's own.

This righteousness in Christ, like the original righteousness it secures, is gift, and so always *iustitia aliena*. But its alien character does not mean that it is wholly foreign to the creature, a fictional quantity. The double ontological rule of creaturely being is: what we are, we are *in God;* and what we are in God, *we are.* There is no other manner in which creatures can have their being. Only in this fellowship, only in this history in which God both creates and recreates creaturely life, can the creature be said to be. This is why the "realization" of the soteriological *extra nos* is not brought about by some work of the creature in which righteousness is appropriated or given form by creaturely enactment. Rather, through the Holy Spirit the fellowship that is secured by the Son's submission to and fulfillment of the Father's will becomes that in which the creature also participates. By the Spirit, the creature enters into the history of reconciliation, not as initiator but surely as participant, as one accounted righteous before God. Righteousness — life and activity in fellowship with God — is *iustitia fidei imputata.*

The foregoing is, in effect, a trinitarian gloss on Psalm 11:7: "The LORD is righteous, he loves righteous deeds; the upright shall behold his face." God is *in se* righteous and because he loves righteous deeds, delighting to see the reflection of his own nature and works in those of creatures, he maintains the life of the upright, so that they may enjoy his presence in unashamed fellowship. In his comment on the verse, Calvin catches this double theme of God's internal and external righteousness: "For inasmuch as [God] is righteous, [the psalmist] shows how it is of consequence, that he should love righteousness; for else would he renounce himself. Also it were a cold speculation, to think that righteousness is shut up in God, if it were not also to our minds that he acknowledges whatsoever is his and shows proof thereof in the governance of the world."[28] God is righteous in his perfect harmony with himself, and just in his dealings with creatures. Because he is righteous he makes righteous. God is "righteous for ever" (Ps. 119:142) — righteous to the eternal depths of his being; his righteousness "is like the deep mountains of God" (Ps. 36:6) — immovably established. This righteousness of his prevails in his jurisdiction of all things in the history of the covenant in which the fellowship determined by the Father is effected by the Son and by the Spirit brought to full fruition. God who is

---

28. John Calvin, *A Commentary on the Psalms*, vol. 1, ed. T. H. L. Parker (London: James Clarke, 1965), p. 133.

righteous rules righteously; and so he justifies sinners that they may behold his face.

IV

Much more could and should be said. In particular, the foregoing sketch of the setting of justification in the history of righteous fellowship between the triune God and his creatures would need to be expanded in conversation with a quite different trinitarian model of justification, one that lays emphasis upon the participation of the justified in the triune life or upon theosis.[29] The task would be to show that the covenantal soteriology presupposed in the foregoing is not, as it is sometimes charged to be, an extrinsicist repudiation of the ontological dimensions of God's relation with creatures, or (Ockhamist? Ritschlian?) retraction of the scope of that relation to mere *Tatgemeinschaft*. Rather, it is an attempt to give expression to the ontological entailments of God's justifying work without falling into the trap of making "participation" into the only way of conceiving of the metaphysics of creaturely being in relation to God. If there is a drastically one-dimensional theology of imputed righteousness, there is a no less one-dimensional theology of koinonia, and neither can serve as the exclusive basis for an account of how the righteous God makes creatures righteous. What is required is a metaphysics in which relation to God is conceived neither in terms of a preconceived conception of ontological union, nor in terms of an abstract opposition between divine and creaturely being, but in accordance with the canon's recital of the differentiated fellowship of the perfect triune life-giver and the creatures of his mercy.[30]

Such a task lies beyond the present sketch. We may close by recalling

29. See Jenson, "Justification as Triune Event." Also, see Tuomo Mannermaa, *Christ Present in Faith: Luther's Doctrine of Justification* (Minneapolis: Fortress, 2005); the essays by Mannermaa, Peura, and Juntunen in *Union with Christ: The New Finnish Interpretation of Luther*, ed. Carl Braaten and Robert Jenson (Grand Rapids: Eerdmans, 1998); Risto Saarinen, *Gottes Wirken auf uns: Die transzendentale Deutung des Gegenwart-Christi-Motivs in der Lutherforschung* (Stuttgart: Steiner Verlag, 1989); Wolfhart Pannenberg, *Systematic Theology*, vol. 3 (Grand Rapids: Eerdmans, 1998), pp. 211-39.

30. Some initial moves in this direction are made in Bruce McCormack, "What's at Stake in Current Debates over Justification? The Crisis of Protestantism in the West," in *Justification*, ed. Mark Husbands and Daniel Treier, pp. 81-117.

that at the beginning of the Schmalkald Articles Luther points briefly to "the lofty articles of the divine majesty" — above all, the doctrines of the Trinity and the incarnation — noting, before he passes on to controversial matters, that "these articles are not matters of dispute or conflict."[31] It is the recovery of just these lofty articles that is required for a good ordering of the church's confession about justification: there is nowhere else to begin.

31. In William R. Russell, *Luther's Theological Testament: The Schmalkald Articles* (Minneapolis: Fortress, 1995), p. 121.

3 Justification and Sanctification: Implications for Church Life Today

John P. Burgess

The words justification and sanctification, so central to the Reformation, are no longer familiar to many North American Protestants.[1] They come to church not on the basis of theological principles, but rather out of tradition or mere habit, a longing for community, or a desire to explore their own spirituality. They expect the church first of all to respond to personal needs that they have defined, not to call them into alternative ways of thinking and living authorized from a source beyond them. In such a world, the most pressing question before the church seems to be *the very question of the church:* What is the church, and what does it mean for people to participate in its life?

These ecclesiological questions are inseparable, however, from the theological concerns represented by the church's classic theological vocabulary of justification and sanctification. The historical vitality of the Reformed tradition lies precisely in its ability to articulate what is at stake, in the relationship of justification and sanctification, for the church and its most basic practices. Reformed thinking has emphasized that the church — and therefore true humanity before God — is the creation of God's justifying, sanctifying Word. Humans cannot truly know themselves apart from the church, and the church cannot know itself apart from the saving work of God in Jesus Christ, to which the Scriptures uniquely testify.

I will first trace Reformed perspectives on the relationship of justifica-

---

1. I will be referring in this chapter primarily to the situation in so-called mainline Protestant denominations, which flow out of the central Reformation traditions defined by Luther and Calvin but also include Anglican and Free Church elements.

tion and sanctification, as articulated and developed with particular force by John Calvin, classic Reformed confessions, and Karl Barth. I will then turn to the vital contribution that Reformed theology can make to the integrity of the one holy catholic and apostolic church today, especially in the North American context. Three dimensions of contemporary church life in particular require clarification in light of God's justifying, sanctifying Word: (1) the character of the Christian life, (2) the sacraments, and (3) church discipline, i.e., how the community of faith orders its life together. In the latter area, I will draw particularly on the thinking of Dietrich Bonhoeffer, whose interest in church practices relates him closely to the Reformed tradition, although he himself was Lutheran.

Union with Christ

Justification and sanctification are two dimensions of one divine gift: the mystical union with Christ that the Holy Spirit effects in us through faith.[2] As John Calvin writes:

> Christ was given to us by God's generosity, to be grasped and possessed by us in faith. By partaking of him, we principally receive a double grace: namely, that being reconciled to God through Christ's blamelessness, we may have in heaven instead of a Judge a gracious Father; and secondly, that sanctified by Christ's spirit we may cultivate blamelessness and purity of life.[3]

Justification means, in Calvin's words, that we do not "contemplate [Christ] from outside ourselves from afar in order that his righteousness may be imputed to us but . . . we put on Christ and are engrafted into his body — in short . . . he deigns to make us one with him."[4] Similarly, sanctification is nothing other than union with Christ. Says Calvin, "When we hear mention of our union with God, let us remember that holiness must

---

2. John Calvin, *Institutes of the Christian Religion,* ed. John T. McNeill (Philadelphia: Westminster Press, 1960), 3.11.10, p. 737. For the centrality of union with Christ in Calvin's theology, see Charles Partee, "Calvin's Central Dogma Again," in *Calvin Studies III,* ed. John Leith (Richmond, VA: Union Theological Seminary, 1986), pp. 39-46.

3. Calvin, *Institutes,* 3.11.1, p. 725.

4. Calvin, *Institutes,* 3.11.10, p. 737.

be its bond. . . . [Only if we are] infused with [Christ's] holiness . . . may [we] follow whither he calls."[5] Both justification and sanctification testify to the fact that in Christ, one is no longer one's own but rather belongs to God.

This rich imagery of union with Christ illuminates first of all the character of Christian existence. But, more fundamentally, it also describes the relationship that God has sought *with all humanity* from the beginning of the creation. The gracious Father of our Lord Jesus Christ is the One who has created all people to call him Father. The life of faithful obedience that Christ evidenced on earth is the way of life to which God called Adam and Eve — and, thus, every human being. Union with Christ, and therefore justification and sanctification, marks out a *history* of salvation.

This history of salvation reveals that God has created humans to trust him, and so to know and obey him (i.e., to engage in theological reflection and moral activity). God has created humans to call upon him, to praise him, and to thank him (and, so, to pray without ceasing). In the famous words of the Westminster Shorter Catechism, "Man's chief end is to glorify God, and to enjoy him forever."[6] God has called human beings into intimate relationship with him and has asked them to pledge themselves to him. The One who is nothing less than the Creator of the universe, the ultimate power by which all things and beings have come into existence and are held in existence, is simultaneously the One who is so gracious and good that he calls each person by name and therefore invites us to know him not as brute, impersonal force, but rather as loving personality.

This relationship is *covenantal*. In contrast to a contract, which sets forth legal stipulations, a covenant rests on free promises. The divine covenant is unique in the respect that the freedom of one party (God) precedes and makes possible the freedom of the other (humanity). God's covenantal love, already manifest in his relationship to Adam and Eve, comes to renewed expression in the explicit covenants that God makes with Noah, Abraham, Moses, and David; in the new covenant that God promises to Jeremiah; and in God's ultimate fulfillment of all these covenants in the life and death of Jesus Christ.[7]

---

5. Calvin, *Institutes*, 3.6.2, p. 686.

6. "Westminster Shorter Catechism," q. 1, in *Book of Confessions* (Louisville: Office of the General Assembly of the Presbyterian Church [U.S.A.], 1994), 7.001.

7. The history of Reformed thinking relating to covenant is complex, and some scholars have argued that in certain of its manifestations (for example, among the Westminster

Our life purpose as humans is neither to merge ourselves into God as though he were an anonymous, cosmic life force nor to lay claim to his personal power and might for our own purposes, as though we could rule on his behalf, but rather — in the words of Karl Barth — to be God's *covenant partners*. We are called to correspond to God's loving, gracious character. We are empowered by God's Spirit to witness to who God has been, is, and will be.

Jonathan Edwards, the great American Puritan theologian of the eighteenth century, sketches a similar vision. God, says Edwards, is like an emanation of light, and human beings were created to be mirrors that would reflect God's glory back to him: "In the creature's knowing, esteeming, loving, rejoicing in, and praising God, the glory of God is both *exhibited* and *acknowledged;* his fullness is *received* and *returned*. Here is both an *emanation* and *remanation*. The refulgence shines upon and into the creature, and is reflected back to the luminary."[8]

Sin is nothing less than separation from God and, therefore, from our true selves before God. For reasons that defy explanation, we turn away from God and even against God. We no longer point to God, but rather to ourselves or to other parts of the creation. We no longer reflect God's glory, but rather become self-preoccupied and self-absorbed. Our relationship to God is no longer right, and so we live un-justified lives. We cannot endure the holiness of God, and so we fall into an un-sanctified state of being. As creatures bound by sin, we are not able to make things right again with God or ourselves. We have violated what is most holy about our humanity: what the Christian tradition has called "the image of God." Only God can restore us, and yet we are unwilling and unable to lay claim to God's mercy on which we so desperately depend.

Puritans) covenant thinking obscured the priority of God's grace. See Holmes Ralston III, *John Calvin versus the Westminster Confession* (Richmond, VA: John Knox Press, 1972). Nevertheless, even where Reformed thinkers distinguished an original Covenant of Works from a postlapsarian Covenant of Grace, their ultimate concern was always to establish the complete insufficiency of the former and the liberating power of the latter offered to God's people from the beginning of time. See the masterful review of Puritan covenant theology in Charles Lloyd Cohen, *God's Caress: The Psychology of Puritan Religious Experience* (New York: Oxford University Press, 1986).

8. Jonathan Edwards, "A Dissertation Concerning the End for Which God Created the World," in *The Works of Jonathan Edwards* (Edinburgh: The Banner of Truth Trust, 1974), p. 120.

The mystery of divine grace is that it does not stand as a force of equal or lesser power over and against the mystery of human sin, but rather that it ultimately absorbs sin and renders it impotent. Athanasius' fourth-century treatise *On the Incarnation of the Word* offers a classic statement of the character of the gracious God in the face of human sin. The One who first called us into relationship with him pursues sinful humanity, seeks us out, and makes accommodation to us. In Athanasius' succinct formulation, only the Creator can be the Redeemer. Only the One who initiated relationship with humanity can restore, confirm, and ratify this relationship. God comes to humanity not only in righteous and holy laws and prophets, but ultimately in vulnerable human flesh. God so loves us that he meets us on our own level. He becomes the Good Teacher who redirects our attention to himself and calls us back into filial relationship with him.

For Athanasius, Christ confronts the human predicament even more fully in his death. Athanasius does not attempt so much to explain the atonement as to confess it, to probe its inner logic as to revel in its paradoxes. The God who becomes human flesh dies, and yet this is a death that miraculously conquers death. The One who descends to hell is the One who springs open its gates. The One who is immortal dies like a mortal so that mortals may receive immortality.

Athanasius concludes, "By so ordinary a means things divine have been manifested. . . . [B]y death immortality has been reached to all. . . . For he was made man that we might be made God; and he manifested himself by a body that we might receive the idea of the unseen Father."[9] Reformed theology, while thoroughly Athanasian in its Christology, has been more cautious in its soteriology.[10] Salvation does not mean that we become God. God remains God, and humans remain human. Nevertheless, the Holy Spirit does intimately unite God and humanity in and through Jesus Christ, the risen Lord. We are joined to Christ in his glorified humanity, which is joined to Christ in his divinity: two natures, distinct yet inseparable in one person. Through the life, death, and resurrec-

9. Athanasius, "On the Incarnation of the Word," in *Christology of the Later Fathers*, ed. Edward R. Hardy (Philadelphia: Westminster Press, 1954), p. 107. The notion of divinization (theosis) has been central to Eastern Christianity.

10. For a helpful discussion, see J. Todd Billings, "United to God through Christ: Assessing Calvin on the Question of Deification," *Harvard Theological Review* 98 (Fall 2005): 315-34.

tion of Christ, we are now as close to the Father as the Son is to the Father.[11] Through Christ, we become truly *human* again.

Union with Christ reaches a high point in the Lord's Supper. Calvin dares to assert that in the Supper, Christ's "life passes into us and is made ours."[12] "Christ pours his life into us, as if it penetrated into our bones and marrow."[13] One is "now quickened by his immortal flesh, and in a sense partakes of his immortality."[14] Genesis' language of the intimacy of male and female serves as an analogy for the even deeper and truer intimacy of human relationship with God. So, the Scots Confession proclaims that we "are so made flesh of his flesh and bone of his bone that as the eternal Godhead has given to the flesh of Jesus Christ, which was by nature corruptible and mortal, life and immortality, so the eating and drinking of the flesh and blood of Christ Jesus does the like for us."[15]

Christ therefore is our justification and our sanctification, and he alone. It is only as we are joined to Christ that we again become what God created us to be: a people in right relationship with God — a holy people, even as God is a holy God. Whatever righteousness we have, whatever holiness, is only by virtue of our union with Christ, and this union is possible only by the work of the Holy Spirit and thus by God himself. Both the objective work of Christ and our subjective appropriation of it through the Holy Spirit take place by God's grace alone. Yet, while our justification and sanctification come to us *extra nos*, they are so joined to us that we ourselves are justified and sanctified. Their reality penetrates into our core identity. They now describe who we really are in the eyes of God.

The Paradox of Salvation

The doctrines of justification and sanctification describe the same reality: believers' union, through faith, with the resurrected Christ who rules from

11. For a recent study of the Reformed understanding of the vicarious humanity of Christ that draws on the work of T. F. Torrance, see Chris Kettler, *The God Who Believes: Faith, Doubt, and the Vicarious Humanity of Christ* (Eugene, OR: Wipf & Stock, 2005).

12. Calvin, *Institutes*, 4.17.5, p. 1365.

13. Calvin, *Institutes*, 4.17.10, p. 1370.

14. Calvin, *Institutes*, 4.17.32, p. 1404.

15. "Scots Confession," ch. 21, in *Book of Confessions* (Louisville: Office of the General Assembly of the Presbyterian Church [U.S.A.], 1994), 3.21.

on high. Neither term can substitute for the other, yet neither can be fully understood or explicated without the other. Together, they describe a series of paradoxes that guard the mystery of salvation.

Alasdair Heron notes that "Reformed thought, like Lutheran, could and did see in this crucial and central doctrine [of justification] the *articulus stantis et cadentis ecclesiae*, the article by which the church stands or falls."[16] Yet, as Alister McGrath reminds us, "Calvin is actually concerned not so much with justification, as with incorporation into Christ."[17] Not only justification but also sanctification is a necessary consequence "of the believer's new life in Christ, and just as one receives the whole Christ, and not part of him, through faith, so any separation of these two soteriological elements . . . is inconceivable."[18] As Calvin himself says, "Christ justifies no one whom he does not at the same time sanctify."[19]

Reformed thinking came to define justification primarily in forensic terms. Calvin asserts that, were we to stand by ourselves before the judgment seat of God, we would hear only words of accusation and condemnation, for we are sinners, and "wherever there is sin, there also the wrath and vengeance of God show themselves."[20] But we do not come alone, but rather through Christ, and therefore God pronounces us innocent.

The Reformed doctrine of justification draws on biblical images of remission of sins, acquittal, pardon, absolution, forgiveness, acceptance, and reconciliation.[21] "For the sake of Christ's reconciling work, God will no more remember my sins or the sinfulness with which I have to struggle all my life long" (Heidelberg Catechism).[22] As we come before the judgment seat of God, God no longer sees us, but rather Christ in whose righteousness we are now "clothed" (Calvin).[23] Christ is the Mediator who stands

16. Alasdair Heron, "Justification and Sanctification in the Reformed Tradition," in *Justification and Sanctification in the Traditions of the Reformation,* ed. Milan Opocensky and Paraic Reamonn (Geneva: World Alliance of Reformed Churches, 1999), p. 113.

17. Alister E. McGrath, *Iustitia Dei: A History of the Christian Doctrine of Justification,* 2nd ed. (Cambridge: Cambridge University Press, 1998), p. 225.

18. McGrath, *Iustitia Dei,* p. 224.

19. Calvin, *Institutes,* 3.16.1, p. 798.

20. Jan Rohls, *Reformed Confessions: Theology from Zurich to Barmen,* trans. John Hoffmeyer (Louisville: Westminster/John Knox Press, 1998), p. 120.

21. See Calvin's discussion in *Institutes,* 3.11.3–3.11.4, pp. 727-29.

22. "Heidelberg Catechism," q. 56, in *Book of Confessions* (Louisville: Office of the General Assembly of the Presbyterian Church [U.S.A.], 1994), 4.056.

23. Calvin, *Institutes,* 3.11.2, p. 727.

between us and God. Through Christ's death, God "covers [our sins] over" (French Confession of 1559).[24] Christ's obedience to the Father did "fully discharge the debt of all those that are thus justified, and did make a proper, real, and full satisfaction to his Father's justice in their behalf" (Westminster Confession of Faith).[25]

Especially important has been the image of imputation. Jan Rohls has noted that for the Reformers, in contrast to medieval Catholicism, "it is precisely not the case that justification consists of God infusing sinful human beings with righteousness as a 'habitual' gift of grace, and declaring them righteous on the basis of this qualitative change."[26] "Instead, grace is a quality of divine relational behavior toward human beings as sinners."[27] As Calvin succinctly states, "Justification consists in the remission of sins and the imputation of Christ's righteousness."[28] Similarly, the Second Helvetic Confession says, "God is propitious with respect to our sins and does not impute them to us, but imputes Christ's righteousness to us as our own."[29] The Westminster Confession of Faith adds, "Those whom God effectually calleth, he also freely justifieth: not by infusing righteousness into them, but by pardoning their sins, and by accounting and accepting their persons as righteous; not for anything wrought in them, or done by them, but for Christ's sake alone."[30]

Drawing on Luther, the Reformed tradition has emphasized that faith is wholly passive and wholly God's gift. It is not something that we do, but is rather a posture of receptivity whereby we are able to trust in God's promise of salvation in Christ. As the Westminster Confession puts it, "The grace of faith, whereby the elect are enabled to believe to the saving of their souls, is the work of the Spirit of Christ in their hearts. . . . [T]he principal acts of saving faith are, accepting, receiving, and resting upon Christ alone."[31]

---

24. *The French Confession of 1559* (Louisville: Presbyterian Church [U.S.A.], 1998), p. 10 (ch. 17).

25. "Westminster Confession of Faith," ch. 11, in *Book of Confessions* (Louisville: Office of the General Assembly of the Presbyterian Church [U.S.A.], 1994), 6.070.

26. Rohls, *Reformed Confessions*, p. 126.

27. Rohls, *Reformed Confessions*, p. 120.

28. Calvin, *Institutes*, 3.11.2, p. 727.

29. "Second Helvetic Confession," ch. 15, in *Book of Confessions* (Louisville: Office of the General Assembly of the Presbyterian Church [U.S.A.], 1994), 5.108.

30. "Westminster Confession," ch. 11, *Book of Confessions*, 6.068.

31. "Westminster Confession," ch. 14, *Book of Confessions*, 6.079.

The grammar of sanctification is markedly different:

[the Holy] Spirit infuseth grace, and enableth to the exercise thereof; in
the former [i.e., justification], sin is pardoned; in the other it is subdued;
the one doth equally free all believers from the revenging wrath of God,
and that perfectly in this life, that they may never fall into condemnation; the other is neither equal in all, nor in this life perfect in any, but
growing up to perfection.[32] (Westminster Larger Catechism)

The Reformed doctrine of sanctification draws on biblical images of
repentance, regeneration, and mortification (dying to the old life of sin)
and vivification (rising to the new life in Christ).[33] Whereas God justifies
us instantaneously by declaring us forgiven in Christ, God sanctifies us
slowly and over a lifetime, as he renews and recreates us in the image of
Christ.[34] Says Calvin,

Indeed, this restoration does not take place in one moment or one day
or one year; but through continual and sometimes even slow advances
God wipes out in his elect the corruptions of the flesh, cleanses them of
guilt, consecrates them to himself as temples renewing all their minds to
true purity that they may practice repentance throughout their lives and
know that this warfare will only end at death.... God assigns to [believ-
ers] a race of repentance, which they are to run throughout their lives.[35]

Justification, as we have noted, is conveyed to us by a trusting, receiving faith. Sanctification too rests on faith, but insofar as faith stirs up good
works in us and makes us active participants in salvation. In the words of
the French Confession of 1559, "Faith does not cool our desire for good
and holy living, but rather engenders and excites it in us, leading naturally
to good works."[36] Similarly, the Second Helvetic Confession emphasizes
that faith "keeps us in the service we owe to God and our neighbor ... and

---

32. "Westminster Larger Catechism," q. 77, in *Book of Confessions* (Louisville: Office of
the General Assembly of the Presbyterian Church [U.S.A.], 1994), 7.187.

33. See Calvin's discussion in Book 3, Chapter 3, of the *Institutes.*

34. "Heidelberg Catechism," q. 86, *Book of Confessions,* 4.086. Calvin notes that this renewal in the image of Christ is also restoration "to the image of God that had been disfig-
ured and all but obliterated through Adam's transgression." See *Institutes,* 3.3.9, p. 601.

35. Calvin, *Institutes,* 3.3.9, pp. 601-2.

36. *French Confession,* p. 12 (ch. 22).

in a word, brings forth good fruit of all kinds, and good works."[37] It is true that sanctification no less than justification depends on God's energizing, guiding Spirit. Nevertheless, we *ourselves* truly grow in holiness through these works, however unevenly.

Contrasted with each other, justification and sanctification pose a series of paradoxes. We have been freed from the power of sin, yet we are still battling it. We are fully united to Christ, yet we are still growing into life in him. We are God's saints, yet our behavior is not yet saintly![38] We are saved by faith, not works, yet there is no faith without works. Rather than simply asserting these paradoxes, however, the Reformed tradition has tried to bring precision to how justification and sanctification interrelate. What is paradoxical must not become confusing, if we are to clarify how justification and sanctification have practical implications for Christian faith and life.

Justification, Sanctification, and the Grace to Confess Our Sins

The Reformers agreed that all of our works fall desperately short of the perfection to which God has called us. Yet, rightly related to sanctification, justification does not paralyze us, but rather frees us to serve God and others. As Charles Cohen has written in relation to Puritan piety, "A person who trusts in God admits weakness and gains strength, asks less of oneself and accomplishes more."[39] Sin no longer controls us, when we are able freely to *confess* it in the assurance that God forgives it.

Justification is more than a momentary declaration that loses its validity as soon as we turn away from God again. To be justified is not to be like a criminal who has been set free only to commit new crimes and be locked up again. Rather, justification extends over our lifetime. It is a reality that has been accomplished once and for all in Christ, yet one that we constantly appropriate anew.

Reformed theologians of the sixteenth and seventeenth centuries, like Luther, believed that medieval Catholicism and then the Council of Trent

37. "Second Helvetic Confession," ch. 16, *Book of Confessions*, 5.114.

38. Note the similar paradox in 1 Corinthians. Paul calls the Corinthians saints (1:2), yet proceeds to upbraid them for their scandalous behavior. So, too, they come together as a church, yet there are divisions among them (11:18).

39. Cohen, *God's Caress*, p. 72.

had failed to grasp the human condition as illuminated by Scripture. Trent declared that baptism truly washed away a person's sin. Although inclination to sin (concupiscence) remained, it could not properly be considered sin. A baptized person really had the ability, with the help of prayer and participation in the sacramental life of the church, to resist this sinful inclination. Even if a baptized person did fall into sin, he or she could return to the innocence of the baptismal state by making use of the sacrament of penance.[40] Trent rejected the Protestant view of justification as imputation. Rather, a baptized person has been *infused* with Christ's righteousness and has therefore become truly righteous.[41] In Jan Rohls's words about Trent, "We not only *are counted* as righteous, but *are* righteous."[42] As the Council itself declared:

> In those who are born again God hates nothing, because *there is no condemnation to those who are* truly *buried with Christ by baptism unto death, who walk not according to the flesh,* but putting off the old man and putting on the new one who is created according to God, are made innocent, immaculate, pure, guiltless, and beloved of God . . . so that there is nothing whatever to hinder their entrance into heaven.[43]

For Trent, Christ's faith, hope, and charity so inhered in the justified person that he or she was now able to do good works. Such a person could obey the commandments and even do good works beyond those required by the commandments (i.e., works of supererogation). All of these works increased a person's justification and ultimately merited God's reward of grace and eternal life.[44]

Reformed theologians, by contrast, maintained that the continuing inclination to sin meant that sin itself remained active within the redeemed. Reformed interpreters typically took Paul's anguished cry in Romans 7 to reflect his condition not prior to, but rather after his conversion:

> I do not do the good I want, but the evil I do not want is what I do. . . . For I delight in the law of God in my inmost self, but I see in my mem-

---

40. "Decrees of the Council of Trent," in *Creeds of the Church,* 3rd ed., ed. John Leith (Atlanta: John Knox Press, 1983), pp. 407, 417.

41. "Decrees of the Council of Trent," pp. 412, 419.

42. Rohls, *Reformed Confessions,* p. 126.

43. "Decrees of the Council of Trent," p. 407.

44. "Decrees of the Council of Trent," p. 424.

bers another law at war with the law of my mind, making me captive to the law of sin that dwells in my members. Wretched man that I am! Who will rescue me from this body of death? (vv. 19, 23-24, NRSV)

Paul's lament was that of every believer. The life of faith did not save the believer from trial and temptation; on the contrary, it intensified his or her experience of them. A person was now more aware than ever of sin's continuing presence, even as he or she struggled against it. In the words of the Scots Confession, "other men do not share this conflict since they do not have God's Spirit, but they readily follow and obey sin and feel no regrets. . . . But the sons of God fight against sin; [and] sob and mourn when they find themselves tempted to do evil."[45] From a Reformation perspective, the Catholic teaching on baptismal grace could only result in self-deception, the sinful pretense that one could be sinless.

The Catholic misunderstanding of sin also meant a failure to grasp the meaning of justification and sanctification. The believer's attention was diverted away from God toward the sinful self. Believers no longer lived by grace alone. Trent agreed with the Reformers that believers could ultimately achieve nothing on their own. Their efforts mattered only because God's grace had healed the will and redirected it. But Trent argued that the believer cooperated with God's grace in such a way as to be able to resist sin, whereas Reformed theologians insisted that the believer's works, even though contributing to his or her sanctification, nevertheless remained "imperfect and defiled in the sight of God."[46]

Reformed theologians were convinced, moreover, that the Catholic view not only took the believer's focus off of God's grace, but also led the believer in the end to despair of his or her salvation. For as hard as one tried, one sooner or later would sin again, and then one's conscience would accuse one of failure. Trent itself had emphasized that believers could fall from a state of grace:

---

45. "Scots Confession," ch. 13, *Book of Confessions*, 3.13.

46. "Westminster Larger Catechism," q. 78, *Book of Confessions*, 7.188. Also, see "Heidelberg Catechism," q. 62, *Book of Confessions*, 4.062. "The Confession of 1967" notes that "all men, good and bad alike, are in the wrong before God and helpless without his forgiveness. . . . No one is more subject to that judgment than the man who assumes that he is guiltless before God or morally superior to others." See "The Confession of 1967," in *Book of Confessions* (Louisville: Office of the General Assembly of the Presbyterian Church [U.S.A.], 1994), 9.13.

Let those who think themselves to stand, take heed lest they fall, and with fear and trembling work out their salvation, in labors, in watchings, in almsdeeds, in prayer, in fasting and chastity. For knowing that they are born again unto the hope of glory, and not as yet unto glory, they ought to fear for the combat that yet remains with the flesh, with the world and with the devil.[47]

By contrast, Reformed theologians insisted that the doctrine of justification, rightly understood, provided believers with firm assurance about their eternal destiny. Paradoxically, a heightened awareness of the continuing reality of sin called forth an equally powerful awareness of one's justification. However much sin might continue to accuse believers, they could take comfort in the fact that they had been pardoned once and for all in Christ. Calvin notes that, "because the godly, encompassed with mortal flesh, are still sinners, and their good works are as yet incomplete and redolent of the vices of the flesh, [God] can be propitious neither to the former nor to the latter unless he embrace them in Christ rather than in themselves."[48]

To live by justifying grace alone is, ultimately, to adopt a posture of continual confession of sin and repentance before the holy God. Christians are not necessarily better than non-Christians, and Christian efforts to do the good never escape the taint of sin. What marks Christians as a distinctive people is not a higher degree of moral perfection, but rather a constant awareness of their utter dependence on God's forgiveness.[49] Calvin finds great significance in the fact that the Apostles' Creed places "the forgiveness of sins" immediately after "the holy catholic church, the communion of saints," for "carrying, as we do, the traces of sin around with us throughout life, unless we are sustained by the Lord's constant grace in forgiving our sins, we shall scarcely abide one moment in the church."[50]

---

47. "Decrees of the Council of Trent," p. 416.

48. Calvin, *Institutes,* 3.17.5, p. 807.

49. Also, note Calvin's great emphasis on the imperfect holiness of the church: "The church is holy, then, in the sense that it is daily advancing and is not yet perfect: it makes progress from day to day but has not yet reached its goal of holiness." See *Institutes,* 4.1.17, p. 1031. For a twentieth-century American theologian who explored what awareness of sin means for Christian involvement in ethics and politics, see Reinhold Niebuhr, *The Nature and Destiny of Man,* vol. 2 (New York: Charles Scribner's Sons, 1947), pp. 244-86.

50. Calvin, *Institutes,* 4.1.21, p. 1035.

Justification impels confession of sin and the honest acknowledgment that our sanctification is never complete.[51]

Justification, Sanctification, and the Grace to Do Good

To grasp the meaning of justification, however, means not only to engage in honest self-examination, but also to do genuinely *good* works (sanctification). Calvin notes that "all the apostles are full of exhortations, urgings, and reproofs with which to instruct the man of God in every good work . . . [and] they derive their most powerful exhortations from the thought that our salvation stands upon no merit of ours but solely upon God's mercy."[52] What God has done for us in Jesus Christ teaches us who we really are. Because our baptismal identity is now our true identity, we are able to act in ways that conform to Christ.

After the Reformation, Lutherans sometimes accused the Reformed of sneaking works righteousness back into the economy of salvation, but Calvin's position was really no different from Luther's: Both called for the "outer person" to be conformed to the "inner person."[53] If our identity is now in Christ, we can truly be ourselves only insofar as we walk in the way of Christ. God's command does not coerce us into external conformity, while leaving our heart and motivations untouched. On the contrary, to live in Christ is to be radically reoriented from the inside out. In the words again of Puritan Jonathan Edwards, "The Spirit of God is given to the true saints to dwell in them, as his proper lasting abode; and to influence their hearts, as a principle of new nature, or as a divine supernatural spring of life and action."[54] Ed-

---

51. The Reformed emphasis on the liberating power of confession of sin has been reflected liturgically. The Confiteor of the Roman Catholic mass — the secret prayer of the priest for his purification — became in Calvin's liturgy a general confession of sin. What had been a clerical act now belonged to the people — and their own confession of sin, once reserved for the confessional box, now had its place here, in Lord's Day worship. What had happened erratically, as infrequently as once a year, became weekly. Furthermore, Calvin's words of absolution were no longer a sacramental act controlled by the church, but rather a public proclamation of God's justifying mercy freely given in Jesus Christ. See Bard Thompson, *Liturgies of the Western Church* (Philadelphia: Fortress, 1961), pp. 190-91.

52. Calvin, *Institutes*, 3.16.3, p. 800.

53. Martin Luther, "The Freedom of a Christian," in *Martin Luther: Selections from His Writings*, ed. John Dillenberger (Garden City, NY: Anchor Books, 1961), pp. 42-85.

54. Jonathan Edwards, "A Treatise on Religious Affections," in *A Jonathan Edwards*

wards speaks of these deep-seated, regenerated springs of action as "holy affections" that find their most vigorous expression in Christian life and practice.[55]

What the Reformed tradition did emphasize (sometimes more strongly than the Lutheran) was that these affections require disciplining and training. They must be exercised and strengthened. Growth in holiness does not come automatically. We can affirm who we are in Christ only as we learn also to resist worldly identities that would claim our ultimate loyalty.[56] Says Edwards, "Godliness is more easily feigned in words than in actions. Christian practice is a costly laborious thing."[57] We will have to work at being who we really are in Christ — and, yet, as Dietrich Bonhoeffer would add two centuries later, "because of our community with [Christ], the yoke of our cross is easy and light."[58]

The Reformed tradition has typically identified two guides to Christian life and practice. The first has been the Ten Commandments, especially as reinterpreted by Christ in the Sermon on the Mount. Here the commandments are understood not as a narrow moral checklist, but rather as a set of broad ethical trajectories. Their spirit is not primarily legalistic and regulatory. Rather, they lay out the way of life that Christ embodies and makes possible for his followers.[59] The commandments of the

---

Reader, ed. John E. Smith, Harry S. Stout, and Kenneth P. Minkema (New Haven: Yale University Press, 1995), p. 157. Prominent nineteenth-century American Reformed theologian Charles Hodge similarly asserted that regeneration involves "the infusion of a new principle of life" in the believer. See Charles Hodge, *Systematic Theology,* vol. 3 (New York: Scribner, Armstrong, & Co., 1874), p. 221.

55. Edwards, "Treatise on Religious Affections," pp. 144-45, 164.

56. Twentieth-century American theologian H. Richard Niebuhr profoundly developed this theme in *Radical Monotheism and Western Culture* (New York: Harper & Row, 1960).

57. Edwards, "Treatise on Religious Affections," p. 168.

58. Dietrich Bonhoeffer, *Discipleship,* trans. Barbara Green and Reinhard Krauss (Minneapolis: Fortress, 2001), p. 208.

59. Like the doctrine of justification, the doctrine of sanctification found liturgical expression. Calvin adopted from Martin Bucer the practice of sometimes placing a recitation of the Ten Commandments immediately after the assurance of pardon. The commandments call a forgiven, justified people to joyful obedience. While retaining a note of accusation, the commandments remind God's people that they can do nothing faithful except by God's grace. The law spurs us not only to make confession of sin, but also to do the good that we really can, as *justified* sinners. The commandments are the identity badge that we wear as a redeemed people. Justification undergirds and impels sanctification. See Thomp-

Second Table are therefore as much positive motivation as negative prohibition. Each "thou shalt not" implies a "thou shalt." "Do not kill" means "respect your neighbor's life." "Do not commit adultery" calls us to practice integrity in marriage and all relationships. "Do not steal" asks us to work for our neighbor's well-being.[60] In sum, in the words of the Second Helvetic Confession, "In [the commandments] is delivered to us the patterns of virtues and vices."[61]

The second means of exercising and strengthening Christian life and practice is the gospel ethic, realized most fully in the life and death of Jesus Christ. As his followers, we are to become living sacrifices and to renounce whatever would separate us from God.[62] In Calvin's famous words, "We are God's: let us therefore live for him and die for him. We are God's: let his wisdom and will therefore rule all our actions. We are God's: let all the parts of our life accordingly strive toward him as our only lawful goal."[63]

---

son, *Liturgies*, p. 191. Note that Bonhoeffer interprets the Sermon on the Mount in a similar way: "'You *are* the salt' — not 'you should be the salt'! The disciples are given no choice whether they want to be salt or not. No appeal is made to them to become salt of the earth. Rather they are just salt, whether they want to be or not, by the power of the call which has reached them. . . . All those who follow Jesus' call to discipleship are made by that call to be the salt of the earth in their whole existence." *Discipleship*, pp. 111-12.

60. The Westminster Larger Catechism even lists these positive duties prior to the negative prohibitions, as if to remind us that the commandments are first of all about the way of life into which Christ calls us, rather than about combating sin. See qq. 103-48, *Book of Confessions*, 7.213–7.258. Also, see Barth's notion that the commandment of God is permission, in *Church Dogmatics* II/2, ed. G. W. Bromiley and T. F. Torrance (Edinburgh: T. & T. Clark, 1957), pp. 592-93. For contemporary Reformed interpretations of key commandments, see John P. Burgess, *After Baptism: Shaping the Christian Life* (Louisville: Westminster/John Knox Press, 2005); and David Willis, *Notes on the Holiness of God* (Grand Rapids: Eerdmans, 2002).

61. "Second Helvetic Confession," ch. 12, *Book of Confessions*, 5.085. It is well known that Calvin places particular emphasis on the "third use of the law," i.e., its role in spurring and guiding the believer in his sanctification. The first use of the law is to accuse us of sin (Luther's principal emphasis); the second, as the foundation for civil law. See *Institutes*, 2.7.6–2.7.12, pp. 354-61.

62. Calvin notes, "The law of God contains in itself that newness by which [God's] image can be restored in us. But . . . our slowness needs many goads and helps" (*Institutes*, 3.6.1, p. 684). Thus, "to awaken us more effectively, Scripture shows that God the Father, as he has reconciled us to himself in his Christ, has in him stamped for us the likeness to which he could have us conform" (*Institutes*, 3.6.3, p. 686).

63. Calvin, *Institutes*, 3.7.1, p. 690. In treating the doctrine of the Christian life, the Reformed tradition as a whole has never given the Beatitudes the same kind of systematic ex-

Casting off all snares of self-love, we should devote ourselves to the well-being of others.

This ethic of self-giving love comes to fullest expression for Calvin in what he calls "bearing the cross," i.e., the particular difficulties and evils that life has given each of us. God, says Calvin, "has destined all his children to the end that they be conformed to Christ. Hence also in harsh and difficult circumstances, regarded as adverse and evil, a great comfort comes to us: we share Christ's sufferings in order that as he has passed . . . into heavenly glory, we may in like manner be led . . . to the same glory."[64]

Both God's law (which nevertheless releases us into grateful service) and God's grace (which nevertheless lays claim to every part of our lives) measure out our lives.[65] We then find that we never achieve the fullness of life that Christ has offered us. But God's law and God's grace do not simply accuse us, they also guide us. They give shape to the gratitude that we offer up to God, now that "we are redeemed from our sin and its wretched consequences by grace through Christ without any merit of our own" (Heidelberg Catechism).[66] They teach us that whatever good we are privileged to do is not of our own making but of God's, and is reason not for pride in self but rather for joyful praise.

Calvin assures us that because we are justified, "our services will be approved by our most merciful Father, however small, rude, and imperfect these may be," just as human parents delight in their children's "childish" efforts to imitate them.[67] Barth makes a similar point:

> The very same command which refers [man] to God's free grace, and therefore humbles him, constantly restores and renews him against all frivolity, laziness and resignation, continually directing him to the aims which are within the limits of his will and are therefore attainable. . . . Thus even where man does not keep the command, the command keeps

---

plication as the Ten Commandments. See B. A. Gerrish, "The French Confession: An Introduction," in *The French Confession of 1559* (Louisville: Presbyterian Church [U.S.A.], 1998), p. 26. Dietrich Bonhoeffer, however, suggests the rich possibilities of the Beatitudes for guiding the Christian life, in *Discipleship*, pp. 100-110.

64. Calvin, *Institutes*, 3.8.1, p. 702.

65. See "The Theological Declaration of Barmen," art. 2, in *Book of Confessions* (Louisville: Office of the General Assembly of the Presbyterian Church [U.S.A.], 1994), 8.14. *Book of Confessions*, 8.14.

66. "Heidelberg Catechism," q. 86, *Book of Confessions*, 4.086.

67. Calvin, *Institutes*, 3.19.5, p. 837.

man. And the fact that it does so, and does so more powerfully than man himself is willing to admit, is from this final standpoint the freedom and righteousness of man.[68]

Justification in Jesus Christ calls us into nothing less than the freedom of the children of God, who do the good that they can within their limitations, and who do it with thanksgiving.

Dangers in Relating Justification and Sanctification

In his *Church Dogmatics* IV/2, Barth offers a brilliant discussion of three ways historically in which justification and sanctification have been wrongly related so as to obscure the gospel message of salvation. In the first case, the Reformed tradition itself has created problems. During the period known as Protestant Orthodoxy, Reformed theologians attempted a more systematic articulation of the faith than Calvin himself had dared. Justification and sanctification became two steps in a larger *ordo salutis,* "preceded by a *vocatio* and *illuminatio,* and followed by the separate processes of *regeneratio* and *conversio.*"[69] The human subject was thought to appropriate God's grace in different stages. Barth critically notes the implications of this position:

> [If appropriation of salvation] consists in a series of different steps, how can it better be made apprehensible than as a series of spiritual awakenings and movements and actions and states of a religious and moral type? The greater and more explicit the emphasis on the *ordo salutis* understood in this way — and this was the tendency in the 17th century — . . . the nearer drew the time . . . in which a religious and moral psychology would take over the leadership and suppress theology.[70]

68. Barth, *Church Dogmatics* III/4, ed. G. W. Bromiley and T. F. Torrance (Edinburgh: T. & T. Clark, 1961), pp. 239-40.

69. Karl Barth, *Church Dogmatics* IV/2, ed. G. W. Bromiley and T. F. Torrance (Edinburgh: T. & T. Clark, 1958), p. 502. The Westminster Standards, for example, discuss salvation according to the following order: effectual calling, justification, adoption, sanctification, and repentance unto life. See "Westminster Confession of Faith," chs. 10-15, *Book of Confessions,* 6.064–6.086; and "Westminster Larger Catechism," qq. 67-76, *Book of Confessions,* 7.177–7.186.

70. Barth, *Church Dogmatics* IV/2, p. 502.

When justification and sanctification are placed in temporal sequence, justification becomes "call" or "gift," followed by sanctification as "response" or "task." Seemingly, then, only when we become aware of how God has acted to save us in Jesus Christ will we be inspired to respond in thankful service and obedience. Justification thus becomes preparation for sanctification; what God has done for us is now complemented by what we resolve to do for God. Barth, however, warns us against focusing on ourselves and our state of mind, rather than on God's continuing work in Jesus Christ through the Holy Spirit *extra nos.*

The second danger has been associated historically with Roman Catholicism and especially the Council of Trent: Justification is collapsed into sanctification. Barth again raises critical questions: "In all the thinking along these lines about the justifiable emphasis on the existential relevance of the atonement, where is the regard for the God who accomplishes it, the bowing before the freedom of His grace, the adoration of the mystery in which He really says an unmerited No to sinful man, the joy of pure gratitude for this benefit?"[71]

Emphasis on sanctification at the expense of justification threatens to make the Christian life little more than moral or ritual activism. Christians easily become obsessed with measuring their progress in faith, and as a result fail to live in the freedom of the gospel. The Christian life becomes a matter of regulation, rather than joyful witness. The church's focus falls on manuals of behavior, rather than on truths of the gospel. The temptation to believe in human perfectibility looms large, diverting our focus from the perfection of God already shared freely and abundantly with us through Christ's death and resurrection.

The third danger is a collapsing of sanctification into justification, a tendency that has manifested itself historically in some strands of Lutheranism. According to Barth, what begins as a legitimate concern to exclude any form of human self-justification ultimately leads to an exaggerated

> *theologia crucis* and the doctrine of justification. In this monism the necessity of good works may be maintained only lethargically and spasmodically, with little place for anything more than indefinite talk about a life of forgiveness, or comforted despair, or Christian freedom, or the

71. Barth, *Church Dogmatics* IV/2, p. 504.

love active in faith. If we do not give any independent significance to the problem of sanctification, do we not necessarily obscure in a very suspicious way the existential reach of the atonement, the simple fact that justification always has to do with man and his action, and that faith in it, even though it is a work of the Holy Spirit, is still a decision of man?[72]

In well-known words to which Barth refers, Bonhoeffer offers a description of the problem of justification without sanctification: "Cheap grace means justification of sin but not of the sinner. Because grace alone does everything, everything can stay in its old ways. . . . The world remains world and we remain sinners. . . . In all things the Christian should go along with the world and not venture . . . to live a different life under grace from that under sin!"[73]

In Barth's view, all three failures rightly to relate justification and sanctification have the effect of focusing us on the sinful self that stands alone, apart from God, and divert us from Jesus Christ. These dangers are especially acute in three areas of North American church life today: the character of the Christian life, the sacraments, and church discipline.

The Christian Life

In recent years, North American Protestants have intensely debated the character of the Christian life as they have become more aware of Protestantism's cultural disestablishment. For generations, the Christian way of life seemed to correspond with good citizenship in an American commonwealth thought to be especially blessed by the Christian God. But as North American society has become more diverse religiously and culturally, Reformation Christians have increasingly sensed that America and Christianity are not synonymous terms.

Efforts to reorient the Christian life in such circumstances face the three temptations that Barth describes. First, North American Protestantism sometimes succumbs to making justification and sanctification stages of a psychological process. Believers become excessively concerned to establish certainty of their salvation through examination of their feelings.

72. Barth, *Church Dogmatics* IV/2, p. 504.
73. Bonhoeffer, *Discipleship*, pp. 43-44. For Barth's reference to Bonhoeffer, see *Church Dogmatics* IV/2, p. 505.

Salvation is reduced to an experience of inner peace or healing ("justification") that should provide a person psychological strength to live rightly in a stressful world of independent, competing egos ("sanctification").[74]

Ironically, Calvin himself opened up this line of thought when he wrote that believers' works, though never grounds for justification, comfort them, since they regard "the fruits of regeneration as proof of the indwelling of the Holy Spirit."[75] Reformed confessions developed this point further, as when the Heidelberg Catechism asserted that good works are means not only by which we express gratitude to God for our salvation, but also by which "we ourselves may be assured of our faith."[76] The Reformed tradition came to speak of the syllogismus practicus: "I know that believers inevitably bring forth good works, and I can see that I do good works, *therefore* I can conclude that I am among the elect."[77]

Max Weber famously argued that this Reformed logic promoted the rise of capitalism in the West (as contrasted to other parts of the world), and especially in Protestant (as contrasted to Catholic) Europe. The syllogismus practicus resulted in a worldly asceticism. Believers lived not for themselves, but rather for their good works. Living frugally, they reinvested their wealth in their worldly enterprises. Subsequent studies have challenged Weber's thesis at several points, but of continuing interest is his attention to the psychological dimension of Reformed faith. Weber helpfully suggests the question: Was the Reformed way driven by thankful obedience or by anxious insecurity about one's salvation?[78]

Among the Puritans, examination of one's works in order to establish the certainty of one's salvation sometimes became a psychological obsession. Believers kept daily journals charting their progress in the Christian life. Church elders examined parishioners for evidence of a saving faith prior to admitting them to communion. The syllogismus practicus seemed

74. For a critique of the therapeutic emphasis of much of North American Protestantism, see David F. Wells, *No Place for Truth; or, Whatever Happened to Evangelical Theology?* (Grand Rapids: Eerdmans, 1993).

75. Calvin, *Institutes*, 3.14.19, p. 786.

76. "Heidelberg Catechism," q. 86, *Book of Confessions*, 4.086.

77. See the discussion in Rohls, *Reformed Confessions*, p. 135.

78. See Max Weber, *The Protestant Ethic and the Spirit of Capitalism*, trans. Talcott Parsons (London: George Allen & Unwin, 1930). For one critique of Weber that emphasizes the Puritans' self-certainty rather than their anxiety, see Michael Walzer, *The Revolution of the Saints* (Cambridge, MA: Harvard University Press, 1965), pp. 300-320.

inevitably to direct attention away from God and his mercy to individuals and their anxious efforts to attain certainty about their salvation. Calvin's deep concern to secure the believer's assurance by God's grace alone began to be undermined by concerns about whether one's works as a believer were indeed good enough.

The syllogismus practicus remains a huge temptation in North American Protestantism today, although it takes less the form of anxiety about one's works than anxiety about one's psychological state. When faith is equated with feelings of inner peace, then their absence becomes grounds for doubting one's salvation. Conversely, the psychologizing of faith leads people to try to relieve their anxiety by creating the right kind of religious experience through music, by adhering to simplistic slogans, or by submitting to a charismatic leader. This "justification" should enable one's "sanctification," i.e., confident living of the Christian life. In contrast, the Reformed tradition at its best has insisted that salvation is first of all an ontological reality in Christ, not a psychological experience in the individual.

The second danger that Barth identifies, the collapsing of justification into sanctification, also has deleterious consequences for the Christian life: an excessive emphasis on techniques for spiritual success. Even though one rarely hears North American Protestants use the language of "merit," the semi-Pelagianism of the Council of Trent manifests itself in new forms in what sociologist Robert Bellah calls "utilitarian individualism."[79] The religion of many North American Protestants is actually that of Deist and Founding Father Benjamin Franklin, who once quipped that "God helps those who help themselves."

The widespread popularity of Christian self-help books and self-help groups reflects many people's concern to improve their "spiritual performance." Activities such as prayer and Bible study are pursued not only for the glory of God, but also for their supposed (again, especially psychological) benefits to the individual.[80] At its best, the Reformed tradition again offers a striking counter-message. In the words of the Second Helvetic Confession, "Whatever reward we receive is also grace, and is more grace than

79. Robert N. Bellah, Richard Madsen, William M. Sullivan, Ann Swidler, and Steven M. Tipton, *Habits of the Heart: Individualism and Commitment in American Life* (New York: Harper & Row, 1985).

80. For a good study of this aspect of North American Protestantism, see sociologist Robert Wuthnow, *The Restructuring of American Religion: Society and Faith since World War II* (Princeton: Princeton University Press, 1988).

reward, because the good we do, we do more through God than through ourselves."[81]

The third danger, the collapsing of sanctification into justification, manifests itself in new versions of Bonhoeffer's "cheap grace." Proclamation of forgiveness of sins easily becomes a therapeutic affirmation of the self, rather than "God's mighty claim upon our whole life."[82] In such a world, the church simply echoes the popular psychological language of the wider culture. People are to be accepted and affirmed for who they are, no questions asked. Although some contemporary North American theologians have declared the demise of Western "Christendom," a culturally accommodated Christianity is still all too present.[83]

In addition, many North American Protestants equate faith with a social, political agenda, whether in the guise of the Religious Right or "progressive Christianity." They associate themselves with churches that do not challenge and reorder their previous ideological loyalties but rather confirm them. Protestant churches in North America desperately need to capture a vision of the liberating obedience that Barth sets forth, in contrast to ways of life beholden primarily to American cultural values.[84]

The Sacraments

Faithful ordering of the sacraments is a second controversial area within contemporary North American Protestant church life. The Reformation practice of baptizing infants has become increasingly problematic.[85] Too often it has become little more than a private ceremony perceived somehow to guard the child from evil, or merely a community welcoming ritual

---

81. "Second Helvetic Confession," ch. 16, *Book of Confession*, 5.123.

82. "Theological Declaration of Barmen," art. 2, *Book of Confessions*, 8.14.

83. Among the most trenchant critics of the North American church's cultural establishment is Stanley Hauerwas. See Stanley Hauerwas and William H. Willimon, *Resident Aliens* (Nashville: Abingdon, 1989). Also, see Douglas John Hall, *The Future of the Church: Where Are We Headed?* (Toronto: The United Church Publishing House, 1989).

84. Note, for example, the Barmen Declaration's call for "joyful deliverance from the godless fetters of this world for a free, grateful service to [God's] creatures." See "Theological Declaration of Barmen," art. 2, *Book of Confessions*, 8.14.

85. For helpful reflections, see Ronald P. Byars, "Indiscriminate Baptism and Baptismal Integrity," *Reformed Liturgy and Music* 31 (1997): 36-40.

indistinguishable from the child dedication ceremonies that Baptist and Free churches practice. Central questions have also arisen about the eucharist. In some churches, music and preaching play such a dominating role that the eucharist is nothing more than an occasional add-on. In other cases, the eucharist functions primarily as a moment for quiet personal introspection, or alternatively as a community-building event of hospitality and mutual affirmation.[86]

Confusion about the sacraments reflects confusion about the proper relationship of justification and sanctification. Calvin and the classic Reformed tradition were careful to demonstrate that *both* sacraments set forth the meaning of *both* justification and sanctification. Baptism does not set forth justification as a first moment in a person's life, followed by his or her participation in eucharistic celebrations that set forth sanctification as a second moment. Nor should one sacrament be understood as emphasizing either justification or sanctification at the expense of the other. Both baptism and the Lord's Supper have aspects of *both* justification (and thus forgiveness) *and* sanctification (and therefore growth in holiness). Both sacraments declare us forgiven, and both spur us to grow more fully into the image of Christ.

The sacraments, like the Christian life, are subject to distortion whenever Christians lose the essential connection between justification and sanctification. When justification and sanctification become two stages of a psychological process, the church tends to neglect its responsibility to baptize infants. All the emphasis falls on (adult) believers' awareness of what is happening to them and for them. Having grasped one's salvation in Christ, one chooses to be baptized as a sign of one's readiness to live the Christian life. Faith in Christ's saving work then becomes the precondition for growth in holiness. Seemingly, only when one has become fully aware of one's justification, can one submit to the demands of sanctification. From a Reformed perspective, however, this position loses a sense of the sovereign God who always chooses us before we choose him. It makes baptism more a matter of what we declare about ourselves than of what God would declare about us before we even know how to respond to him.

In relation to the Lord's Supper, psychologizing of the faith has tended

---

86. For incisive reflections on these matters, see Joseph D. Small, "A Church of the Word and Sacrament," in *Christian Worship in Reformed Churches Past and Present,* ed. Lukas Vischer (Grand Rapids: Eerdmans, 2003), pp. 311-23.

historically to overemphasize the question of one's worthiness in coming to the table. Calvin argued that, while faith is a prerequisite for communing, the faith that we bring is always "weak and feeble," and needs to be awakened, aroused, stimulated, and exercised by the Supper itself.[87] Under the influence of Puritanism and pietism, however, people became increasingly concerned with how to demonstrate a right faith. In some cases, church authorities determined whether one came to the table rightly disposed. As with baptism, an awareness of sin and forgiveness were seen as preceding the sacrament, with a commitment to a holy life being its fruit. Justification was the first stage, sanctification the second.

Today, perhaps as a reaction against this past, the psychologizing of the Supper takes a different form. The concern is less for whether a person approaches the table in right faith, and more for how the meal can elicit and sustain feelings of personal value and corporate respect. The Supper is expected to produce a personal experience of "justification," on which basis one might then commit oneself more fully to holy living. Union with Christ again becomes a psychological experience rather than an ontological reality.

The second danger that Barth notes — justification being swallowed up by sanctification — tends to result in humans' overestimation of their ability to possess holiness. If the sacraments are understood primarily as physical matter infused with supernatural holiness, mere physical contact with them is thought somehow to enable us to become holy, too. Baptismal water becomes holy water that ensures cleansing from sin. Eucharistic bread and wine become holy food and drink that offer us eternal life here and now. The sacraments come to be regarded as having miraculous, healing power (perhaps physically as well as spiritually) and as guaranteeing one's personal salvation.

The Reformers vigorously critiqued this position as manifested in medieval Catholicism and defended by the Council of Trent. By carefully distinguishing yet interrelating justification and sanctification, Reformed theologians insisted that the sacraments truly unite us with Christ, yet in such a way as to maintain the essential difference between Christ's holiness and our own. While the sacraments invite us to participate in Christ's holiness, we remain sinners who must make confession of sin ever again. Through the sacraments, we live in Christ and receive his holiness, and yet

---

87. Calvin, *Institutes*, 4.17.42, p. 1420.

we never possess holiness apart from him. The material of the sacraments undergoes no magical change, and yet precisely because of their materiality they impress more fully upon us the change in status that God has wrought in us through the life, death, and resurrection of his Son.[88]

Some North American Protestants, in their desperation to renew churches that seem moribund, find themselves attracted to Catholicism and Eastern Orthodoxy, precisely because these two traditions promise the possibility of experiencing, especially in the liturgy, a sanctified, holy world in place of the thoroughly disenchanted world that Protestantism itself helped to create. But the Reformation critique still holds true. Our attention must not be diverted by "holy things," but must remain focused on God's liberating Word in Christ. In classic Reformed thought, the sacraments serve the Word, intensify it, and seal it. They are holy only insofar as they bear witness to the One who alone is holy.

The third distortion that Barth criticizes — sanctification collapsed into justification — has results just as deleterious for worship and sacraments, also evident in contemporary North American Protestantism. When baptism is simply a declaration that we are justified, and does not draw us into a transformed way of life in Christ, it soon loses its power even to set forth justification and becomes, instead, a mere social expectation, an empty ritual. When the Lord's Supper is understood only as forgiveness and not also as call to holiness, it loses its essential connection to self-examination and repentance. It becomes, as we have noted, merely the individual's personal moment with God or, alternatively, a community celebration in which we accept each other as we are. But then we fail to comprehend that the church is something infinitely more: the body of Christ. Again, the implications of "cheap grace" that Bonhoeffer saw for worship and sacraments unfortunately characterize too much of North American Protestant life today: it "is preaching forgiveness without repentance; it is baptism without the discipline of community; it is the Lord's Supper without confession of sin; it is absolution without personal confession."[89]

---

88. Calvin says, "Because we are of flesh, [the sacraments] are shown us under things of flesh, to instruct us according to our dull capacity, and to lead us by the hand as tutors lead children." *Institutes*, 4.17.6, p. 1281.

89. Bonhoeffer, *Discipleship*, p. 44.

Church Discipline

Perhaps even more problematic than discipleship or sacraments in contemporary North American Protestant church life is the question of church discipline. When people join congregations on the basis of personal taste, the church becomes little more than a consumer choice. People view the church as a service center, rather than as a disciplined community that authorizes a way of "life together." They want the church not to make demands on them, but rather to help them to explore their own spiritual path. If North American Protestants think of church discipline at all, they associate it with punitive measures against persons (most often, pastors) who have violated church rules (very often, in relation to sexual conduct) that reflect the legal requirements of the wider society.

Ironically, North American Protestantism, although having few forms of binding communal life, is characterized by contentious efforts to regulate church life. Denominations are divided into political parties that fight, by means of church legislative and judicial measures, for competing visions of a rightly ordered church. Each side sees the church as an institution to shape in its own theological, moral image. Even in a consumer-oriented world, much seems to be at stake in terms of who will control church power and money.

Calvin has high regard for discipline, even calling it the sinews of the church body.[90] Yet, in contrast to several later Reformed confessions (such as the Scots Confession), he does not make it a third mark of the church. For Calvin, discipline is never simply for the sake of institutional order. Rather, it should support the church's ministry as marked out by Word and sacrament. The Christian life is a matter not of mere conformation to external moral norms, but rather of intimate union with the living Christ, who becomes present to us through Word and sacrament insofar as Word and sacrament are set forth faithfully by the church and are received by its members in faith.

Because church discipline has to do with union with Christ, we can also say that church discipline should aim at rightly relating justification and sanctification. It must steer the narrow but liberating way between "cheap grace" and legalism, between excessive psychological introspection and insufficient self-examination and confession. Although Calvin's

---

90. Calvin, *Institutes*, 4.17.1, p. 1230.

Geneva has sometimes been depicted as a grim, unbending theocracy, recent scholarly analysis of disciplinary cases suggests that the Consistory's principal goal was reconciliation between aggrieved parties.[91] Calvin himself warns the church against "unaccustomed rigor."[92]

A Reformed conception of church discipline is best understood primarily in terms of key practices and disciplines that strengthen life together, rather than as disciplinary proceedings that inevitably impose punitive measures on particular individuals. Drawing from his experience at the *Predigerseminar* in Finkenwalde, Bonhoeffer sketches out what some of these practices and disciplines might look like: reading Scripture together, praying together, listening to each other, helping each other, bearing with each other, confessing sin to each other, and proclaiming God's forgiveness to each other.[93] For Bonhoeffer, as for Calvin, reconciliation stands at the center: a reconciliation that becomes possible only as members of the community live out both their justification and their sanctification in Christ.

Unless justification and sanctification, forgiveness and holiness, are properly related, church discipline inevitably deteriorates into one or another caricature of its true purpose. Three dangers are evident again. First, when justification and sanctification are separated and made two stages of a psychological process, justification tends to be reduced to human experiences of mutual acceptance, and sanctification to human feelings of moral superiority. Church life then becomes obsessed with abstract theological and moral causes set forth in the name of mutual acceptance or moral

91. See Robert M. Kingdon, "Efforts to Control Hate in Calvin's Geneva," in *Calvin Studies IX*, ed. John Leith and Robert Johnson (1998). Also, see *Registers of the Consistory of Geneva in the Time of Calvin*, ed. Robert M. Kingdon (Grand Rapids: Eerdmans, 2000). For an interesting essay that relates insights from the Consistory to church practice today, see Charles Wiley, "Ordinary and Extraordinary Discipline," Church Issues Series No. 6 (Louisville: Office of Theology and Worship, Presbyterian Church [U.S.A.], n.d.).

92. Calvin, *Institutes*, 4.17.11, p. 1238.

93. See Dietrich Bonhoeffer, *Life Together* [together with *Prayerbook of the Bible*] (Minneapolis: Fortress, 1996). For a sampling of recent North American theological explorations of the importance of church practices and disciplines, see Stanley Hauerwas, *The Peaceable Kingdom* (Notre Dame, IN: University of Notre Dame Press, 1983); *Practicing Our Faith*, ed. Dorothy C. Bass (San Francisco: Jossey-Bass, 1997); *Knowing the Triune God: The Work of the Holy Spirit in the Practices of the Church*, ed. James J. Buckley and David S. Yeago (Grand Rapids: Eerdmans, 2001); and *Practicing Theology: Beliefs and Practices in Christian Life*, ed. Miroslav Volf and Dorothy Bass (Grand Rapids: Eerdmans, 2002).

righteousness. In North American Protestantism, "progressives" typically call for the church to celebrate a "diversity" that simply secures their own power. "Conservatives," for their part, insist that the church represent "traditional standards" but give inadequate attention to how they will minister to those who fall short.

Life together in such a church is crippled. People become obsessed with the psychological wounds that "the others" have inflicted upon them, failing to recognize their own self-righteous adherence to one cause or another. The Christian community as a whole loses the joyful freedom of the children of God. Efforts by one side to discipline the other seem punitive. Church discipline fails to invite both sides into common, shared training in discipleship. Instead, what results most often is anxious conformity by one church party to another, out of fear of losing power and privilege. But the suppression of conflict as often as not later explodes into angry, destructive opposition. Again, the Reformed tradition suggests a different way forward. It reminds us that faith is not first of all about having the right ideas about one human cause or another, but rather about obedient trust in the risen Lord.

Second, when sanctification is emphasized at the expense of justification, the church becomes obsessed with trying to guarantee and guard its holiness. Here too the result is the loss of evangelical freedom. The church no longer sees itself honestly for what it really is: a fallible human institution that is the body of Christ only as it lives by God's justifying, sanctifying grace. The church again deteriorates into warring camps, each anxious to assert its own vision of justice and righteousness, failing to remember that there is no holiness other than God's. The current battles within North American Protestantism today are remarkable by their inability to call all sides into a season of confession of sin and repentance, in contrast to the teaching of classic Reformed theology, which understands confession of sin and repentance as key characteristics of the church on earth.

Third, when justification is emphasized at the expense of sanctification, church discipline easily falls away altogether. Church life becomes unbinding and fragmented, with nothing more than "I'm o.k., you're o.k." to hold us together. Such a church may have a friendly spirit, but it will not yet have experienced genuine unity and reconciliation in Christ. Its members may succeed at raising money for the poor and donating time to charitable causes, but they will not yet humbly and gratefully participate in the life of the One who died and rose for their salvation. Such a church simply accedes to the consumer spirit, no longer sure that it has any other purpose than to find paying customers and to keep them happy. Reformed theology could again challenge such a church to rediscover its identity in God's justifying, sanctifying Word.

Justification, Sanctification, and Divine Reality

This brief analysis of contemporary North American Protestantism confirms that the doctrines of justification and sanctification are inextricably linked and interrelated. Each doctrine implies and conditions the other. If the Reformed tradition has sometimes appeared to give more attention to sanctification, it has done so, as Calvin notes, only so that "it will better appear how man is justified by faith alone, and simple pardon; nevertheless actual holiness of life, so to speak, is not separated from free imputation of righteousness."[94] Justification is not the theological principle from which we then derive sanctification secondarily. Rather, reflection on sanctification and the shaping of the Christian life should help to clarify what is at stake in the doctrine of justification, and vice versa. Neither doctrine can take absolute precedence one over the other.[95]

Because the doctrines of justification and sanctification are always Christological in character, they also have ecclesiological implications.[96] When justification and sanctification are reduced to psychological categories, or where one of these doctrines is emphasized at the expense of the other, the church can neither proclaim Christ rightly nor live rightly as the body of Christ.

94. Calvin, *Institutes*, 3.3.1, p. 593.

95. Karl Barth observes that Calvin's discussion of sanctification is preceded by his major chapter on faith, which anticipates his discussion of justification. Barth argues that Calvin's doctrines of justification and sanctification are integrally interrelated. It is only a question of one's particular angle of view on the economy of salvation whether justification or sanctification seems to have precedence over the other. See Barth, *Church Dogmatics* IV/2, p. 510.

96. Luther insisted that justification is the article by which the church stands or falls *(articulus stantis et cadentis ecclesiae)*. Reformed theology would agree, but only (1) if we understand justification as essentially related to sanctification, and (2) that both justification and sanctification point us to a more fundamental reality: the church's union with the living, resurrected Christ. See McGrath, *Iustitia Dei*, p. 225. Also, see Michael Weinrich, "The Reformed Reception of the Joint Declaration," *Reformed World* (March 2002): 22.

Where classic Reformed doctrines of justification and sanctification avoid these confusions, they contribute to the integrity of the one holy catholic and apostolic church. They impel holy living, while guarding against new forms of "works righteousness"; they guarantee that both declaration of forgiveness and call to obedience will come to full expression in both of the sacraments; and they shape church discipline in ways that promote mutual encouragement and mutual admonition, mutual forgiveness as well as mutual accountability.

At the same time, Reformed theology at its best teaches us to be aware of theology's limitations. Getting our theology right on matters of justification and sanctification will not by itself renew the church. The only thing that would ever make our theology "right" is God's gracious Word, which points us surely and joyfully again to God's freely given grace in Jesus Christ, a grace that surrounds us and sustains us each day whether we are aware of it or not. What matters ultimately are not our *ideas* about justification and sanctification, but rather the *realities* to which they humbly point, namely, God's justifying, sanctifying work for us and our salvation through Christ in the power of the Holy Spirit.[97] Only when these divine realities take hold of us can faithful theological reflection lead us into profounder ways of living the faith, of celebrating the sacraments, and of shaping "life together." Only then will the gospel guard us in the faith, even as we struggle to express its truths with the language of justification and sanctification.

---

97. As Michael Weinrich powerfully argues, "Justification as an expression of God's justice is not a doctrine but the basic prerequisite of every substantial doctrinal insight." See Weinrich, "The Reformed Reception," p. 22. Brian Gerrish notes, "Calvin names but one fundamental doctrine . . . that we cleave to Christ [which] is not strictly a doctrine at all [but rather] the habit of mind on which every Christian doctrine, without exception, rests." See Brian Gerrish, "Tradition in the Modern World: The Reformed Habit of Mind," in *Toward the Future of Reformed Theology*, ed. David Willis and Michael Welker (Grand Rapids: Eerdmans, 1999), p. 12.

4 Justification and Divine Justice?

Dirkie Smit

1. "For Us and Our Salvation"?

> It is not enough to affirm that the reconciling activity of the Son of God has its ground in the divine love if we are not then able to affirm in a coherent way that that love is operative at every step along the way in the accomplishment of our redemption. We must show how the divine love comes to expression precisely in the outpouring of wrath and judgment. If we do not, we introduce a contradiction into the being of God between God's mercy and His righteousness. We make God's mercy the prisoner, so to speak, of His righteousness, until such time as righteousness has been fully satisfied.[1]

With these words, Reformed systematic theologian Bruce McCormack describes the challenge facing any faithful and convincing presentation of the Christian understanding of reconciliation. Through the centuries, Christian witness and reflection have often failed in this regard — for a variety of reasons, born in diverse spiritualities and sensibilities, and leading to a variety of often contradictory accounts of reconciliation and the gospel. Many historical and continuing controversies in the church are related to the difficulties of this task.

One of the most common failures has been a presentation of reconciliation in which, in McCormack's words, divine mercy is made the prisoner

---

1. Bruce L. McCormack, *For Us and Our Salvation: Incarnation and Atonement in the Reformed Tradition* (Princeton: Princeton Theological Seminary, 1993), p. 27.

of divine justice, until such time as the divine justice has been fully satisfied. The thrust of McCormack's argument is to show that the Reformed tradition, including Calvin and sixteenth- and seventeenth-century Orthodoxy, stood in a longer tradition that made it difficult for them to escape the problems inherent in this seeming contradiction between mercy and righteousness, between love and justice.

This longer tradition is popularly attributed to the influence of Anselm and his doctrine of so-called satisfaction or substitution. According to many, this tradition, which became the classic and pervasive account of reconciliation in the Western church, is to blame for the failure of theology, church, and piety to fully appreciate how "God's love is operative at every step along the way in the accomplishment of our salvation."

Of course, such critics often disagree fundamentally among themselves about the proper ways to correct this failure, sometimes even rejecting all language of wrath and judgment, clearly appeasing contemporary cultural sensibilities.

Even the story of this dominant tradition is, however, more nuanced and complex than often portrayed, and the efforts of representatives of this tradition — including Calvin, Reformed confessions, and contemporary Reformed theology — to struggle with the difficult challenge described by McCormack have been more intense and serious than often appreciated.

2. Justification and Divine Justice?

There is no doubt that a major part of the Reformed tradition stands in the tradition of Anselm, including Calvin, early Reformed confessions, and Karl Barth in his influential restatement of the doctrine of reconciliation in the last century. There is, however, also no doubt that most of these figures and documents were deeply aware of the difficulties and tensions in this tradition of presenting the gospel, and in diverse ways attempted to escape the temptation of "making mercy the prisoner of justice" while at the same time refusing to give up the biblical language of wrath and justice and the judicial frame of understanding the truth of Jesus Christ.

A brief review of the broad outline of this story may prepare the way for some concluding remarks pointing out central concerns regarding the understanding of divine justice in relation to the good news of reconciliation, justification, and redemption.

Anselm? — "Not God, but the structure of justice"

There is, in fact, ample reason to doubt whether Anselm's own version of the satisfaction theory was so "vulgarly Anselmian" as it nowadays is often said to be, and as it was indeed appropriated in much of popular piety in Western Christianity. Michael Welker summarizes this popular reception as follows:

> God requires a compensation for human beings' deficiency. Since no sinful human being is in a position to produce this atoning compensation, the sinless Son of God, the Lamb of God, must be sacrificed. Only this sacrifice can pacify God's anger. . . . This has propagated a latent image of God that is deeply unchristian, indeed demonic: This God is always seeking compensation; it takes a sacrificial victim to calm and pacify this ultimately merciless and vengeful God.[2]

Welker quite correctly calls this view "nothing less than destructive of faith."[3] Yet, while several of its elements indeed find their background in Anselm, other elements are alien to him and even distort his intentions. The latent image of God represented here indeed becomes "unchristian," but this popular reception does not do justice to Anselm's own presentation.

Long before Anselm, of course, the Christian tradition struggled to interpret and proclaim the reconciliation achieved in and through the life and particularly the cross and resurrection of Jesus Christ. The famous historian von Harnack pointed out, very critically, that many of the early Latin theologians had been lawyers and were therefore predisposed to interpret and portray relations between God and humanity in the legal terms well known to them: "It was of the highest moment that Tertullian, the jurist, and Cyprian, the ecclesiastical ruler, were the first Latin theologians."[4] Questions of justice therefore played a major role in theological reflection on the atonement in the West. In the East it has always been different, which is wonderfully expressed in the seeming perplexity of Valerie

---

2. Michael Welker, *What Happens in Holy Communion?* (Grand Rapids: Eerdmans, 2000), p. 109.

3. Welker, *What Happens in Holy Communion?*, p. 109.

4. Adolf von Harnack, *History of Dogma, vol. VII*, trans. Neil Buchanan (Boston: Little, Brown, 1902), p. 310.

Karras's informative and insightful Orthodox response to the *Joint Declaration:* "Orthodox have never quite understood what all the fuss was about to begin with."[5]

Justice, however, could mean many different things during the complex and confusing scene of the early medieval period. Around 1100, Anselm, Archbishop of Canterbury, offered the first "definitive systematic treatment of the atonement in terms of satisfaction."[6] According to Alister McGrath, two closely related questions would from now on determine discussions.[7]

First, how is it possible, given the limitations of human language, to speak of God as "righteous" (or "just" or "unjust")? In other words, given the limited nature of our understanding (and today theology is again deeply aware of the radical nature of this limitation), how is it possible to claim that we know what justice is, and then to use our definition as a grid by which to describe, understand, and even critique God's actions? Should we not rather proceed in the opposite direction, letting God define what justice and especially divine justice are, and then simply follow God's definition, irrespective of how just or unjust it may seem from a human perspective?[8]

Second, *if* we somehow claim that we know and use a concept of justice appropriate to characterizing God's dealings with us, what concept of justice would that be? Anselm saw people using different notions of justice

---

5. Valerie A. Karras, "Beyond Justification: An Orthodox Perspective," in *Justification and the Future of the Ecumenical Movement,* ed. William G. Rusch and George A. Lindbeck (Collegeville, MN: Liturgical Press, 2003), p. 99.

6. Colin E. Gunton, *The Actuality of Atonement: A Study of Metaphor, Rationality and the Christian Tradition* (Edinburgh: T. & T. Clark, 1988), p. 87.

7. See Alister E. McGrath, *Iustitia Dei: A History of the Christian Doctrine of Justification,* 2nd ed. (Cambridge: Cambridge University Press, 1998), pp. 55-60.

8. A major part of the controversies between the so-called nominalists and voluntarists (the debates concerning William of Occam and Duns Scotus) depended on these critical concerns. Was God subject to an existing judicial, legal framework of justice, one that we know and can describe, so that God ultimately was not free, but if he wanted to save us, had to save us in a way that satisfied *this* understanding of justice? Anselm's own position came very close to reflecting such convictions. The voluntarist position on the other hand would be that God is God precisely in that he is sovereign and free, also to define what is good and therefore what is just and unjust. We are saved by God's action in Jesus Christ, which also thereby defines and reveals to us what divine justice is, irrespective of whether it contradicts our previous human understandings and linguistic formulations of good and moral and just. This position may lead to problematic situations where the seemingly arbitrary actions of God appear to us to seriously contradict, even affront, our sensibilities concerning morality and justice, thereby making it difficult for us to hear the gospel as good news "for us and our salvation."

common to their time in their effort to understand and describe God's dealings with and for us. He attempted to bring clarity to this confusion by rejecting some of these understandings of justice, including the very influential and popular understanding of the *ius diaboli*, the justice of the devil. Anselm then made use of a concept of justice built on the role of honor, legal satisfaction, and compensation for honor that has been violated.

For Anselm, God is wholly and supremely just — and therefore *morally* just — which raises questions of how such a God can then give eternal life to people who deserve eternal death, and how such a God can justify sinners. McGrath rejects the widespread criticism of Anselm as "legalist" and "typical of the Latin impulse to carry religion into the legal sphere." Such comments are "misguided and discredited."[9] The central questions facing Anselm in *Cur Deus Homo* (1098) and already earlier in the *Proslogion* (1079) are moral, not legal, questions.

For Anselm, the apparent contradiction between divine mercy *(misericordia)* and divine moral justice *(iustitia)* must be solved in such a way that God's mercy is grounded in his moral justice. Otherwise his mercy would be morally unacceptable to us, who operate with a moral understanding of justice learned from "the moral rectitude of the created order, established by God at creation, and in itself reflecting the divine will and nature. This moral ordering of the universe extends to the relationships between human beings and God, and between human beings amongst themselves."[10] Anselm's move is exactly the opposite from McCormack's. For Anselm, mercy must be a form of justice. For McCormack, justice must be a form of mercy. The current attraction of McCormack's position may be the result of changed cultural sensibilities from the time of Anselm, but it may also be more faithful to the scriptural witness concerning our salvation and the nature of God.

Anselm's primary question is determined by his historical context and his understanding of justice. Drawing on medieval ideas of morality, expressed in honor and shame, Anselm explains that we owe God all possible honor and obedience. When that honor is morally violated, it must not only be restored, but also compensated in some way satisfactory to the dignity of the one who has been dishonored, namely God. Only the one who violated the honor can make restoration by paying the debt and offering

9. McGrath, *Iustitia Dei*, p. 55.
10. McGrath, *Iustitia Dei*, p. 56.

compensation, yet sin renders human beings unable to do so. God alone is able to pay the debt, which means that we need a Mediator who is both human and divine to accomplish our reconciliation and salvation. Only in that way could mercy be done to us, while divine moral justice is fulfilled. In Jesus Christ, both human and divine, this debt is paid, not only in the death on the cross, but also in the incarnation and through his life of obedience and honor to God.

According to this understanding, God's freedom in will and action is limited by his own nature, which includes his moral justice. God is not free to do anything that violates his own nature. God's character — as *summa iustitia* — is expressed in the moral order of creation, and free forgiveness of sins through mercy alone would violate this order. Anselm was convinced that such a presentation of the atonement could explain to *his* readers, with *their* sense of moral justice, how the whole event of reconciliation was an act of divine moral justice.[11]

But does Anselm's explanation of the *why* of the cross work for readers with different sensibilities and different notions of justice? Was it a convincing way of reading the scriptural witness to make mercy subservient to moral justice, rather than the other way around? Does it lead to a faithful understanding of the God of the Bible? Is mercy here not indeed made the prisoner of one particular human understanding of justice? These are critical questions to Anselm and the dominant soteriological tradition of the West, which built on his work.

But it is also clear that Anselm's own presentation is not as vulgar and crude as often depicted, that it is certainly not a matter of an angry, wrathful, and merciless God looking for revenge and suffering. Robert Jenson wisely comments:

> It is easy to caricature this (Anselmian) teaching, making it picture God the Father as a hanging judge who can only be appeased by his own Son's death, and some proponents and most opponents have done so. In Anselm's own teaching, however, what must be "satisfied" is *not God directly but the structure of justice he has built into creation*, without which

11. The essential point is that Anselm considers, presumably on the basis of the established satisfaction-merit model of the penitential system of the contemporary church, that the payment of a satisfaction by the God-man would be regarded by his readers as an acceptable means of satisfying the demands of moral rectitude without violating the moral order of creation (see McGrath, *Iustitia Dei*, p. 57).

life as a creature would be meaningless, and which God, therefore, precisely for the sake of creatures, cannot allow us simply to undo.[12]

God is not ultimately merciless and vengeful, but there is *a* particular human notion of justice related to the moral order of justice in creation that cannot be ignored, not even by God. Somehow issues of justice and injustice, of sin and wrath, of judgment and a judicial framework, all belong in the scriptural account of our salvation.

Whether Anselm's theory was successful in showing that and how this injustice is related to God's mercy — in other words, whether his theory of substitution and satisfaction was successful in following the scriptural testimony that "it is never God who is reconciled to us; it is always God who reconciles us to himself" (Jenson), or again whether this dominant theory of atonement successfully achieves what McCormack pleads for, "showing how the divine love comes to expression precisely in the outpouring of wrath and judgment" — that is indeed another question.

Calvin? — *"Since our mind cannot lay hold of the mercy of God unless impressed by fear"*

Anselm drew on medieval ideas about honor, lords, and vassals. Calvin used imagery of the law courts and business transactions of his time. Both, however, used their respective contemporary conceptual tools to express roughly the same idea, namely that we owe a debt to God and that Christ alone can pay this debt.[13] Calvin's idea is often depicted as a prime example of a penal substitutionary view, but that may be a gross and inaccurate generalization.[14] Because he was a jurist, with a background and training in law, one would expect a judicial framework and judicial terminology

---

12. Robert W. Jenson, "The Person and Work of Jesus Christ," in *Essentials of Christian Theology*, ed. William C. Placher (Louisville: Westminster John Knox, 2003), p. 203 (my emphasis).

13. William C. Placher, "How Does Jesus Make a Difference?," in *Essentials of Christian Theology*, p. 190. He continues that "the risk of this account is that, if distorted, it can make 'God' or 'God the Father' seem like the villain of the story, with Christ the hero who wins our freedom."

14. See Brian A. Gerrish, *Grace and Gratitude: The Eucharistic Theology of John Calvin* (Eugene, OR: Wipf & Stock, 2002 [Minneapolis: Augsburg Fortress, 1993]), p. 55.

from him. The thrust of his discussion of the divine justice may then come as a surprise.

There is namely no doubt at all that Calvin did not want believers to see any conflict within God between divine justice and mercy, or between the wrath of the Father and the self-sacrificial grace of the Son. Brian Gerrish convincingly argues this point:

> For Calvin . . . the language of reconciliation had to be used circum-spectly: there must be no suggestion that God was not good or loving before Christ came into the world, as though Christ initiated his love. Titus 3:4 reads, "When the goodness and loving kindness of God our Saviour appeared. . . ." Does this mean that the goodness of God was un-known before the appearance of Christ in the flesh? Not at all. The in-carnation was not the first manifestation of his fatherly love, but the pledge of it. "That the world was reconciled to God by the death of Christ is the familiar way of speaking in the scriptures, although we know that he was a kindly father throughout the ages." To be reconciled to God through Christ means, in short, to "have in heaven instead of a judge a kindly-disposed father." . . . In the precepts of the law God is only the rewarder of perfect righteousness and the severe judge of evildoing, but in Christ God's face shines full of grace and mildness even on poor, unworthy sinners. The work of Christ is, quite simply, to give us access to a gracious, fatherly God.[15]

Faith, for Calvin, is the lifelong contemplation of this gracious face of the Father in our Lord Jesus Christ.

In his systematic treatment of the atonement in the *Institutes* (1559), Calvin makes two crucial and remarkable moves. The first is in line with the overall thrust of his theology. As recent scholarship has increasingly re-alized, Calvin seeks to be rhetorical, or more specifically edifying or *pastoral*. He is concerned with practical piety, with the actual experience and re-sponse of gratitude. In this specific case his explicit intention is to ensure that the presentation of the atonement offered by theology and the church should be pastoral. It should serve the rhetorical function of leading read-ers and hearers to experience gratitude and to delight in the sovereign and free grace of God.[16] For this purpose, he deliberately adjusts and nuances

---

15. Gerrish, *Grace and Gratitude*, pp. 59-60.

16. Many scholars have demonstrated the importance of rhetoric for Calvin's theology,

the penal substitutionary model so that his readers and hearers, given *their* understanding and sense of justice, will be "the more deeply moved" to appreciate how much they owe to the mercy of God.

Our initial experience, says Calvin — in other words, the fundamental, pervasive, and common human experience known to him and his contemporaries — is that of "feeling that God is angry and at enmity with (us)," such that we are "anxiously longing for the means of regaining (God's) favour."[17] Human beings, according to Calvin and his contemporaries, know themselves as "sinners, until freed from guilt . . . always liable to the wrath and curse of God, who, as he is a just judge, cannot permit his law to be violated with impunity, but is armed for vengeance" (p. 434). "No man," says Calvin, "can descend into himself, and seriously consider what he is, without (this) feeling" (p. 434). It reflects people's basic understanding of self, of justice, of divine justice, and indeed of God himself, perhaps as the result of the longstanding teaching and practices of the medieval church, but, nevertheless, as true for every human being.

But is this sense of God true? Is it correct? Does Scripture teach us to see ourselves as well as God and divine justice like this? Does this sense of God reflect the proper relationship between divine justice and divine mercy, based on Scripture? Or does it suggest "some appearance of a contradiction" between the divine mercy and justice? In Calvin's own words:

> But before we proceed further, we must see in passing, how it can be said that God, who prevents us with his mercy, was our enemy until he was reconciled to us by Christ. For how could he have given us in his only-begotten Son a singular pledge of his love, if he had not previously embraced us with free favour? As there thus arises some appearance of contradiction, I will explain the difficulty. (pp. 434-35)[18]

---

e.g., Serene Jones, *Calvin and the Rhetoric of Piety* (Louisville: Westminster John Knox, 1995); and specifically dealing with his doctrine of sin, Don S. Compier, *John Calvin's Rhetorical Doctrine of Sin* (Lewiston, NY: Edwin Mellen Press, 2001); and Rachel S. Baard, *Constructive Feminist Critiques of Classical Sin-Talk* (Princeton Theological Seminary, unpublished doctoral thesis, 2004). For a helpful revisioning of atonement theology in terms of Calvin's rhetorical purposes, see Leanne van Dyk, "How Does Jesus Make a Difference?," in *Essentials of Christian Theology*, pp. 205-20.

17. John Calvin, *Institutes of the Christian Religion*, trans. Henry Beveridge (Grand Rapids: Eerdmans, 1953), 2.16.1. p. 434. Subsequent page numbers to the *Institutes* are provided in the text.

18. 2.16.2.

Calvin explains this difficulty by pointing out to his readers "the mode in which the Spirit usually speaks in Scripture" (p. 435). He offers a rhetorical explanation. The Scriptures (and thus the Spirit) use "modes of expression accommodated to our capacity" (p. 435). Why? Because the Spirit (through the Scriptures) has a pastoral purpose. What is this pastoral purpose? The Spirit wants us to have a deeper feeling for our misery *so that our appreciation of grace* may also be deeper. The better we "understand how miserable and calamitous our condition is without Christ" (p. 435), the more adequate will be our gratitude for the divine mercy. Our limited capacity of understanding is unfortunately such that "were it not said in clear terms, that Divine wrath, and vengeance, and eternal death, lay upon us," we should be "less disposed to value the blessing of deliverance" (p. 435).

Calvin illustrates his point by comparing two fictitious people, one with only a limited awareness of divine wrath and therefore only "sensible in some degree" of how much we owe the divine mercy, and another deeply impressed by the powerful scriptural depiction of divine justice and therefore "moved much more deeply":

> Let a person be told, Had God at the time you were a sinner hated you, and cast you off as you deserved, horrible destruction must have been your doom; but spontaneously and of free indulgence he retained you in his favour, not suffering you to be estranged from him, and in this way rescued you from danger, — the person will indeed be affected, and made sensible in some degree how much he owes to the mercy of God. But again, let him be told, as Scripture teaches, that he was estranged from God by sin, an heir of wrath, exposed to the curse of eternal death, excluded from all hope of salvation, a complete alien from the blessing of God, the slave of Satan, captive under the yoke of sin; in fine, doomed to horrible destruction, and already involved in it; that then Christ interposed, took the punishment upon himself, and bore what by the just judgment of God was impending over sinners; with his own blood expiated the sins which rendered them hateful to God, by this expiation satisfied and duly propitiated God the Father, by this intercession appeased his anger, on this basis founded peace between God and men, and by this tie secured the Divine benevolence toward them; will not these considerations move him the more deeply, the more strikingly they represent the greatness of the calamity from which he was delivered? (p. 435)

Rhetorically, pastorally, it is by the fear of God that our minds best lay hold of the mercy of God, which should be the intention of all proclamation and theology.

> In short, since our mind cannot lay hold of life through the mercy of God with sufficient eagerness, or receive it with becoming gratitude, unless previously impressed with fear of the Divine anger, and dismayed at the thought of eternal death, we are so instructed by divine truth, as to perceive that without Christ God is in a manner hostile to us, and has his arm raised for our destruction. Thus taught, we look to Christ alone for divine favour and paternal love. (p. 435)

Calvin's strategy, however, raises a key question regarding all rhetorical theories, namely, whether they deal with truth or merely with ways of speaking. Here we come to Calvin's second strategic move. Calvin himself explicitly asks this question, as if critically directed against his own presentation, and responds that, though this mode of speaking by the Spirit (in Scripture) is for the purpose of moving us, one should not therefore conclude that what is said is powerful, but not true — persuasive, but not accurate and reliable. No, "though this is said in accommodation to the weakness of our capacity, it is not said falsely" (p. 435).[19]

How is this possible? Calvin points to the seriousness of sin. We should never underestimate human iniquity. Its extent, depth, and radical nature violate not only a human sense of justice but God himself. Therefore, although we must certainly affirm the continuing and radical love and grace of God, we should not interpret this love and grace of God in such a way that our sin and injustice become unimportant, something that God could easily ignore and forget about.[20]

All this sin, however, is expiated and abolished in the death of Christ, precisely because of the love of God for us. It is impossible not to hear Calvin's emphasis here on the mercy and love of God as the real motivating power behind the righteousness given to us in and through Christ.

> As the Lord wills not to destroy in us that which is his own, he still finds something in us which in kindness he can love. . . . He created us for life.

19. 2.16.3.

20. "God cannot love the iniquity which he sees in all. All of us have that within which deserves the hatred of God. . . . [W]e are all offensive to God, guilty in his sight, and by nature children of hell." Calvin, *Institutes*, 2.16.3, pp. 435-36.

Thus, mere gratuitous love prompts him to receive us into favour. . . . Accordingly, God the Father, by his love, prevents and anticipates our reconciliation in Christ. Nay, it is because he first loves us, that he afterwards reconciles us to himself. (p. 436)

And then, "to give additional assurance to those who require the authority of the ancient Church, I will quote a passage from Augustine to the same effect":

Incomprehensible and immutable is the love of God. For it was not after we were reconciled to him by the blood of his Son that he began to love us, but he loves us before the foundation of the world, that with his only-begotten Son we too might be sons of God before we were anything at all. Our being reconciled by the death of Christ must not be understood as if the Son reconciled us, in order that the Father, then hating, might begin to love us, but that we were reconciled to him already, loving, though at enmity with us because of sin. To the truth of both propositions we have the attestation of the Apostle, "God commendeth his love toward us, in that while we were yet sinners, Christ died for us" (Rom. 5:8). Therefore he had this love towards us even when, exercising enmity towards him, we were the workers of iniquity. Accordingly, in a manner wondrous and divine, he loved even when he hated us. For he hated us when we were such as he had not made us, and yet because our iniquity had not destroyed his work in every respect, he knew in regard to each one of us, both to hate what we had made, and to love what he had made. (pp. 436-37)[21]

Put differently, Calvin attempts to affirm the grace and mercy of God, without negating the serious nature of human sin. He develops a doctrine of God and of the saving grace of God in which a judicial framework still finds its proper place. The radicality of evil is remembered and acknowledged, and the proper role of judgment is therefore retained, but there can be little doubt that it remains rooted in the divine mercy.

Calvin's theology is a theology of grace, his doctrine of God a doctrine of grace, and his doctrine of the atonement an attempt to remain faithful to this proclamation of grace, although he may not be fully successful in achieving the latter, according to many critics. There can be no doubt as to

---

21. 2.16.4.

the overall thrust of his theology, as many Calvin scholars have demonstrated. Perhaps the account by Gerrish can suffice to make the point.

Gerrish argues that Calvin's whole theology is eucharistic, also in the sense of grace and gratitude. At the heart of Calvin's theology is God as "the Father and fountain of good."[22] Gerrish shows how this image of a loving, gracious, familial God is present in every part of Calvin's systematic thought, thereby rejecting all those portrayals of Calvin's God as an absolute monarch, an autocratic will with a horrible decree, a merciless judge, and a wrathful punishing tyrant, so often uncritically accepted both in scholarship and popularly. It would probably come as a surprise, says Gerrish, to many people, both theologians and ordinary believers, "to learn that scholars who have devoted a lifetime to Calvin research have arrived at exactly the opposite reading of his doctrine of God."[23] This fundamental image of God as Father and fountain of all good has major implications for the relative weight of the image of God as judge within Calvin's overall theology of grace.

> The work of Christ is, quite simply, to give us access to a gracious, fatherly God. . . . [T]here really is a sense in which the legal language of justification by faith "self-destructs": the point of the doctrine is to move us out of the legal domain into the world of family relationships, and it is just this point that so often gets lost in theological controversy over satisfaction, substitution and imputation. Calvin certainly held that God is a just judge who cannot cast aside his governance of the universe. And yet he also held that it is not God's judicial person but God's fatherly person that determines the life of true piety. The familial imagery runs alongside the forensic imagery and finally supplants it. In the end, Christ saves us, reconciles us, justifies us as God's Son who takes us for his brothers and sisters. . . . Calvin cannot allow that the Father was ever really angry with his beloved Son in whom he was well pleased.

---

22. Gerrish, *Grace and Gratitude*, pp. 22-31. Gerrish argues that the crucial passage at the beginning of the *Institutes* describing God as the fountain of all good must be taken as regulative for everything that follows. Calvin's fundamental definition of God or his fundamental image of God is the *fons omnium bonorum*, the spring or fountain of all good. Correlatively, piety is a response to this Father or Fountain of All Good. Central to this piety is gratitude, thankfulness, and reverence for the goodness, mercy, and love of this Father and Fountain of Good.

23. Gerrish, *Grace and Gratitude*, p. 23.

Quite the contrary, the meaning of our reconciliation is that we are drawn, as Christ's brothers and sisters, into the Father's delight in his one true Son.[24]

Calvin's discussion of the relation between divine mercy and justice nevertheless raises difficult questions.[25] What if human experience and self-knowledge and cultural sensibilities change, so that people no longer share this initial experience on which his whole discussion rests? What if shared understandings of justice and mercy change, so that people no longer experience a deeper appreciation of divine mercy when powerful rhetoric is employed to impress them with the wrath and anger of God, but rather the opposite occurs? What if the truth of the scriptural account of justice and God is in fact different from Calvin's own?

It is in regard to the last question in particular that Calvin has often been criticized. Even McCormack is not convinced. He acknowledges Calvin's rhetorical strategies and the role of language "accommodated to our capacity." He also acknowledges that Calvin was convinced that the grace and mercy of God are the effective ground of the atonement; the atonement did not give rise to grace and mercy as its effect. Nevertheless, according to McCormack, Calvin's account still suffers from major weaknesses.[26]

One weakness is that Calvin wrongly interprets passages such as Romans 5:10, "which do not say that God was our enemy until Christ reconciled us to Him, but rather that we were His enemies. The enmity spoken of lies on the human side, not on the divine side." The "real source" of Calvin's problem, McCormack argues, is his "tendency to make the righteousness of God, abstracted from his love, the object toward which the atoning work of Christ is directed." In spite of Calvin's awareness of this "apparent contradiction" and his attempt to address it — and in spite of his efforts to build his whole theology on divine mercy — he makes "God's mercy the prisoner . . . of his righteousness."[27]

---

24. Gerrish, *Grace and Gratitude*, pp. 60-61.

25. Attention to the many other expressions that he used in the variety of his writings and to his many other rhetorical and pastoral depictions regarding the atonement and the mediating work of Jesus Christ would further confuse the issue and lead critics to endless discussions of his role in the tradition of Western soteriology.

26. McCormack, *For Us and Our Salvation*, pp. 26-34.

27. Other Calvin scholars disagree and attempt to show that Calvin did not think in terms of such a contradiction within God. Sometimes they contrast Calvin with Luther, of

That is the final outcome of Calvin's version of the satisfaction theory. By appealing to the idea of accommodation, he had allowed the (apparent) contradiction between mercy and righteousness to stand. He had taken the position that on the conceptual level, these things cannot be resolved: all the while hoping that somehow, in a way incomprehensible to us, a resolution does exist in God Himself.[28]

For McCormack, the theological task is to demonstrate that this contradiction is only an apparent, not a real, contradiction within God. It is a contradiction on our side, because we apply our inadequate ideas of justice to God, thereby misreading the scriptural account of the reconciling activity of the Son of God. We must, says McCormack, rethink our understanding of God and divine justice.

Reformed Confessions? — "Merciful justice and righteous mercy"

How does this story continue in the Reformed confessional tradition? Here McCormack has even more objections than with Calvin, since Reformed confessions fail, according to him, to reflect adequately on the doctrine of God and the classical problem of the attributes of God: "Seventeenth-century Reformed theology was scarcely able to overcome this defect. If anything, its treatment of the atonement as a satisfaction of the divine wrath was even more abstract than Calvin's. Calvin at least

---

whom many claim that he indeed worked with such a contradiction, even a conflict or struggle, between divine justice and grace, sometimes expressed as a conflict between Father and Son. Many Luther scholars for their part reject this portrayal. George Hunsinger offers helpful material in "What Karl Barth Learned from Martin Luther," in *Disruptive Grace* (Grand Rapids: Eerdmans, 2000), pp. 279-304. He says that Barth, "unlike Luther, recoiled from any suggestion that the cross entailed a contradiction or conflict in God's being itself, an idea he regarded as supremely blasphemous," but then adds "although Luther surely did not go as far as some recent theologians who appeal to him, he did at times seem to project a conflict between God's righteousness and God's mercy, God's curse and God's blessing, God's wrath and God's love back into God's being itself. With reference to Christ's cross he once wrote: 'There God enters into conflict with God.'" Hunsinger argues that several scholars, such as Aulen (Luther effectively locates the conflict in the divine being), Moltmann (Luther posits a dichotomy in God), and Gollwitzer (in the cross a cleavage goes through God, God is forsaken by God, God rejects himself), are less careful than Barth, who does not see in Luther a rupture within the divine being.

28. McCormack, *For Us and Our Salvation*, p. 27.

sensed that there was a problem. The later Reformed theologians, from Ursinus on, did not."[29]

It is of course difficult to interpret the Reformed confessional tradition as a whole, or to evaluate any of its specific teachings. There are simply too many documents, figures, and events, with too many socio-historical and cultural contexts, and too many theological and ecclesial backgrounds.[30] Perhaps, however, one specific confessional document can illustrate the problem. McCormack's reference to Ursinus draws our attention to the Heidelberg Catechism, as widely known, influential, and representative as any of the sixteenth- and seventeenth-century Reformed confessions. Is it accurate to claim that the Heidelberg Catechism did not even sense a problem concerning the divine wrath and punishing justice within the scriptural account of the mercy of God?

The catechism seems to follow an Anselmian logic of presentation.[31] The discussion begins with the divine law as summarized by Jesus in Matthew 22. We know our misery from this law, since we find that we cannot keep the law perfectly and are prone by nature to hate God and neighbor (3-5). Did God create us such? By no means, but rather good, in the divine image, in true righteousness and holiness, to know, heartily love, live with, and praise God. We, however, are corrupt and disobedient, incapable of the good and inclined to wickedness, "except when we are regenerated by the Spirit of God" (6-8).[32] Is God therefore not unjust to us, expecting what we cannot do? Not at all. Will God let this disobedience go unpun-

---

29. McCormack, *For Us and Our Salvation*, p. 28.

30. Studies offering overviews and summaries of this tradition are nevertheless useful. They discern general trends and common characteristics, family resemblances within the shared tradition, thus making it possible to reflect on a particular theme, like the atonement, and even the operative understanding of the relationship between divine mercy and justice. See Jan Rohls, *Reformed Confessions: Theology from Zurich to Barmen*, trans. John W. Hoffmeyer (Louisville: Westminster John Knox, 1998), pp. 86-101, esp. 117-29.

31. Many critics find this abstract, formal, and unconvincing, and following Anselm rather than Scripture. However, such a critical judgment presents a problem of interpretation, because in fairness it should be said that in the first question and answer — the famous presentation of our only comfort in life and death, namely that we belong to Jesus Christ — the full gospel, in fact a full trinitarian account of it, has already been offered. It is therefore indeed possible to read the seemingly abstract 3-17 in the light of 1-2, which makes them appear in a radically different light. Ignoring the interpretive framework provided by 1-2 for the moment, however, we will focus on the discussion that follows.

32. A very remarkable turn of phrase at this early stage of the presentation.

ished? By no means, for he "punishes sin in his just judgment, temporally and eternally" (9-10).

The catechism shows that it is fully aware of the "apparent contradiction," since it immediately asks: Is God then also merciful? (11). The problem is already clear from the order of the argument. The catechism has first and foremost, on the basis of the law in a judicial, legal, and punitive sense, established that God is "just." Now it asks: Is there not something good to be expected from this stern, just, and punishing God? The answer is almost surprising, since it once again affirms the divine justice, rather than the divine mercy: "God is indeed merciful, but also just; therefore his justice requires, that sin which is committed against the most high majesty of God, be also punished with extreme, that is, everlasting punishment of body and soul" (11). The divine mercy seems to be taken for granted, while the divine justice is defended at length.

How should the catechism's intention be understood? Is it employing the same rhetorical strategy as Calvin? Yes, mercy is in the name of God, Father, Son, and Holy Spirit, and yes, the gospel is all about good news, grace, goodness, justification, adoption, comfort, forgiveness, and regeneration, as we heard in answer 1 and shall hear again at the end of the catechism. But we should not move too quickly to mercy, before we have properly considered, even if only for a moment, the seriousness of our sin and the seriousness of divine justice. Otherwise we shall never properly understand, sense, experience, and appreciate the incredible wonder of the divine grace.

Or is Heidelberg offering a different account from Calvin's? Is it based on a different framework, i.e., on a doctrine of God in which a particular understanding of divine justice, namely a legal and punitive one, calling for satisfaction and therefore substitution, dominates the logic and the account given of the scriptural message?

With question and answer 12, the catechism moves from human misery to the way of deliverance: "Since then, by the righteous judgment of God, we deserve temporal and eternal punishment, is there no way by which we may escape that punishment, and be again received into favour?" It almost sounds in strong Anselmian fashion as if the divine justice (though understood now more legally than morally, in contrast to Anselm) forms the framework, the point of existential departure, in which human beings begin to look for a means of escape.

Given the legal nature of the human predicament, that way of escape would have to take the form of a theory of satisfaction, argues the catechism: "God will have his justice satisfied: and therefore we must make this full satisfaction, either by ourselves, or by another." But can we by ourselves then make this satisfaction? "By no means, we in fact daily increase our debt." Can there be found anywhere a mere creature to pay this debt (because only a creature can satisfy what creatures have violated, according to Anselm)? No. What sort of mediator and deliverer must we then seek? The underlying doctrine of God is again threatened here by the catechism's use of Anselmian logic: God is clearly the Judge, the One who is against us, and we are looking, somewhere, for someone, who will be able and willing to save us from this God, from this wrath, someone who will be on our side in this legal process. This one will have to be both human (but perfectly righteous) and divine. Why human and perfectly righteous? Because the justice of God requires that the same one who sinned also make satisfaction (again, it is the divine justice that must be satisfied, because it is understood legally). Why also divine? So that by his power he may bear the burden of divine wrath, thereby obtaining and restoring for us righteousness and life (12-17). Again, it is the divine wrath that must be borne before we can escape our misery.

Who is this Mediator (18)? The answer is known, namely our Lord Jesus Christ whom God has made our wisdom, righteousness, sanctification, and redemption (1 Cor. 1:30). The scriptural quotation is, however, quite remarkable, since it affirms precisely the divine initiative behind all of this, which according to many critical interpreters is lacking in this presentation.

One interpreter who has seriously engaged these interpretive problems is Eberhard Busch.[33] In what he calls "a conversation with" rather than "an interpretation of" the catechism, Busch demonstrates that a fair and proper interpretation and appraisal of the catechism's argument may be more difficult than at first apparent. In particular, Busch shows that it is possible to read answer 11 as the key: "God is indeed merciful, but also just." Because we do not know the content of these two characteristics beforehand — in other words, because we must not apply common cultural assumptions about either mercy or justice to the divine mercy and justice — the history of Jesus Christ described in answers 18 and following must

---

33. Eberhard Busch, *Der Freiheit zugetan: Christlicher Glaube heute — im Gespräch mit dem Heidelberg Katechismus* (Neukirchen: Neukirchener Verlag, 1998), pp. 79-110; see also pp. 142-75 and 219-42.

determine our understanding. It then becomes possible to see that the divine justice and mercy do not exclude one another. God is both, and both of these attributes and forms of God's action are important and positive. The divine mercy and the divine justice qualify one another. They do not succeed, replace, or follow one another in time, and they do not contradict or threaten one another. God practices mercy in the form of righteousness and justice as a form of mercy. God is merciful justice and righteous mercy at one and the same time in Jesus Christ.

Busch is arguing that the catechism is attempting precisely what McCormack expects of a faithful and convincing presentation of the Christian understanding of reconciliation. Not everyone would agree with such an evaluation of the Reformed confessional tradition, but at least Busch and McCormack agree on what would constitute a proper account because they have both been inspired by Karl Barth's doctrine of reconciliation and his influential account of atonement.

Barth? — "The redemptive fire of His love"

A brief but moving account by Busch helps to summarize Barth's major contribution.[34] Busch's presentation moves through four paragraphs. In the first, called "Repressed Sin," Busch points out, in ways reminiscent of the logic of both Calvin and the Heidelberg Catechism, that Barth wrote his doctrine of sin in the face of "an excess of wickedness" (pp. 199ff.).[35]

34. Eberhard Busch, *The Great Passion* (Grand Rapids: Eerdmans, 2004), pp. 199-218. The four volumes of Barth's doctrine of reconciliation, *CD* IV/1–IV/3, were written between 1951 and 1959, while IV/4 and the unrevised fragments published as *The Christian Life* were written between 1959 and 1961. Together they involve nearly 3500 pages of text. Volumes 1-3 spell out the saving history that is Jesus Christ. Salvation as divine act is the topic of *CD* IV/1. In *CD* IV/2 the focus shifts from God acting as reconciler to the one who is reconciled in him, to humanity reconciled. In *CD* IV/3, which covers two volumes, the focus is on the mediatorship of Christ, being both divine and human. Among other helpful accounts of Barth's position, see Colin Gunton, "Salvation," in *The Cambridge Companion to Karl Barth*, ed. John Webster (Cambridge: Cambridge University Press, 2000), pp. 143-58; John Webster, *Barth's Ethics of Reconciliation* (Cambridge: Cambridge University Press, 1995); and Timothy Gorringe, *Karl Barth: Against Hegemony* (Oxford: Oxford University Press, 1999), pp. 217-67. Gorringe's book argues for the contextuality of Barth's theology. His comments situating the doctrine of reconciliation against a historical backdrop are very helpful.

35. Page numbers in the text refer to Busch, *The Great Passion*.

Collective humanity took on "a terrifying and monstrous appearance" by way of large-scale murder and destruction, and by massive "lostness and condemnation," as though "fire fell down from heaven." Barth believed that humans had failed to come to grips with the enormity of this reality, the deep nature of human failure, rebellion, injustice, violence, and horror. In short, humans had no proper awareness of sin as sin. Says Busch, "Barth composed his doctrine of sin in the face of this alarming disconnect between the gigantic nature of the violence committed in our century and contemporary humanity's loss of a consciousness of guilt" (p. 199).

Why are we not aware of sin? Because we do not know God, says Barth. The decline in our knowledge of sin goes along with the decline in our knowledge of God (p. 201). For Barth, the highest accomplishment of sin, the "sin of all sins," consists in "refusing the name of the sinner," in denying, contesting, or repressing sin and our involvement in sin (p. 200). A certain form of theology may have contributed to this decline in our knowledge of God, and therefore to our involvement in sin (p. 201).

In this regard, Busch reminds readers of two crucially important citations from Barth, and briefly develops their relevance for an account of reconciliation. The first is that "there are few heresies so pernicious as that of a God who faces nothingness more or less unaffected and unconcerned, and the parallel doctrine of man as one who must engage in independent conflict against it" (p. 201). In Barth's estimation, this heresy has become popular in modern theology, and the Reformation is partly to blame, since it did not fully appreciate the importance of relating the law of God to the gospel. If the law is emptied from the gospel, isolated from it, and seen as merely preceding it, then we may be led to think that God stands over against evil as unaffected and unconcerned. This is a fundamental misunderstanding with disastrous consequences. Once this law emptied from the gospel as God's gracious involvement with us becomes a mere standard by which to judge what is sinful, and a standard available to us in our natural and moral laws, then we very easily begin to evaluate ourselves, to measure and judge ourselves, and indeed to pardon ourselves. We become able, in our own eyes, to deal with sin, according to the standards of the formal law that we possess and understand. We are no longer confronted by the gracious God himself, who is deeply concerned with us and therefore deeply affected by what happens to us (p. 201).

The second citation is that "there is no doctrine more dangerous than the Christian doctrine of reconciliation . . . if we do not consider it with this warning in view . . . that the fact that it speaks of God making good what we have spoiled does not mean that we can call evil good" (p. 202). The fundamental error here, Busch explains, would be to think that God's reconciliation is reconciliation with sin, that God by making good our evil deeds is calling our evil good. According to Barth, Reformation thought contributed to this error by allowing a form of "double bookkeeping" (p. 202). Sin and grace were seen not in radical conflict and contradiction, but as mutually compatible entities. Badness became tolerable, inevitable, part of who we are (p. 203).

By allowing these two heresies to become widespread, Reformation thought contributed to the very dangerous situation we face today. Sin has become harmless. If it becomes very disruptive, we think we can deal with it ourselves, by "engaging in independent conflict against it" (p. 203). If it is not very disruptive, we easily make allowance for it.

Against this backdrop, Busch continues to his second paragraph, "The Sympathetic Judge" (pp. 203ff.). We learn to recognize and name our sin precisely there where God not merely forbids it, but in fact engages it, actively confronts it, and shows himself to be deeply affected by it and involved with it. No law that is divorced from *this* gospel message — namely, that God subjects himself to sin in order to contend with it — will ever be able to show us the sinister reality of sin. The event in which God wrestles with sin is the reconciliation of the world with God in Jesus Christ on the cross. Busch calls this insight "Barth's decisive discovery" (p. 204).

The starting point of theological reflection on reconciliation should be our knowledge of the reality of this reconciliation (p. 204), which again raises the critical question of whether the Heidelberg Catechism starts (epistemologically) with this reality (as expressed in questions 1 and 18), allowing it to determine the logic of the presentation of the sections in between, or whether it employs, as critics claim, a logic based on human needs determined independently of this reality. For Barth and Busch, but also for most of the Reformed tradition since Calvin, the reality of the reconciliation makes us see its necessity, not the other way round. The cross demonstrates the serious and terrible nature of human corruption, not the law as a formal standard against which to measure ourselves, whether legal, moral, or natural.

There are, however, major implications for our knowledge of God and our doctrine of God, if we take seriously and follow the presupposition of Calvin's whole theological project, seeing God in the face of Jesus Christ, meditating on this face, and letting this experience define and determine our image of God. Says Busch,

> The fact that God is not uninvolved in his encounter with our sin, in that he reconciled us to himself in the suffering of Jesus Christ, means further that God himself, in unity with the One who suffers there, is in the lowliness of this suffering, and is so without "any alteration or diminution of His divine nature" yet also without any weakening of the gravity of his humiliation. In this regard we must "learn to correct our notions of the being of God," notions that are deeply rooted. (p. 205)

Busch cites a crucial passage in which Barth declares that "God is not uninvolved when he faces the dreadful character of the cross":

> With the eternal Son the eternal Father has also to bear what falls on the Son as He gives Himself to identity with the man Jesus of Nazareth, thus lifting it away from us to Himself in order that it should not fall on us. In Jesus Christ God Himself, the God who is the one true God, the Father with the Son in the unity of the Spirit, has suffered what it befell this man to suffer to the bitter end. It was first and supremely in Himself that the conflict between Himself and this man, and the affliction which threatened this man, were experienced and borne. What are all the sufferings in the world, even those of Job, compared with this fellow-suffering of God Himself which is the meaning of the event of Gethsemane and Golgotha? (p. 205)

These words come from *CD* IV/3, i.e., toward the latter part of Barth's massive exposition of the doctrine of reconciliation, and they presuppose and summarize central convictions and concerns of the whole discussion. They represent a major attempt to do exactly what McCormack has called for, to demonstrate that the love of God, deeply affected and engaged, is operative at every step along the way of redemption, coming to expression also in the cross, as the outpouring of God's wrath and judgment, but *for* us and our salvation.[36] There is no contradiction between God's mercy and God's righteousness here. Rather, in the passion of Jesus we see the ac-

---

36. "The decisive point is that the mercy of God toward us and his participation in relation to evil mean that the Humiliated One suffered '*for us.*'" See Busch, *The Great Passion*, p. 206.

tive passion of God's very self. This is what Barth calls "the revolution of God" (p. 206).[37]

We should never think that reconciliation merely means that God's attitude toward us is conciliatory. Instead, the reconciliation of the world with God in Christ takes place in the form of a real conflict, Busch says, a conflict with sin and sinners (p. 206). It takes place in the form of "the ruthless nonreconciliation of God with the wrong" (p. 206). Otherwise it would be cheap grace, but in reality — look at the cross! — it is "negation and not affirmation, condemnation and not validation, indeed destruction of sin and of the subject who has fallen victim to it and now practices it" (p. 206).

In Barth's own words, "the very heart of the atonement is the *overcoming* of sin . . . [but] *not* 'out of any desire for vengeance or retribution on the part of God'" (p. 206).[38] God does not seek satisfaction through some sacrificial victim, in order then to become more conciliatory. No, the wrath of God does not extinguish the love of God; it is in fact *"the redemptive fire of his love."*[39] Says Busch:

> The wrath of God . . . expresses the *righteousness* that is the will of his love. His love . . . practices righteousness. It is a distorted love that labels the wrong as, in fact, right. It is graceless to become an accomplice of the wrong. . . . The reconciling mercy of God, Barth stresses, is an incomparable right act in which God graciously overcomes sin through the exercise of the right. The issue is not that wrong should be "punished"; what is at stake is its removal. . . . *We do not know either grace or right if we do not see that in the reality of reconciliation grace and right are not two things, let alone an antithesis, but they are one and the same thing.*[40] (p. 207)

In order to explain this gracious act of God's right, Barth uses the expression "The Judge judged in our place" (*CD* IV/I, pp. 211-83). Here the influence of the tradition since Anselm, and all its associated problems concerning divine justice, are clearly at work. "Barth's answer to the age-

---

37. Referring to *CD* IV/I, pp. 546, 562.
38. Referring to *CD* IV/1, p. 253.
39. Referring to *CD* IV/I, p. 490 (my emphasis).
40. In this last sentence, Busch emphasizes only the word "one"; the remainder is my emphasis.

long question of why God became human is that he did so 'in order to *judge* the world,'" says Busch (p. 207). The Crucified is the true Judge, not judging according to a norm external to himself or according to a moral, legal, or cultural understanding of justice to which he is subjected. Rather, he himself is "the measure of all righteousness" (p. 208). In his suffering "for us," "taking our place," the true Judge "acts toward us as the divine and definitive and 'last day' Judge, making and executing his ultimate judgment" (p. 207).

In an astonishing way, the Savior of the world is also its Judge, but the judgment that he passes on sinners is their pardon. The divine yes is hidden in the divine no. The Judge is judged in our place. The verdict that ought to have been ours is pronounced and executed on him. We are now no longer in the place we occupied when we were sinners. He occupies that place. Our sin has become his sin. In him we have been judged already (p. 208). One hears in all these words and descriptions the richness of the scriptural account as well as the problems and questions of the Western theological tradition, but now framed in such a way that divine mercy and justice no longer conflict.

This love of God seen in the reality of the reconciliation on the cross is the justification of us sinners. Yet it is more, says Barth, since it is also the justification of God. In this work of the justification of unrighteous human beings, God also and in the first place justifies himself (p. 209).[41] Sin is menacing the whole work of God, the world as created by him, and his covenant that he made with the world that he created, and this menace is quite intolerable to God. The questions have therefore radically changed. The question raised by sin is not whether we can appease an angry God, but whether God is really the world's Creator and Lord in view of the chaos that has broken into creation. Has God chosen us in vain as covenant partners? Since it is ultimately God's own work that is threatened by sin, only God can contend with it. Through the reconciliation on the cross, God answers these questions and justifies himself (p. 209).

How does this judgment become the justification of the sinner? How does it actually reach and affect us? Busch considers such questions in a third paragraph, "The Justice of Grace" (pp. 209ff.). Reconciliation has the purpose that human beings be justified, before God. But what does that actually mean? Is it only nominally, "as though"? Or is it real, in any sense

41. Referring to *CD* IV/1, p. 561.

of the word? Here the second citation from Barth becomes important, says Busch, so that we do not call evil good (p. 209).

Busch first stresses that for our justification the judgment of God is very important (pp. 210ff.). In Barth's understanding, judgment is not opposed to grace, but is in fact the form of grace. It is namely *that* form of grace that cannot be reconciled with human wrong. It is that element in *this* God's grace that makes grace an act of opposition against our evil, including our self-destruction. The grace of *this* gracious God would not be grace without his judgment over the sin that destroys, denies, and violates. The judgment of *this* God is never without grace, but it is the redemptive fire of his love, judging *because* it is merciful (pp. 210-11).

Busch then stresses a second point, namely that the message of justification according to Barth proclaims the wonder that on the other side of this judgment human beings are, as it were, raised from the dead (pp. 211ff.). They are taken from death to life; they are created anew. Justification means — *also* means — the establishment of the right, the lordship of *this* God over us. Therefore, for Barth, everything depends on our not regarding this justification, including this killing of sinners, as "only nominal" (p. 211).

In descriptions very much like Calvin's portrayals of the *mortificatio* and the *vivificatio* of the Christian life, Barth stresses that the death of the sinner and the resurrection of the justified are real, that they actually take place, in Jesus Christ. It is a strange righteousness, but is also our righteousness, a history that concerns and involves us. The core of our sin is our resistance, our hostility to this grace (pp. 211-14).

In his fourth and final paragraph, Busch considers Barth's views on "The Validity of Reconciliation" (pp. 214ff.). This discussion reminds one of the comprehensive framework of Calvin's eucharistic theology. Barth's central definition of reconciliation, says Busch, is the fulfillment of the covenant between God and humanity (p. 214). If we should ask, like Anselm, why God became human, the answer should be, as the Old Testament discloses, that the covenant became threatened, because the human partner broke it, and that the coming of Jesus Christ was to fulfill it through reconciliation. Reconciliation therefore means that the covenant grace of God shows itself to the undeserving, as grace for lost sinners.

In sum, these four paragraphs raise four issues concerning our understanding of divine justice: (1) divine justice faces the seriousness of radical evil and sin; (2) divine justice is merciful; (3) divine justice establishes justification; it is real and active, renewing and life-changing; and (4) this saving and renewing divine justice establishes a richer and more comprehensive understanding of salvation, more in accord with the scriptural accounts, than that which the discourse of legal justification and judicial acquittal captures. These four themes have also been characteristic of diverse attempts of the Reformed tradition to understand the divine justice active in and through the gospel of justification.

3. Divine Justice and Legal Justice?

These last comments point to a very important issue. In reviewing the Western tradition since Anselm, at least as seen through Reformed eyes, I have made repeated references to the fact that the prevailing understandings of human justice, whether legal, moral, or cultural, often — perhaps always — played a major role in the theological and ecclesial discussions of the divine justice. It is as if people applied their own preferred understandings to God and to divine justice. But were these understandings adequate?

Over the last century, scholars from diverse disciplines have posed this question in one specific form: Has not the legal understanding of the Western world, influenced by its Greek and Latin judicial roots, been a major hindrance in the way of appreciating the scriptural accounts of justice, including also divine justice?

This concern has also caused major debates — exegetical, historical, and systematic — concerning Luther's views on justification and the role of divine justice. Many have argued that his existential experience of 1545 — of how he hated the divine justice and could not understand what Romans 1:17 could possibly mean, until his eyes were opened — was based on just such a legal or judicial understanding of the divine justice. The next question, then, has been about the adequacy of that position — both before and after Luther's experience of anxiety and his newly found insights of paradise — in relation to Paul's position.[42]

Many other scholars, and again from a variety of disciplines, have argued that typically legal or judicial understandings of the Old Testament

---

42. For an informed overview, see Martien E. Brinkman, *Justification in Ecumenical Dialogue: Central Aspects of Christian Soteriology in Debate* (Zoetermeer: IIMO, 1996), pp. 57-77; also, see McGrath, *Iustitia Dei*, pp. 376-87.

traditions concerning justice, both divine and human, and concerning the nature and role of the law, both divine and human, have missed the mark completely. Old Testament ideas of justice, as evidenced both by studies of expressions most commonly translated with words related to justice, and by studies of the covenant, of the laws, and of the divine character and actions, are worlds apart from typical Western legal understandings of justice. For the Old Testament, justice has to do with the order of the world, an order based on covenantal relationships of trustworthiness, fidelity, and reliability. Such justice is therefore concerned with actions, both divine and human, that embody covenantal reliability, demonstrated in acts of grace, salvation, healing, protection, compassion, and care.

Michael Welker, together with scholars like Jan Assmann and Bernd Janowski, have drawn on these insights to show that "judging" *(Richten)* and "saving" *(Retten)* belong inextricably together in the biblical conception of justice. Biblical justice is a saving justice *(rettende Gerechtigkeit)*, and the divine justice should be understood as a saving justice.[43] Under the influence of Western juridical, legal conceptions of justice, theologians have not always been true to the Scriptures, however complex, rich, and varied this alien influence has been, as McGrath's historical overview of *iustitia Dei* shows.

Although many of these viewpoints are still debated, a growing consensus can no longer be denied. The Western legal or judicial framework did not help the Christian tradition to appreciate the nature of divine justice and its integral role within the divine mercy and covenantal love, by which God has created us for covenantal life in abundance, and actively saves us from all forms of destruction and self-destruction, misery, evil, and threats.

This insight is particularly relevant to those traditions in which the law has been understood primarily, sometimes even exclusively, as a standard of measurement and therefore an instrument of accusation and punishment, calling for satisfaction and substitution, an expression of the divine anger and wrath, in open or hidden contradiction to divine grace and

---

43. See Jan Assmann, Bernd Janowski, and Michael Welker, *Gerechtigkeit* (München: Wilhelm Fink Verlag, 1998); also Michael Welker, "Dynamiken der Rechtsentwicklung in den biblischen Überlieferungen," in *Rechtsnorm und Rechtswirklichkeit*, ed. Aulis Aarnio (Berlin: Duncker & Humblot, 1993), pp. 779-95. For practical implications, see Michael Welker, "Moral, Recht und Ethos in evangelisch-theologischer Sicht," in *Ethik und Recht*, ed. Wilfried Härle and Reiner Preul (Marburg: N. G. Elwert, 2002), pp. 67-82.

mercy. Other traditions, such as the Reformed, where the whole of the Old Testament was taken seriously and seen in a positive light, and where the relationship between law and gospel was regarded as complex, rich, and complementary, have more easily appreciated that divine justice — most certainly *also* in a judicial form and as accusation, judgment, and punishment, but by far *not only* in this form — is closely related to mercy and grace, even if they have not always seen that justice as a manifestation of mercy and grace themselves.

4. Popular Piety and the Doctrine of Justification

The four major themes that have been present throughout the Reformed history of the doctrine of justification can frame a few concluding observations:

1. **Divine Justice Facing the Seriousness of Evil**
   a. The understanding of the divine justice dominant in popular piety in the Western church, especially in evangelical circles, reflects a serious caricature of the scriptural account of reconciliation in Jesus Christ and of the saving love and mercy of God active in reconciliation, including justification.
   b. Although the historical developments were complex and rich, and cannot be reduced to a simplistic and linear development, it is fair to say that this popular piety is based on an understanding of divine justice and accordingly of justification that is primarily moral and legal. The Western tradition has made it difficult to appreciate the biblical view of divine justice, especially the integral link between judging and saving.
   c. Luther's existential discovery that the justice of God was not something to hate and fear, but rather a saving, effective, and gracious justice, was still based primarily on such a legal, juridical framework.[44]

44. "I greatly longed to understand Paul's Epistle to the Romans and nothing stood in the way but that one expression, 'the justice of God,' because I took it to mean that justice whereby God is just and deals justly in punishing the unjust. . . . I did not love an angry God, but rather hated and murmured against him. . . . Night and day I pondered until I saw the connection between the justice of God and the statement that 'the just shall live by faith' (Romans 1:17). Then I grasped that the justice of God is that righteousness by which through

d. The tradition has acknowledged that human sin is extremely serious. Evil and injustice cannot simply go unpunished or be ignored. To act as if they do not matter would be a gross contradiction of the biblical views of divine justice. Even where a legal or juridical framework is no longer imposed on the scriptural account, sight should not be lost of the aspect of *Richten,* of judgment, of punishment of evil.

e. The Reformed tradition, including Calvin, Reformed Orthodoxy, influential Reformed confessions, and Barth, moves in the tradition of Anselm but has tried to take the scriptural and particularly the Old Testament accounts of divine justice and the law seriously. There has been an ongoing struggle about how to do justice to the integral link between divine mercy and divine justice, between God's own acts of salvation and grace and God's rejection and punishment of sin and evil.

f. In the *Joint Declaration* the dominant theory of the Western tradition plays no explicit role. It is still possible to point out, from an Orthodox perspective, that the whole problematic has historically been caused by, and in that sense still presupposes, a Western preoccupation with judicial and legal justice and justification. On the surface, however, the language of the declaration reflects nothing of the issues, emphases, and problems traditionally associated with the legal understanding of divine justice, with satisfaction and substitution, with a possible tension between God's grace and justice, or with a possible contradiction or conflict within the triune God. Rather, the biblical background of justification receives sustained attention, and the declaration's key formulations underline the divine grace at work and the fact that God is the active subject in our justification.[45]

---

grace and sheer mercy God justifies us through faith. Thereupon I felt myself to be reborn and to have gone through the gates of paradise. The whole of Scripture took on a new meaning, and whereas before the 'justice of God' had filled me with hate, now it became to me inexpressibly sweet in greater love. This passage of Paul became to me a gate of heaven." See Luther's account in James D. G. Dunn and Alan M. Suggate, *The Justice of God* (Grand Rapids: Eerdmans, 1993), p. 6.

45. See the key paragraph 15 in The Lutheran World Federation and the Roman Catholic Church, *Joint Declaration on the Doctrine of Justification* (Grand Rapids: Eerdmans, 2000).

2. Divine Justice Done by the Merciful God

g. A full account of the doctrine of justification and reconciliation calls for serious reflection on the doctrine of God.[46] The critical question has always been the operative doctrine of God at work in and behind views of the atonement. Some theologians therefore call for an account of the attributes of God, although others warn of the danger of speculation. Some argue that the doctrine of reconciliation calls for a trinitarian account of God, while others ask for an account of God's election.[47]

h. This fuller account of divine justice at work in our justification has pneumatological and ecclesiological implications. If justification is indeed the work of the triune God, involving the active and full salvation of human beings, including our renewal and regeneration, then attention should also be paid to the work of the Spirit in and through the church and in and through believers. One could argue that an awareness of these dimensions has traditionally been present in Reformed theology.[48]

3. Divine Justice Establishing the Actuality of Justification

i. A full account of the doctrine of reconciliation also calls for an account of sanctification.[49] It is not without reason that Calvin, the Heidelberg Catechism, and Barth all took the Christian life so seriously. If justification is not merely nominal, but actual, not only "as though," but somehow real, the doctrine of reconciliation should involve an account of the ethics of reconciliation. A scriptural understanding of divine justice necessitates nothing less.

46. In itself this claim does not solve the problems involved, since everything depends on the content of the doctrine of God involved. This point has been aptly illustrated by a recent study of justification within the theological projects of five major contemporary theologians, namely Jüngel, Pannenberg, Moltmann, Jenson, and Bayer. See Mark C. Mattes, *The Role of Justification in Contemporary Theology* (Grand Rapids: Eerdmans, 2004).

47. See the essays by John Webster and Katherine Sonderegger in this volume. Also, see the very relevant discussion in Bruce McCormack, "Grace and Being: The Role of God's Gracious Election in Karl Barth's Theological Ontology," in *The Cambridge Companion to Karl Barth*, pp. 92-110, esp. 98-110.

48. Colin Gunton is critical of a lack of attention to pneumatological and ecclesiological aspects of reconciliation in Barth, arguing that they do not receive enough "weight." See Gunton, "Salvation," in *The Cambridge Companion to Karl Barth*, pp. 155-57.

49. See the essay by John Burgess in this volume.

Many responses to the *Joint Declaration,* also many from a Lutheran background, emphasized this point and sometimes indicated disappointment that it is not already part of the consensus.[50]
j. In an ethics flowing from justification, attention should be given
to notions of human justice.[51] Barth powerfully related justification and justice.[52] In his ethics of reconciliation in the *Church
Dogmatics,* in which he portrays the Christian life in the form of an
exposition of the Lord's Prayer, the struggle for "small forms of
human righteousness" occupies central place.[53] Several responses
to the *Joint Declaration* argued that justice should have been considered.[54] In views of divine justice where *Richten* and *Retten* together describe God's saving work, doing justice has a proper

50. See the strong argument by the Lutheran ethicist from Marburg, Michael Haspel,
"Justification and Justice," in *The Doctrine of Justification,* ed. Karen L. Bloomquist and
Wolfgang Greive (Geneva: Lutheran World Federation, 2003), pp. 171-86; also Wolfgang
Huber, *Rechtfertigung und Recht* (Baden-Baden: Nomos Verlag, 2000), esp. pp. 21ff.

51. For consideration of some practical implications, see Duncan B. Forrester, *Christian
Justice and Public Policy* (Cambridge: Cambridge University Press, 1997), pp. 205-29; for an
overview of debates, see Brinkman, *Justification in Ecumenical Dialogue,* pp. 37-55.

52. See his three short essays on law and gospel, on justification and justice, and on the
Christian community and the civil community, that together demonstrate his thinking
about this relationship just before and after World War II, in *Community, State and Church,*
ed. Will Herberg (Garden City, NY: Doubleday, 1960). Also, see the essay by George
Hunsinger in this volume.

53. Recent years saw several helpful studies of Barth's ethics and of his ethics of reconciliation, e.g., the work by John Webster, including *Barth's Ethics of Reconciliation; Barth's
Moral Theology* (Grand Rapids: Eerdmans, 1998); and *Barth* (New York: Continuum, 2000).
Webster uses different expressions to describe this pervasive role of ethics in Barth, including "moral ontology" (borrowing from Charles Taylor), "an intrinsically ethical dogmatics,"
"our moral space," "the moral field," "a morally textured reality," and "the room of the gospel in which there is room for us" (all from *Ethics*); it is "intrinsically an ethical dogmatics, a
description of the human covenant partner as agent," "a counter-ontology" (borrowing
from John Milbank — see *Barth's Moral Theology*); it is "a trinitarian moral ontology of the
command of God," describing "the moral field," "the situation in which human agents
stand," "the moral nature of reality" *(Barth).* Also, see Dirkie J. Smit, " 'The Doing of the Little Righteousness' — On Justice in Barth's View of the Christian Life," in *Loving God with
Our Minds,* ed. Michael Welker and Cynthia Jarvis (Grand Rapids: Eerdmans, 2004), pp. 120-
45.

54. See the argument by H. Russel Botman calling it "a scandal" if we should break "the
doctrinal connection of justification with justice," in "Should the Reformed Join In?," *Reformed World* 52, no. 1 (2002): 12-17.

place. The notion of restorative justice from recent South African discussions of truth and reconciliation could prove useful.[55]

4. Divine Justice Bringing the Fullness of Salvation

k. Such an understanding of divine justice calls for combining the rich, varied, and complex descriptions of salvation in the biblical accounts with rich, varied, and complex analyses of the human condition, its lostness, and the need and suffering of the groaning creation. The scriptural portrayals go beyond the notion of justification, especially if their eschatological aspects are taken seriously. The content of the divine justice is much richer than the notion of justification can express, especially if heard only with judicial overtones.[56]

l. It is therefore unwise to regard the doctrine of justification as an adequate summary of divine justice — this saving mercy and grace of the triune God — active in all aspects of salvation. Not only are there many other powerful metaphorical descriptions of salvation, but even those with strong aspects of justification may simultaneously possess a wealth of other meanings and associations.[57]

m. In particular, we need a fuller and more positive account of the law of God in order to appreciate the richness of divine justice. This point has been important traditionally to Reformed theology and

55. See the essay by Sándor Fazakas in this volume. Also, see Desmond Tutu, *No Future without Forgiveness* (London: Rider, 1999); John W. de Gruchy, *Reconciliation: Restoring Justice* (London: SCM Press, 2002).

56. Barth comments on this point when he considers the miracles of Jesus and the too narrow understanding of them in the Western theological tradition. "Looking back we may well ask with amazement how it was that the Reformation, and (apart from a few exceptions) the whole of earlier and especially more recent Protestantism as it followed both Luther and Calvin, could overlook this dimension of the Gospel which is so clearly attested in the New Testament — its power as a message of mercifully omnipotent and unconditionally complete liberation from φθορα, death and wrong as the power of evil. How could Protestantism as a whole, only too faithful to Augustine, the 'father of the West,' orientate itself in a way which is so one-sidedly anthropological (by the problem of repentance instead of by its presupposition — the kingdom of God)?" Karl Barth, *CD* IV/2 (Edinburgh: T. & T. Clark, 1958), p. 233. Also, see Dirkie J. Smit, "Paradigms of Radical Grace," in *On Reading Karl Barth in South Africa*, ed. Charles Villa-Vicencio (Grand Rapids: Eerdmans, 1986), pp. 17-44; and the essay by Michael Weinrich in this volume.

57. As Hunsinger has demonstrated regarding "the blood of Christ." See his "Meditation on the Blood of Christ," in *Disruptive Grace*, pp. 361-63.

has also become important in recent ecumenical reflection.[58] In this regard, Welker's work on law and gospel is helpful. Welker shows that justice, compassion, and truth are interwoven in the legal codices of the Old Testament, in the preaching of Jesus, and in the work of the Holy Spirit, and should remain closely interwoven for church and theology today. A positive understanding of the law — as justice between equals, compassionate reintegration of the marginalized, and the knowledge and worship of God as the enduring foundation and critical source of this justice and compassion — does not contradict gospel and Spirit, but rather informs and structures knowledge and practice of the gospel.[59] Divine justice involves compassion; it is caring justice for the helpless and suffering.[60]

In this regard, Michael Weinrich strongly expresses his disappointment with the *Joint Declaration,* claiming that its use of the Old Testament falls below standards achieved long ago in both Catholic and Lutheran the-

---

58. As the bishop and widely respected social ethicist Wolfgang Huber has argued at length. See Wolfgang Huber, *Gerechtigkeit und Recht. Grundlinien christlicher Rechtsethik* (Gütersloh: Chr. Kaiser, 1996), pp. 107ff. Huber describes the positions of the different confessional traditions very well.

59. Michael Welker, "Security of Expectations: Reformulating the Theology of Law and Gospel," *Journal of Religion* 66 (1986): 237-60; "Righteousness and God's Righteousness," *The Princeton Seminary Bulletin* (1990): 124-39.

60. It is in this spirit that the South African Reformed *Confession of Belhar* confesses: "We believe that God has revealed Godself as the One who wishes to bring about justice and true peace among human beings; that in a world full of injustice and enmity God is in a special way the God of the destitute, the poor and the wronged and that God calls the Church to follow in this; that God brings justice to the oppressed and gives bread to the hungry; that God frees the prisoner and restores sight to the blind; that God supports the downtrodden, protects the stranger, helps orphans and widows and blocks the path of the ungodly; that for God pure and undefiled religion is to visit the orphans and the widows in their suffering; that God wishes to teach his people to do what is good and to seek the right; that the Church must therefore stand by people in any form of suffering and need, which implies, among other things, that the Church must witness against and strive against any form of injustice, so that justice may roll down like waters, and righteousness like an ever-flowing stream; that the Church as the possession of God must stand where God stands, namely against injustice and with the wronged; that in following Christ the Church must witness against all the powerful and privileged who selfishly seek their own interests and thus control and harm others." See *A Moment of Truth,* ed. G. D. Cloete and D. J. Smit (Grand Rapids: Eerdmans, 1984).

ology, thereby at risk of going wrong. He summarizes many of the central aspects of the Reformed understanding of justification and divine justice that we have also reviewed here:

> If justification is not fundamentally based on God's election and God's steadfast faithfulness to his covenant we cannot grasp the theological depth of its biblical meaning. God's election of those poor and enslaved Hebrew people in Egypt is an act of justification. The gift of the covenant is an act of justification. The law was never a way to salvation but it was grounded on justification. Renewing the covenant which was broken by the people was an act of justification. Justification is not just a matter of the New Testament, it is the matter of the whole Bible. To believe in justification by God is basically to believe in God's faithfulness. God's justice was never in contrast to his mercy. There is a mutual implication of justice and mercy: if we put justice over against mercy everything will go wrong.[61]

---

61. Michael Weinrich, "The Reformed Reception of the Joint Declaration," *Reformed World* 52, no. 1 (2002): 22-23.

5 Called to Salvation in Christ: Justification and Predestination

Katherine Sonderegger

To students of the doctrine of predestination it will come as no surprise to hear that the 1999 *Joint Declaration on Justification* says nothing on election or reprobation. It is one of the truisms of the modern era in Christian theology that the question of predestination has lost its hold on pulpit and pew. In *The Courage to Be,* Paul Tillich famously divides the theological eras into categories of existential struggle: over death, in the early period (ontic anxiety); over worthiness, in the late medieval period and Reformation (moral anxiety); and finally over meaning, in our time (spiritual anxiety).[1] Luther's quest was characterized by Tillich as the existential question, "How can I appease the wrath of God? How can I attain divine mercy, the forgiveness of sin?" (p. 59). And that question, Tillich concluded, had lost its power as a central religious quest, or, in Tillich's idiom, as a "symbolic expression of one's ultimate concern" (pp. 189, 190). We moderns are gripped by the search for meaning in our lives, but such a quest does not touch on or spring from a doctrine of divine foreknowledge and predestination. Rather, it is the Lord God himself — the symbol of Ultimate Meaning — who must be affirmed and elected in a world of anomie and suffering.

One need not be a follower of Tillich in all things to see the power of his analysis here. The theological systems of the First World — the Atlantic cultures of Europe and North America — have not placed the doctrine of predestination at the foundation of their dogmatics — with Karl Barth, perhaps, as the lone exception. (We will address that "perhaps"

1. Paul Tillich, *The Courage to Be* (New Haven: Yale University Press, 1952).

later.) More striking still is the silence in our art and our preaching about the quest for the certainty of one's election and the fear of reprobation. Indeed we might distinguish the large-scale, catholic denominations from the sectarian churches in the First and developing world on this very matter: what is for the mainline and Roman Catholic Christian a largely historical artifact is for the emerging Christian a vital drama, the eschatological act of God's election of sinners to grace and glory. Little wonder that the preaching of only a century or two ago sounds so foreign to our modern ears! Consider Jonathan Edwards's "Sinners in the Hands of an Angry God," not so anomalous a sermon in Edwards's corpus as is sometimes confidently asserted. Here is a major doctrinal sermon, delivered by the leading Puritan divine of his day, to a prominent congregation of the Connecticut River Valley. To our near ancestors, election and reprobation were considered natural, significant, and weighty themes for congregational preaching.

Several centuries more divide us from the murals, frescoes, and miniatures of religious art that depict the Final Judgment, Harrowing of Hell, and Dance of Death. To be sure, there are historical and sociological elements at work in the widespread and vivid scenes of divine predestination; such rich and evocative depictions of human hopes and fears cannot be devoid of material causes. But we overlook the striking theological power of these images if we do not see that the eschatological fate of one's life gripped Christians from elites to commoners, and on the strength of these hopes and fears spring the towers, chantries, shrines, monasteries, and pilgrimages of Europe. Little wonder that the polemics of the Reformers, among themselves and against Rome, turned on debates about predestinating grace and the liberty of the predestinate will. Among the seventeenth-century Protestant dogmaticians, Lutheran and Reformed, predestination remained a centerpiece of orthodoxy, even at the price of polemic between the two Confessions. This doctrine was the common idiom of Christian theology in the pre-modern era; and between us and them a great gulf is fixed.

So, little wonder that the *Joint Declaration on Justification,* signed by the World Federation of Lutheran Churches and the Roman Catholic Church, two unimpeachable citizens of the catholic, developed world, spends no time in controversy or agreement about election and reprobation. This is just as we expect, after all. The document appears to share and simply reflect the modern theological culture of indifference toward the doctrine of divine decrees. Perhaps this makes the *Joint Declaration* an odd place to begin Reformed reflections on the place of election in God's justifying work. We do not ordinarily expect to learn anything substantial from silence: it seems hardly promising to expect to learn something new from something missing. Nor does it appear promising to examine yet more closely the cultural assumptions of an age that seems to effortlessly detach doctrines of justification, merit, and grace from their origin in God's predestinating and electing will. Yet, surprisingly, the *Joint Declaration's* silence on predestination is not quite as straightforward or prosaic as all this might lead us to believe. This chapter explores the surprising implications of examining the doctrine of justification apart from its context in election — implications that touch on the history of doctrine, the legacy of the Reformation, and the modern commitment to ecumenical theology.

It is well worth pausing a while to consider how startlingly new it is to separate justification from the divine decrees. The doctrine of justification in the pre-modern world was fully integrated into the doctrine of predestination: only the elect were called; only the called were justified. Justification could no more be discussed as a fully separate *locus,* distinct from election, than could ordination, distinct from ecclesiology. The Augustinian structure of redemption — God's determination of the elect, his gifts of grace to turn the sinner's heart, to justify, and to persevere to the end — stood in the near background of every debate, Catholic, Lutheran, and Reformed, about justification. The *ordo salutis,* which moved from divine decision to creaturely glorification, formed the larger context that gave meaning and force to the doctrine, much as shadows define figures. New in our era is the conviction that predestination need no longer be part and parcel of the *ordo salutis:* justification can now stand alone as a doctrine of the creatures' status before the Creator.

The silence about election in the *Joint Declaration,* then, casts in bold relief the contemporary view of the history of doctrine and its place in ecumenical theology. This history will form the heart of my essay, exploring the Reformed and Lutheran controversies in the scholastic era over electing grace and the order of the predestinating decrees. The framework for this history will be set by the insights gained about the genre of ecumenical agreements, their composition and premises. The conclusion will offer a Reformed assessment of this modern willingness to detach justification from its broader context in predestination — and its cost. To anticipate the argument of the whole: Predestination forms the necessary context to justification, as shadow to light; without it, justification itself loses definition, rigor, and force.

We begin with the genre of ecumenical agreements, as it frames and introduces the historical and systematic questions that lie deeper within the theological matter of the text.

The *Joint Declaration on Justification* as Ecumenical Theology

The signatories to the *Joint Declaration* seek to find common expression to those doctrines that have been church-dividing: only those confessions and dogmas that give rise to declarations of condemnation fall within the scope of this document. The major sources for these church-dividing condemnations are the Decrees of the Council of Trent and the Formula of Concord, and within those, only those anathemas that touch on justification explicitly. Seven areas are brought out for discussion: Justification and cooperative grace; Justification as forensic and inherent; Justification as *sola fide;* Sin in the Justified; Law and Gospel; *Certitudo;* and Justification and meritorious works (JD 4.1–4.7). Predestination and election have no place on this list as they are not explicitly under debate at Trent — those debates are reserved for the dawn of the seventeenth century when Molinism becomes prominent, and controversial, in Jesuit theology — nor in the Formula, though they are discussed in the appendix. Indeed: "There has been no public, scandalous, and widespread dissension among the theologians of the Augsburg Confession concerning the eternal election of the children of God" (FC, Article XI). The framework of this genre, then — the exclusion of all topics that do not divide the church — isolates and sharply focuses the doctrinal light, bringing the controverted matter into high relief, but also casting in shadow the doctrines that, in surrounding the polemical doctrines, give them strength and meaning.

This loss of the greater, surrounding context to doctrine is the cost of ecumenical irenicism. *Mutatis mutandis,* we may be reminded of the philosophical example of the wink: the twitch of an eyelid becomes the expression of irony, affection, or teasing not through the motion itself, but through the larger environment, custom, and unstated practice of human culture. The loss of the greater context is the loss of the wink as a wordless form of human exchange. Perhaps we catch a glimpse of the worry about loss of context in the *Joint Declaration* itself. Commenting on the prominence of justification as the "indispensable criterion" by which church teaching is "oriented" — the article by which the church stands or falls — the Catholic writers do not want to lose the larger theological environment: they "see themselves as bound by several criteria" and underscore the "internal relation of all truths of the faith" — an emphasis Lutherans do not deny (JD 3.18). It may well be that the ecumenical theologians would have said more on other doctrines and their integrated, holistic relation to one another than the ecumenical genre allows, for they no doubt recognize that, like the gesture of the wink, the unsaid assumptions disclose the meaning, force, and reach of what is said explicitly. But in this genre, only justification is "said"; predestination, which conditions, grounds, and gives meaning to the doctrine of justification, stands in the shadows. Readers of ecumenical documents must supply the rest, for without context the force of the doctrine and the doctrinal agreement remain obscure.

Church history, too, is sharply focused and isolated by the ecumenical genre. Indeed, the very engine that drives the agreement is the willingness to archaize the condemnations that divide the church: those anathemas belong to the churches that issued them, but do not "strike at" the churches of the present-day (JD 5.42). We see here some of the quiet acceptance of John Henry Newman's idea of the development of doctrine, where the essence of the "Christian Idea" is preserved in "notes of true development" amidst real change of idiom, expression, and form.[2] In Newman's famous maxim: "In a higher world it is otherwise, but here below to live is to change, and to be perfect is to have changed often." In the *Joint Declaration,* the Catholic and Lutheran partners acknowledge that they no longer teach the "chief article" as they once did, such that the condemnations remain valid for those churches that did and do teach justification under the idiom and form of medieval doctrine, but not for those who express the original idea in the new, developed form. In Newman's phrase, the anathemas do not define the doctrine or conclude its development. Rather, like other church controversies, they belong to the development itself. These anathemas function much as do heresies and doctrinal strife in Newman's system: they clarify and animate the central Idea; the old and corrupt is shaken off and the vital and true, strengthened and preserved.

2. John Henry Newman, *An Essay on the Development of Doctrine* (Garden City, NY: Doubleday, 1960), part II, ch. 5, p. 63.

There is genius in this ecumenical irenicism. The condemnations of the Reformation era need not be retracted in order for ecumenical work to go forward; indeed, they are expressly affirmed (JD 5.43). In this way, the theologians — some of them martyrs — are allowed their judgments, fitting for their day. But the church today can leave those quietly behind, without — it is hoped — reducing theological argument to equivocation. The formula adopted for this ecumenical development of doctrine is the statement of common confession, followed by "differing emphases": theological differences not deep or sharp enough to be church-dividing, yet not so antiquated as to be otiose. Significantly, predestination does not belong to either church's distinctive "emphasis."

Yet this silence about predestination hardly means that the history of this doctrine vanishes without a trace on the *Joint Declaration*. On the contrary! Its silence rests on a quiet agreement on the seventeenth-century Lutheran and Catholic developments in doctrine. Following the exegetical section of the declaration, the framers turn to the heart of the agreement, Section 3, the "Common Understanding of Justification." Paragraph 16, while seemingly summary in nature, tacitly rests on the achievement of post-Reformation Lutheran and Catholic teaching on election: "All people are called by God to salvation in Christ. Through Christ alone are we justified when we receive this salvation in faith. Faith is itself God's gift through the Holy Spirit who works through word and sacrament in the community of believers and who, at the same time, leads believers into that renewal of life which God will bring to completion in eternal life." Lying behind this allusion to 1 Timothy is a century of polemic between Lutheran and Reformed divines — the "Protestant scholastics" — on the extent, aim, and foundation of the divine decree on election of sinners to grace and glory.

Predestination in the Older Protestant Divines

Seventeenth-century Protestant divines inherited a complex debate over the multiple forms of Augustinianism that governed the Latin church in the medieval era; to this, they added their own sophisticated stock of conceptual distinctions that linked the doctrine of God to soteriology and ecclesiology. Not surprisingly, all sides affirmed a robust doctrine of divine simplicity, the hallmark of "classical theism." God, without parts, or potency, or change, or matter, must know and will and decree with a single, pure act that is his own being. On the whole, the Protestant scholastics side with Thomas Aquinas in his claim that God's attributes are identical to his essence — the highest form of divine simplicity — but some, especially in the Lutheran camp, accepted Duns Scotus's tolerance for a certain conceptual diversity with the divine simplicity, such that the attributes need not be strictly identical to the essence. We might consider this a broader form of divine simplicity. Such transcendental distinctions matter to scholastic theology because the divine foreknowledge, providence, and predestination of creatures join the multiple with the utterly Simple and severely test the boundaries of divine sovereignty and creaturely autonomy.

Because God is utterly and always God, the relation God has to his creatures must be unique: God does not receive from creatures knowledge of their state, aims, or acts but rather knows them from his own being as Creator. Thus, the unfolding of the world's course, from inorganic to organic and human history, must be known by God immediately, perfectly, and eternally. Stemming from Augustine's systematic work on the doctrine of Trinity, the Protestant doctrine of divine knowledge and will was assimilated to the persons of the Trinity: the Son, the Logos, as God's knowledge; the Spirit, God's will. These acts of the divine intellect were entirely *a se:* the only object of divine agency — strictly speaking — is God himself. Medieval debates over the divine knowledge of particulars or of future contingents in the creaturely realm turned on the complex relation of God's own inner thought and will to the world *ad extra;* but never by loosening the strictures on divine sovereignty and aseity.

Into this systematic structure of divine act and attribute fell the Reformation debate over justification, human liberty, and divine election. Certainly, the humanism of the magisterial Reformers allowed a breadth of rhetorical expression denied scholastics, early and late. While Luther clearly knew and used ably the conceptual distinctions of the schools, he did not debate the doctrines of election and human agency in dialectical form, but rather he debated exegetically, using literary modes in turns medieval and startlingly modern. So too Calvin shows his scholastic training in the *Institutes* but does so warily, and favors instead the rhetorical and exegetical style of the renaissance classicists. But this greater literary freedom of expression never destroyed the scholastic and logical underpinnings; indeed the seventeenth-century divines, under the impress of new Aristotelian and Ramist logics, made explicit and systematic the doctrines of divine perfection and immutability assumed by an earlier generation.

All sides to the sixteenth-century debates, then, agreed that predestination was a central act of God with his creatures; all agreed that election was the larger doctrinal context for the work of justification. This allowed the signers of the Formula of Concord to quietly announce their consensus on the divine decrees. Even Erasmus in his public debate with Luther could not bring himself to repudiate God's sovereign electing act, however much he hoped to find an agreeable *via media* in matters of merit, grace, and choice. Human agency, and its place within the *ordo salutis,* sparked the fiery Reformation debates; election remained the common coin for Calvin, Luther, and Trent.

We may well wonder about this broad, pre-modern consensus. Why was everyone so confident about the common background to the doctrine of justification? To say that the doctrine of predestination was considered scriptural and ineliminable from Augustine's legacy to the church only begs the question. It is these certainties of the age, and their undoing, that attracted Paul Tillich's eye; his theory of the living symbol was designed to reflect upon — though probably not to explain — history's changes. Perhaps the most that we can say is that Calvin and Luther and the Tridentine theologians simply agreed with Augustine in his anti-pelagian writings: to deny electing grace is to "empty the cross of Christ of power." The collapse of that background agreement is the story of modern theology in the West.

The seventeenth century finally brought conflict over election to the Protestant camp. Lutheran and Reformed did battle over election in the scholastic era, a battle that laid the groundwork for the implicit doctrines of the *Joint Declaration.* We turn first to the Reformed; then the Lutheran.

Turretin as Exemplar of Reformed Teaching on Election

Francis Turretin sums up with particular rigor this seventeenth-century development in his late compendium, *Institutes of Elenctic Theology* (1696).[3] Here, a Reformed dogmatician sets out the consensus position of European Calvinists after the Synod of Dort: neither Lutheran nor Roman, neither Arminian nor Socinian. This is a systematic work aimed at clarity and precision in controversy — "elenctic" (refutative) rather than irenic or

---

3. Francis Turretin, *Institutes of Elenctic Theology,* trans. G. Giger, ed. J. Dennison (Phillipsburg, NJ: P. & R. Publishing, 1992).

ecumenical! After opening sections on the genus of theology itself and Scripture as its foundation, the *Institutes* moves through the classical doctrine of God, his unity, attributes, and Trinity, to the long, central section on the divine decrees and predestination. Unlike many earlier scholastics, Turretin does not treat predestination as a species of the general doctrine of providence but rather views election, as does Barth, as a development of the doctrine of God.

Significantly, for Turretin and the Reformed dogmaticians in general, the simplicity of God thus governs the doctrine of the decrees, *realiter*. The distinctions and ordering controverted with other churches cannot belong to God's being as *essential* distinctions — only the triune persons form real relations in the Godhead — but rather belong to the realm of human conceptions: "For we are compelled to divide into various inadequate conceptions what we cannot compass in one single conception; however this is not said on the part of God himself who decreed with himself all these things by a single and most simple act" (ET, p. 430, 4th Topic, section XXIV). Spread over the whole treatment of predestination, then, is a modesty and horror of "idle curiosity" Calvin would recognize and approve. Ramist logic echoes a theme in Thomas's doctrine of analogy: the essence of God, utterly simple and unique, cannot be known as such, through an act of direct intellection, but must rather be understood through dialectical pairs of terms, through an act of discursive reason. Temporal sequence, contrasting attributes, and logical ordering are not, then, for the Scholastics a direct description of the divine life — but neither are they empty distinctions. What is one transcendentally is *necessarily* multiple and diverse in human thought. Scholastic concepts refer to divine realities, but under the conditions of creaturehood. Moreover, the doctrines of the divine decrees are to be studied for their fruitfulness for the Christian life — the life "lived for God" as William Ames would have it — and are to be treated not as technical points of systematic theology but instead as mysteries, simple and utterly one in themselves, yet diverse, ordered and determined for us.

Turretin, like all Reformed divines, holds that God decrees or wills his own Being: God decrees his "good-pleasure" *(eudokias)* as an internal and essential act of his nature. This divine good pleasure or counsel, then, cannot be other than the divine essence and *ratio* itself, a simple, rational will, which takes the divine nature as its Object but "terminates" in the creature. Much as Thomas argued that God knew creatures through knowing himself as their Cause and End, so Turretin argues that God wills the end of all creatures through the knowledge of himself as the Good Pleasure, Justice, and Glory of the world. Thus, God's relation to the world is a "schematism" *(schesis)*, a term that finds its modern uses in Kant's critical vocabulary. God's counsels are absolute; they cannot be altered by the acts of the creature nor can they depend on anything outside the divine good pleasure itself. From this follows the Reformed divines' confident assertion that there is a "fixed and immovable end" to each human life, "determined by the decree of God" (ET, 4th Topic, Q. v, the End of Life). The *decretum absolutum* and the "necessity of future events" follow directly from the theological claim that the divine decree is in God *realiter* and partakes of the divine simplicity.

Now, this absolute decree is realized in the acts *ad extra* of election and reprobation, the doctrine of predestination. Turretin reports the consensus of the Reformed divines, against Trent and the Remonstrants, that the sole cause of predestination is the mercy and justice of God, or, echoing Romans, the demonstration of his glory. So absolute is this purpose that even the Incarnate Word cannot be the "impulsive cause" or "foundation" of predestination — neither his merits nor his passion nor his exemplary obedience — for no creature can act upon or determine a divine counsel. From out of his own good pleasure, God determines for himself some creatures for grace and glory, some for rejection and damnation; election does not mark out anything in the creature as such, nor is the sin and infidelity of the reprobate the ground — though it is the correlate, the *"sine qua non"* — of rejection. God does not foresee merits in the creature, neither works nor faith, nor does he abandon only those *(preterition)* who disobey and harden their hearts. Rather, the divine Ruler *(autokratoros)* autonomously and royally determines vessels for wrath and for glory, some to set forth his justice by being left in their sins, and others to exhibit his mercy by being delivered by his grace.

This Augustinian focus on Romans 9–11 gives rise to the Reformed debate over the ordering and *scopus* — aim or end — of the divine decrees. Turretin follows the pattern of Dort in making the human being, "created and fallen" *(creatus et lapsus)*, the *scopus* of election, an infralapsarian ordering of the decrees. That is, predestination logically follows on and assumes the doctrines of creation and fall. Turretin does not consider the supralapsarian ordering church-dividing, though he finds it less persuasive exegetically and systematically. Supralapsarians hold that the object of predestination is the human being capable of being created and fallen (*creabilis et labilis*) and in this way precedes in human thought both the doctrines of creation and fall. The Infralapsarian majority saw ethical reason vindicated in its ordering: God's electing will extends to what is, not merely to what is possible, and more tellingly, God's justice extends to those already dead in sin, denying sinners — not the innocent — the grace of saving faith and justification.

But in either ordering of the decrees, the Reformed held in unison that God did not decree the universal salvation of all, either "antecedently" or absolutely: God was no universalist. The Reformed shared with Christians of all schools in that generation that some human creatures were not saved; no one denied the reality of damnation. Indeed the very debate so vital to Luther's life before God — can I be certain of my election? — turned on the acknowledgment that damnation was a steady and present threat to every creature, even — perhaps especially to — every believer. What *was* open to debate was the range of divine grace: Did God proffer grace universally? As the Reformed from Calvin to Turretin acknowledge, 1 Timothy 2:4 ("God wills all human beings to be saved") appeared to teach just such a universal offer. "Antecedently," it was said by opponents of the Reformed, God willed universal salvation through Christ; "subsequently" God applied this grace effectively to the elect. Or, for Arminians and some Lutherans, God wills universal grace; only those who accepted it — perhaps through grace itself — would receive the salvation God offered. Such variants on the doctrine of election occasioned strong polemic from the Reformed from Calvin forward, who held, against their opponents, that grace extended only to the elect, and did so irresistibly. But neither Reformed nor Lutherans, Roman Catholics nor Arminians of the seventeenth century assumed that this verse taught universal, effective *salvation*. All sides agreed that there were many, perhaps most, who spurned the gospel and grieved the Holy Spirit. All taught a form of the divine decree.

The debate over universal offers of grace, then, stemmed not from their threat to the doctrine of reprobation but rather from their threat to the believer's hard-won certainty of election: Reformed divines held that should salvation extend to all on condition of acceptance, faith, or good works, certainty could only apply to the *condition* of the offer, not to the gift of election itself. The goal prized by Luther — *certitude* — could be won, the Reformed argued, only if the decrees shared in the sovereign surety of God himself; only the *decretum absolutum*, working irresistibly by grace, offered refuge to troubled souls.

Karl Barth as Exemplar of Modern Reformed Doctrine of Election

Famously, Karl Barth in his magisterial second volume of the *Church Dogmatics* disputes nearly all the certainties of the Reformed teaching on election.[4] Such disputes did not spring, however, from any distaste for the Protestant scholastics. On the contrary! It was otherwise with Barth's teachers. Fashionable among Protestant academic theologians in the nineteenth century was the view that the "Older Orthodoxy" was unusable and fatally rationalistic, a theology handed over to "arid metaphysics and speculation." Not so the young Barth, however much he later saw seeds of Protestant modernism in their work. Through Heppe and Dorner,[5] Barth discovered with delight the rigor and "objectivity" of these seventeenth-century divines, and learned how doctrine could be rendered coherent through careful method. Indeed it would be difficult to overestimate the shaping influence of the Reformed divines in the *Church Dogmatics* as a whole. Never is this clearer than in Barth's doctrine of election.

For Barth, Christ must be the true ground and object of election; he alone the true Elector and Elected, the One elected for rejection. From this central act of self-determination within the Godhead, election itself moves first to the community — Israel and the church — and then only, through the medium of community, the individual, taken up into Christ. This makes election, Barth argues, a doctrine of joyous good news, the herald of the Book of Life, not the warning of a hidden and awesome *Decretum Absolutum*. To be sure, there is rejection, penalty, and death! But these are Christ's properly and truly, as he has elected them for himself. The doctrine of election, in Barth's hands, is no timeless and static counsel, but rather a "history" and an "event" of God's covenant with humanity in Jesus Christ. Barth rehearses here his major themes in his opposition to scholastic, natural theology: God's sovereignty and trustworthiness are compatible with the temporality, movement, and direction that the divine covenant with historical beings implies. Only a lifeless God, Barth claims, could

---

4. Karl Barth, *Church Dogmatics* II/2, ed. G. W. Bromiley and T. F. Torrance (Edinburgh: T. & T. Clark, 1957).

5. Heinrich Heppe, *Reformed Dogmatics, Set Out and Illustrated from the Sources* (London: Allen & Unwin, 1950); Isaak Dorner, *History of Protestant Theology, Particularly in Germany, Viewed According to Its Fundamental Movement and in Connection with the Religious, Moral and Intellectual Life* (Edinburgh: Clark, 1871).

remain impassible and immutable in decree, election, and reconciliation. In a lengthy excursus, Barth lays out the seventeenth-century debates on the ordering of the decrees, much of this still under the influence of Heppe and Dorner. He favors the supralapsarian position as more congenial to a Christological center for God's electing act. Yet, in his focus on Christ as savior to the lost, and one determined from divine eternity to assuming and expiating sin and its penalty, Barth conforms his doctrine to the Infralapsarian focus on the created and fallen human life. Overarching his treatment of the doctrine as a whole stands the notion of gracious covenant — itself dear to Puritan divines — as the divine *pactum* initiated by God with Israel, with King David, and realized in the Royal Son, Jesus Christ, himself as such, the reconciliation of God with rebel humanity. Election, in Barth's eyes, teaches the gospel of grace as it sets out the universal reach of Christ's reconciling work: all human creatures are elect in him, as he is the head of all humanity, the Lord of the whole church, the call and the content that is to reach every ear, Jew and Gentile — that death, sin, and the devil are defeated in Christ.

That Barth's treatment of this doctrine is fresh, innovative, and remarkable, one can scarcely doubt: *Church Dogmatics* II/2 is rightly prized as a hallmark of rigorous, historical, and synthetic theological imagination. But we may well wonder if Barth's doctrine is not *sui generis*, a doctrine of divine reconciliation that so transforms the central pillars of predestination that it strains membership in that family. Here is truly a universal election — not, to be sure, a doctrinaire universalism — in which all take their part, witting or not, and stand oriented toward the destiny of life in Christ, an utterly gracious fact founded on the happy exchange of the Incarnate Lord for the sinful world. Such transformations in doctrine make Barth's own theology of election more modern than his sources may suggest — indeed, a fitting companion to Schleiermacher's — and in an irony perhaps welcomed by Barth himself, more Lutheran than Reformed.

Lutheran Scholastics on the Doctrine of Election

In the seventeenth-century debates with the Reformed, the Lutherans developed a doctrine of the *decretum conditionatum*, a decree conditioned — not absolute — by God's foreknowledge of faithful apprehension of Christ's justifying work. Those whom God foreknew to receive Christ with faith constituted the elect; those who turned aside were hardened. These notes, certainly, are not lacking in the Reformed *ordo salutis:* the elect are graciously called through the means of the church, Word and sacrament, and justified through the divinely appointed executive of salvation, Jesus Christ, who dies for our sins. Yet, for the Lutherans — and this was decisive — divine grace was universal and resistible, positions acceptable to Trent. The certainty of election cannot then rest upon the immutable simplicity of God's will; rather, certainty stems from faithful assent to divine assurance. Such certainty must be held distinct from base *securitas*, a "carnal" security in one's own merit and act. We might even say that a pious insecurity is compatible with a conditioned decree. Believers look away from themselves to the *speculum electionis*, Christ, the mirror of election. Yet, their status as believers, while a gift of grace, remains contingent upon an offer accepted and embraced, and until death, that status is fallible. Faith is the free, self-involving assent to the divine promise; just so, the "gift of perseverance" or "final faith" is simply belief that in fact perseveres to the end.

In the seventeenth century, talk of a conditional decree and foreseen faith raised specters of synergism and semi-pelagianism in the minds of the orthodox Reformed — and some Lutherans as well. Seventeenth-century Lutheran divines, no strangers to scholastic precision, offered refinements to these terms, affirming that faith could never be the "impulsive cause" of the divine gracious willing. The Lutherans entered the eighteenth century confident that their movements toward resistible grace remained Augustinian, Lutheran, and clearly anti-pelagian. But the subtleties of scholastic doctrine could never withstand Enlightenment rationalism or overcome modern self-confidence about creaturely life before God. Faith, once the work of the Holy Spirit, now drew dangerously near to the pelagian moralism of a choice of the will liberated by a universal and benevolent "common grace," a power present in every human heart. "Salvation" was universal gift, made effective through the "risk of faith," a reaching out and grasping close the golden ring.

The *Joint Declaration* as Exemplar of Modern Universalism

The *Joint Declaration*, in Section 3.16, seems to share this modern confidence about creaturely life before God; it extends salvation to all: "All people are *called* to salvation in Christ." The "golden chain" of Romans 8:30

appears to form the environment and context here: those whom God pre-destinated, he called; those he called, he justified. The *Joint Declaration* then joins effective calling to faith, which in turn comes to life in the community and in the world through acts of love. To be sure, this document nowhere *explicitly* affirms universalism in salvation: the doctrine of election is not so prominent as to warrant this affirmation! Yet this catena of effective calling, justification, and sanctification by effective sacraments, testified to by faith active in love, form the traditional ingredients in the doctrine of election and seem to confirm the *Joint Declaration* as a document of quiet universalism. But we should not move too quickly here. These universalist strains are balanced by the Lutheran and Tridentine themes of resistible grace.

As the *Joint Declaration* expresses it, "In trust in God's promise believers are assured of their salvation, but are never secure looking at themselves" (JD 4.6, 35); or, in the Catholic emphasis, "No one may doubt God's mercy and Christ's merit. Every person, however, may be concerned about his salvation when he looks upon his own weaknesses and shortcomings" (JD 4.6, 36). Though a document of the modern era, the *Joint Declaration on Justification* rings the changes on medieval and sixteenth-century debates on merit and gracious election. It never falls into pelagian moralism of the modern kind. "As sinners persons stand under God's judgment and are incapable of turning by themselves to God to seek deliverance, of meriting their justification before God, or of attaining salvation by their own abilities" (JD 4.1, 19). We might ask, then, whether any document that raises, as this one does, the insecurity of believers before God, especially when they examine their own failings, could be considered universalist in tone.

The answer lies, I think, in an ironic effect of the doctrine of resistible grace. The premises of seventeenth-century teaching on predestination, both Catholic and Lutheran, were assuredly not universalist. The context that defined justification was explicit and well understood. To resist grace on one's own strength alone sounds pelagian — so near in fact that most pre-modern theologians assigned blame to the resisting human will only within the larger schema of divine permission or willing. But in our day — unlike in our forbearers' — when the resisting will is considered, the larger schema is universalism. The fear about one's salvation becomes a bare counter-factual: we *would* be terrified for our salvation were we to consider our own unworthiness apart from Christ. Again, resistance to such a great good appears to recede into a counter-factual: we *could* resist this grace; but seeing for ourselves this true good, we do not. In our time, the love and mercy of God is thought to be better served by speaking of God effectively willing faith to all: all are called to salvation in Christ. So strong is this presupposition in our era that only an explicit rejection of universal election, or an express doctrine of predestination, could clarify that a universal call to salvation in Christ does *not* entail universalism. Once again, we see how the silence about predestination in this document renders obscure the particular force and range of the express doctrine of justification. Without the larger context, the doctrine of justification is like the blink of a human eye: the movement remains, but the meaning is indeterminate. Predestination was in times past the environment of justification: can it speak clearly without its background language?

A Reformed Assessment

A Reformed theologian might well ask whether the doctrine of justification, shorn of its relation to the doctrine of predestination, can successfully ward off both the confident striving and the anxious insecurity of our age. Or, to adopt Newman's idiom: Have the "notes of true development" been sounded when justification is defined apart from its correlate doctrines of predestination and election? When universalism forms the backdrop of Christian teaching, faith is vulnerable to becoming a work of the human will with little at stake. We may no longer be able to see why justification became church-dividing in the first place. Nor may we be impelled to "make the common understanding of justification bear fruit in the life and teaching of the churches" (JD 5.46) as justification has little work to do for our easy consciences. The "practical syllogism," much maligned among academic theologians, loses its power, to either reassure or torment, as reprobation falls away as threat to our life before God. To "stand under God's judgment" loses its sting when believers cannot believe it applies to them — truly, existentially, or finally. And, oddly, the freedom of human creatures to believe the gospel, much as they might assent to a worldview, is prey to the anxious frailties of all our achievements: we cannot seem to stand still for long under any one party banner.

Can the Lord's mighty arm — strong to save — comfort, restore, justify, and beat down Satan under our feet when there is and has always been nothing but election to life that awaits us? No ecumenical document could answer all these questions in one agreement, and no church tradition can revive a doctrine by its own will or for the sake of its history. Indeed, a doctrine as awesome as predestination could hardly be affirmed simply because its absence is a loss. But it may well be that an analysis of justification apart from predestination casts light on the risks of such a separation in the doctrinal unity of the faith, and reminds us that the rugged peaks of the doctrine of predestination may still have lessons to teach us, strengths to test us, to comfort, and to warn.

6 Justification and Sacrifice

Laura Smit

In order to possess what you do not possess
You must go by the way of dispossession.

T. S. Eliot, "East Coker" III

In 1993, Delores Williams, a professor at Union Theological Seminary, New York, spoke at an interdenominational Re-Imagining Conference and announced: "I don't think we need folks hanging on crosses, and blood dripping, and weird stuff."[1] Although her language was especially provocative, her basic perspective is increasingly common. Many people — even those who consider themselves Christians, even those who consider themselves Christian theologians — find the violence and bloodshed of the cross to be problematic and would prefer an understanding of justification that did not implicate God in something that, on the face of it, appears to be so primitive and even barbaric. It is not fashionable in academic circles to think of the atoning work of Christ in terms of sacrifice.

Some feminist thinkers point to the danger of a sacrificial model for Christ's work, in that the model of sacrifice may be used to justify the oppression of women, who have often been asked to reflect the model of Christ by sacrificing themselves on behalf of church or family.[2] Others are

1. "Paganism at the Re-Imagining Conference in Minneapolis (1993)," *BRF Witness* 29 (May/June 1994). Accessed online at http://www.brfwitness.org/Articles/1994v29n3.htm on 6/8/2006.

2. See especially Valerie Saiving's classic article, "The Human Situation: A Feminine View," *Journal of Religion* 40 (April 1960): 100-112. For a more modern treatment of this per-

more concerned that such a model might justify the totalitarian requirements of extreme nationalism, in which people are called to sacrifice
themselves without question for the good of their country.[3] In the after-
math of 9/11, there is new discomfort with any theology that might seem to
condone religious violence and self-immolation.[4] All in all, the language of
sacrifice has fallen on hard times in theological circles.

Those who *do* discuss sacrifice are typically influenced by the work of
René Girard, who understands sacrifice as a phenomenon occurring across
cultures, explainable in terms of societies' need for a scapegoat on whom
to channel all the tensions and hostilities that would otherwise tear civili-
zation apart. Girard sees scapegoating as a way for those who perpetuate
violence to avoid facing their own culpability by presenting the victim of
violence as the guilty one. Under this view, the point of sacrifice is to restore harmony in the community. Girard understands the Old Testament
sacrificial system as fitting this scapegoating pattern, but believes that Jesus' sacrifice on the cross was a subversion of this pattern, rejecting all violence in a sharp break with the Old Testament, rupturing old patterns and
making it newly possible to hope for a non-violent society. Those theologians influenced by Girard typically understand the cross as a human act
to which Jesus submitted, not an act initiated by or even desired by God,
since they hold that by definition a God of love cannot initiate violence
and would not desire such a sacrifice.[5] James Allison says, "Girard has

---

spective, see Darby Kathleen Ray, *Deceiving the Devil: Atonement, Abuse, and Ransom*
(Cleveland: Pilgrim, 1998).

3. This is especially Magadelene Fettlöh's concern (though she also is sensitive to the
feminist issue). See "Braucht Gott Opfer?," in *Ich glaube an den Gott Israels,* ed. Frank Crüsemann and Udo Theissmann (Gütersloh: Chr. Kaiser, 1998), pp. 49-54; and "Gottesfleish —
Impulsreferate zu 'Theologie im Gespräch,'" in *Neue Musik in der Kirche IV: Gottesfleisch*
(Frankfurt: Peter Lang, 2005), pp. 58-84.

4. Consider the "Non-Violent Atonement Conference," which says in its promotional
material: "In today's world with our growing awareness of the dangers of violence, sacrifice,
and militant religion, the death of Jesus need no longer be construed with divine violence."
Accessed online at http://girardianlectionary.net/Atonement%20Conference%20Two%20
Day%20Schedule.doc on 08/15/2006. Interestingly, there is also new appreciation in some
quarters for sacrifice, in light of the self-sacrifice of police officers and fire fighters responding to 9/11, but this perspective does not (yet?) appear to have made many inroads into academic theology.

5. For an example of a Girardian theologian, see James G. Williams, *The Bible, Violence,
and the Sacred: Liberation from the Myth of Sanctioned Violence* (San Francisco: Harper
SanFrancisco, 1991).

[shown] how Jesus gave himself up to a typical human lynching so as to undo the world of violence and sacrifice forever."[6]

This Girardian analysis is problematic, both in its understanding of the Old Testament sacrificial system and in its understanding of the cross. It is true that there is violence in the Old Testament that could reasonably be understood in a Girardian light: think, for instance, of the slaughter of the Canaanites. However, the Levitical system of temple sacrifice does *not* fit Girard's pattern, in that such sacrifices are meant to heighten an offerer's awareness of guilt and dependence, not mask such awareness. There is no blaming of the victim in the Levitical sacrificial system, no sense that the offered animal somehow deserves to die rather than the person making the offering. In fact, the animal must be perfect and without blemish. Already in the Old Testament, the sacrificial system designed by God subverts the human patterns of scapegoating and violence that Girard identifies as typical of (fallen) human societies.

Those who take the biblical witness seriously cannot avoid the idea, *pace* Girard, that in both testaments the act of sacrifice is something God institutes and blesses. Sacrifice is central to the Old Testament witness, and God is clearly the initiator of the sacrificial system (Lev. 1–9). When people sacrifice to him it is because he has told them to do so (Gen. 15:9; 22:2; Exod. 12:1-20). The act of sacrifice is meant to provide a safe means of access to God's presence (Lev. 16:2). Markus Barth observes: "Initiative and effective will, power and result lie only and entirely with God. The High-Priest makes all his careful preparations to enter behind the veil *not in order* that God appear over the mercy seat . . . , *but because* God has promised to appear there."[7] Sacrifice is not some sort of magical ritual by which human beings summon God; rather, sacrifice is the means by which sinful human beings enter safely into the presence of the transcendent God.

Girard is certainly right in understanding the cross as a rejection of human patterns of vengeance and violence; however, he is wrong to construe the New Testament as rejecting the Old Testament sacrificial system. Instead the New Testament presents that system as transformed and fulfilled in the work of Jesus, still and always at God's initiative. The work of Christ

6. Interview with James Allison, "Violence Undone: James Allison on Jesus as Forgiving Victim," *Christian Century* 123 (Sept. 5, 2006): 30.

7. Markus Barth, *Was Christ's Death a Sacrifice?*, Scottish Journal of Theology Occasional Papers No. 9, ed. T. F. Torrance and J. K. S. Reid (Edinburgh and London: Oliver & Boyd Ltd, 1961), p. 23.

is consistently construed in terms of sacrifice, and God is credited with initiating the sacrifice of the cross (John 3:16; Rom. 3:24-25; 8:3, 32; 2 Cor. 5:21; Gal. 4:4-5). Jesus is portrayed, not as a victim of human violence, but as one who voluntarily lays down his own life (John 10:18; Eph. 5:2).

Sacrifice is a popular theme in contemporary continental philosophy, though again the act of sacrifice is not generally affirmed. Dennis Keenan represents this perspective in his book *The Question of Sacrifice,* in which he enters into dialogue with thinkers such as Kristeva, Bataille, Levinas, Irigaray, Lacan, and Derrida, all of whom have written on the nature of sacrifice.[8] Keenan defines sacrifice as complete, consuming self-giving, assuming that real sacrifice requires giving without hope for reward. Given this definition, he suggests that sacrifice is not possible in a Christian context, because Christianity has introduced a promise of reward in exchange for sacrifice. This, Keenan claims, introduces the element of "calculation," creating a "transcendent economy," and subverting sacrifice into an economic transaction that is no longer a sacrifice at all.[9]

Keenan's assumption about the nature of sacrifice does not match biblical definitions. Most Old Testament sacrifices are not fully consumed, but rather involve shared meals, with covenant-making and feasting as immediate benefits. Further, every sort of biblical sacrifice has as its *telos* the restoration or maintaining of a right relationship with God. Sacrifice opens a portal of safe access to the transcendent God. In a biblical context, sacrifice simply does not mean supremely disinterested annihilation.

But Keenan seems to think that it should. If the one making sacrifice (or being sacrificed) anticipates any positive outcome as a result of the sacrifice, such as the achievement of some good that makes such sacrifice reasonable, then as far as Keenan is concerned there is no real sacrifice because the act has been commodified. "Sacrifice has come to be understood as a necessary passage through suffering and/or death (of *either* oneself *or* someone else) on the way to a supreme moment of transcendent truth. Sacrifice effects the revelation of truth. Sacrifice is the price to be paid for this gain."[10] In Anselm's *Cur Deus Homo,* Keenan sees an "understanding of Christ as a token of exchange that restores the balance of payments be-

---

8. Dennis King Keenan, *The Question of Sacrifice* (Bloomington and Indianapolis: Indiana University Press, 2005).

9. Keenan, *Question of Sacrifice,* pp. 1, 2.

10. Keenan, *Question of Sacrifice,* p. 10.

tween the divine and the human." Keenan is offended by Anselm's use of the language of a debt owed to God, since he does not believe that sacrifice should be tainted by a suggestion of exchange or economy.

Christian theology must challenge Keenan's assumptions, both his definition of sacrifice and also his assumption that any language of exchange is inherently illegitimate. God did not institute the practice of sacrifice so that human beings could be annihilated, but in order to channel the blessings of access to his presence. Sacrifice is meant to be an experience of radical dependence, acknowledging God's sovereignty, not an experiment in maximal negation. It is indeed meant to be a wonderful exchange, in which we give up lesser goods in exchange for lasting goods. As Paul says, "I consider that the sufferings of this present time are not worth comparing with the glory about to be revealed to us" (Rom. 8:18).[11] The value of sacrifice is not found in seeing how much we can suffer; rather, sacrifice clears space in our lives so that we may be filled by God's glory.

The real danger is not so much that an offerer will understand sacrifice as an exchange, but rather that the offerer will believe it to be an exchange between equals, as if through the act of sacrifice a human being could control or compel God to conform to the human will. When a sacrifice is offered in such a spirit of control, it ceases to be an offering and becomes an attempt at magic instead. The difference between a right sacrifice and a magical abuse of sacrifice is internal or attitudinal, not easily discernible from without. The blessings that are properly associated with sacrifice and that proceed from sacrifice are the blessings associated with acknowledging one's complete dependence on God and God's complete authority over all of life, an acknowledgment not compatible with an attitude of magic and control.

Old Testament Patterns

Already in the Old Testament, especially in the psalms and prophets, we find that the most important component of sacrifice is not the ritual but a broken spirit, an attitude of dependence acknowledging God's sovereignty. Already in the Old Testament "the power of the cultic sacrifice is spiritualized, ethicized, and internalized so as to transfer the rich theological mean-

---

11. All Scripture citations are from the NRSV.

ing of the sacrifice to the offering of a person's or a group's own life."[12] Sacrifice is never meant to be a means of evading guilt, but rather is a means of acknowledging guilt and failure, in a spirit of humility, brokenness, and dependence. The psalms are full of statements about God's lack of interest in sacrificial animals and the need to adopt a humble and contrite attitude instead (Pss. 40:6; 50:12-15; 51:16-17; 116:12-19). From the beginning, the Old Testament sacrificial system is aimed at cultivating people who have the law written on their hearts, whose covenant with God is internal rather than external, leading to a relationship with him that is based not on fear but on knowledge (Jer. 31:33-34; Heb. 10:14-18). Over and over the prophets condemn the performance of sacrifice in a spirit of control, asserting that what really matters to God is that we care for those who are helpless and cultivate a spirit of dependence on God's mercy (Isa. 1:11-17; 66:1-2; Jer. 7:22-23; Hos. 6:6; Amos 5:21-24; Micah 6:1-4, 6-8; 1 Sam. 15:22). Jesus himself repeatedly cites such passages, warning his hearers that God "desires mercy not sacrifice" (Matt. 9:13; 12:7; Mark 12:33; Heb. 10:5-9).

This has led some biblical scholars to postulate a division between the priestly and the prophetic religion of Israel. But it seems more accurate to understand the priestly religion as the norm and prophetic religion as an emergency intervention made necessary when sacrifice became detached from dependence on and personal knowledge of God. When sacrifice functions as it is meant to function, as a means of fellowship with God through which offerers are enabled to conform themselves to God's will, then the mercy, humility, and contrition that the prophets call for will naturally flow from the act. It is only when sacrifice is performed in a spirit of barter as if between equals — or, worse, as if God is an impersonal power to be manipulated and controlled by human beings — that it is rejected by God.

Prior to the Exodus, sacrifice is not institutionalized in the Old Testament but is located within the family. Cain and Abel offer sacrifice, demonstrating that from the beginning sacrifice took diverse forms and did not always involve the shedding of blood (Gen. 4:4-5). Cain's sacrifice is unacceptable, while Abel's is accepted, apparently because of an attitudinal difference, later revealed in Cain's attitude of resentful entitlement. Noah offers burnt offerings after he emerges from the ark, and the Lord is said to

12. Philip Hefner, "The Cultural Significance of Jesus' Death as Sacrifice," *The Journal of Religion* 60 (Oct. 1980): 417.

have "smelled the pleasing odor," a motif that then recurs in the Levitical sacrificial system (Gen. 8:20-21). Abraham offers sacrifices (Gen. 12:8; 14:17-20), including the puzzling sacrifice that institutes the covenant with God (Gen. 15) and the terrifying near-sacrifice of his son Isaac (Gen. 22). Here the lesson of dependence is underlined in that acceptable offerings are provided only by God himself.

The first institutionalized sacrifice is the Passover lamb, which is not a burnt offering, since it is eaten by the family rather than consumed by fire on an altar. It is only the blood of the Passover lamb that is the sacrifice, painted on the doorposts of the people of Israel, given in place of the blood of the eldest son of each family (Exod. 12). Blood is a sign of the life of the sacrificed animal and the power of life in general, which is why God makes a special claim on blood. Covenants are sealed in blood (Exod. 24:8), and the people of Israel are told not to eat any blood, because the power of this life force belongs to God alone (Lev. 3:17). He is the Lord and Giver of Life, and so it is right that the symbol of life be offered to God in recognition of his lordship.

The Old Testament book that gives us the most information about sacrifice is Leviticus, which begins with a careful description of the sacrificial system in the tabernacle. Leviticus lays out procedures for five different sorts of sacrifices. The burnt offering, or holocaust, is sometimes also called the "whole offering," because the offering is given in its entirety and completely burned. The offerer lays his hand on the head of the offering, and it is described as "atonement" for the one offering it (Lev. 1:4). The cereal offering, or oblation, is an alternative to the offering of blood, a mixture of grain, oil, incense, and salt, sometimes baked, sometimes not. The grain offering is not entirely consumed, but is shared with the priests (Lev. 2). In the sacrifice of thanksgiving, or the peace offering,[13] only the fat of the animal is burned on the altar, and its blood is sprinkled. The rest of the offering is shared with those giving the offering, as a meal shared with God (Lev. 3). In this offering, too, the offerer lays his hand on the head of the offering before it is slaughtered, though it is not described as atonement. The sin offering may be an animal (different sorts of animals are prescribed depending on the wealth of the offerer) or, for those who cannot afford even turtledoves, it may be a grain offering instead. But the sin covered by this

---

13. The NRSV has "sacrifice of well-being," but this term is not widely used in the literature.

offering must be an unintentional violation of God's statutes (Lev. 4, 5). The guilt offering is for sins against another person and includes reparation as well as sacrifice (Lev. 6, 7). It is possible to see all five of these types of sacrifice reflected in New Testament teaching on the sacrificial work of Jesus.

In all these sacrifices, there is meant to be a parallel between what is happening to the offering (being surrendered to God) and what is happening to the offerer. Whether the offering is meant to be an acknowledgment of guilt or an expression of praise, it is always an expression of dependence and submission to the claims of the transcendent Lord. Sacrifice exposes the truth about the offerer (his or her sinfulness and creatureliness) and also elicits certain appropriate attitudes (gratitude, dependence, and penitence).

The culmination of the sacrificial hierarchy is Yom Kippur, the Day of Atonement (Lev. 16:29-34; 23:26-32). This is an annual day of atonement for all the sins that the people of Israel — both individually and collectively — have committed against God. The existence of this day makes clear that the sacrificial system was never understood as a failsafe way to atone for or make payment for all the sins of Israel. At the heart of the sacrificial system is a recognition that the system is inadequate, that ultimately the people of Israel must throw themselves on God's mercy, sending their representative into his presence to intercede on their behalf. The high priest offers sacrifice on behalf of the community, and each individual is required to fast and abstain from work, so that the day is described as a sabbath (Lev. 16:31). All of these sacrifices are decreed, in great detail, by God himself, clearly establishing that God is the initiator in the act of sacrifice. On this day, the sacrifices and indeed all the rituals of the day, including the fasting and the enforced rest, combine into one great prayer of confession, which God has promised to hear and answer with forgiveness.

According to Leviticus, once Moses and Aaron receive God's instructions about the new sacrificial system, they make extensive preparations for Aaron's installation as the high priest and his first official sacrificial acts. When Aaron finally offers his very first sacrifice before God under the new liturgical rubrics, God demonstrates his satisfaction with the sacrifice by consuming it entirely with fire from heaven (Lev. 9:24). But almost immediately Aaron's two sons, Nadab and Abihu, decide to practice some liturgical innovation. They offer unsanctioned fire before the Lord, and the same fire from heaven consumes them, just as it had consumed the offering (Lev. 10:1-2). Nadab and Abihu do not come before God in a spirit of obedience and submission, and so they forfeit the protection that Aaron and Moses enjoy in coming before the presence of this fearsome God.

It is the same fire that consumes the sacrifice in approval and consumes Nadab and Abihu in — what? wrath? punishment? There is no explanation of God's motivations for this action. It seems that Nadab and Abihu have simply wandered into God's power in an unsafe way, without using the safety measures laid out in the sacrificial system, and so they are incinerated much as two people might be who wandered into a high-voltage electrical fence. They are not so much culpable as foolish. The story makes clear that our God cannot be domesticated. He is love, but he is also power and glory. He is in fact "a consuming fire" (Deut. 4:24; Heb. 12:29). Sacrifice and its accompanying bloodshed are initiated by God, for he is the one who makes the offer of atonement.[14] There is certainly a sense in which the God we worship is a God of violence, a dangerous God, who cannot be tamed. To deny this is to make God over in accordance with our own dreams, to prefer the illusion of our imagination to the fully actualized reality of God's own presence.[15]

Sacrifice is part of the created world, a way that the creature interacts with the Creator. The point of sacrifice is to establish contact with God, to gain access to God. Sacrifice presupposes that there is a gap between humans and God that needs to be bridged, because God is understood as transcendent, awesome, terrifying, truly and utterly Other.[16] There is no thought of sacrifice between the three persons of the Trinity. Although they give themselves to one another freely and eternally, it would be improper to refer to that self-giving as sacrifice. The act of sacrifice only

---

14. Barth, *Was Christ's Death a Sacrifice?*, p. 23.

15. Hans Boersma makes this point in his helpful book, *Violence, Hospitality, and the Cross: Reappropriating the Atonement Tradition* (Grand Rapids: Baker Academic, 2004). Boersma takes issue with Girard and others by insisting that all traditional Christian understandings of the atonement must implicate God in the violence of the cross. We cannot avoid this implication simply by turning away from Anselm in favor of Abelard. Boersma challenges the notion that all violence is morally reprehensible, pointing out that all reasonable people can be brought to see that there are instances, for example, when it would be appropriate to inflict physical harm on someone in order to save his or her life.

16. Perhaps one reason that sacrifice is so distasteful to many contemporary Christians is that for the most part we have a far more domesticated, immanent understanding of God's nature, seeing him as being pretty much just like us, only bigger. Since we do not typically share the existential problem that the sacrificial system attempted to answer, we do not understand the function of sacrifice.

makes sense in the context of creation.[17] Sacrifice is essentially the response of dependence from creature to Creator, a response acknowledging the creature's next-to-nothingness and the Creator's full actuality, a response acknowledging the creature's joyful and life-giving duty to conform to the Creator's will. As such, in an extended sense, sacrifice would have made sense also in an unfallen world and will make sense in the eschaton. We can easily imagine offering to God the most beautiful flower or the most melodic song quite apart from any need to make reparation for sin, simply as a function of being a creature.

Priesthood is likewise inherently a creaturely act, the act of human beings who are placed between heaven and earth with the task of mediating the one to the other. As priests, human beings stand between the material and the spiritual, channeling God's blessing to the creation and offering the creation back to God through acts of knowing, naming, enjoying, and praising. As George Herbert puts it, human beings are made "Secretary" of God's praise, the only creatures with pen and voice to use in expressing praise to God on behalf of all the trees and beasts who would sing to God if only they could. "Man is the world's high Priest: he doth present/The sacrifice for all; while they below/Unto the service mutter an assent/Such as springs use that fall, and winds that blow."[18] In the absence of sin, the primary priestly act would be paying loving attention to the creation, naming the particularities of the creation, and giving God praise for them and on their behalf, such that the creation flourishes under the priestly gaze.

In the event of sin, humanity needs a new sort of priest, one whose loving attention restores what was damaged. The book of Hebrews attests to the fact that a sinful human cannot fill this function. The Aaronic priesthood can at best testify to the brokenness of the human condition and beg for mercy, for Aaron is himself in need of healing, as he well recognizes. The book of Leviticus frequently calls on the priest to turn the specified offering "into smoke on the altar," evoking the "vanity" or "smoke" of Ecclesiastes. Sacrifice reveals the ephemeral nature of the world in which we live, a world in which life can be reduced to smoke and pass away into nothingness.

---

17. J.-M. Buathier, *Le sacrifice dans le dogme catholique et dans la vie chrétienne*, 6th ed., rev. (Lyon: Vitte and Perrussel and Paris: Victor Lecoffre, circa 1890), p. 38. "Le sacrifice naît avec la creation."

18. George Herbert, "Providence," in *The Country Parson; The Temple* (The Classics of Western Spirituality), ed. John N. Wall, Jr. (New York: Paulist Press, 1981), p. 238.

This nothingness is precisely the issue. The sin for which we need redemption is a fall away from actuality into illusion, into the life of smoke and shadow. The eighteenth-century preacher and pastor William Law suggests that "wrath" simply describes the natural state of human beings who are cut off from a relationship to God, such that all their longings and desires, which are properly fulfilled in God, are left unfulfilled, plunging them into a state of chaotic yearning and confused desire. In such a state, interactions with God become painful and punishing, not because God has changed or become anything other than Love itself, but rather because the person is not properly aligned to God's power, not in a proper relationship of dependence and receptivity. Wrath is a name for the restless unfulfilled desire of the human person apart from God, and the only antidote for such wrath is the insertion of a Mediator who is capable of restoring proper access to God, directing all the desires of the human heart toward their proper end.[19] Given such an understanding, sacrifice is indeed a wonderful exchange, the letting go of lesser objects of desire in order to acknowledge God as the one true end toward whom all desires point.

The grounds for this exchange are established in Leviticus 10:10: "You are to distinguish between the holy and the common, and between the unclean and the clean." This proper ranking of loves and values is necessary so that wounded humanity, with all perceptions of reality distorted by sin, will begin approximating the priestly task of right naming and loving attention. It is necessary to notice that some things are holy, whereas others are not, to make distinctions between God's ways and the ways of rebellion and sin. But Zechariah 14:20 looks forward to a day when such distinctions will be obsolete because everything will be holy, a day that is inaugurated by Christ's resurrection. The New Testament people of God will then be holy, not merely clean. Holiness will no longer be the province of a few special people who are set apart for God, but will rather be the property of all believers, since all believers will participate in the divine nature (2 Pet. 1:4; 1 Pet. 2:9). The holiness of the Law (and so, the Logos/Son), which was once external on tablets of stone, will be internal, written on the heart (Jer. 31:31-34; Heb. 8:6-13).

19. William Law, *The Spirit of Love* (London: G. Robinson and J. Roberts, 1752/1754). Accessed online at http://www.ccel.org/l/law/love/ on 08/15/2006.

New Testament Patterns

The language of sacrifice was adopted by Christians from very early in the life of the church, as is clear from the fact that already in the book of Mark Jesus speaks of his death in sacrificial terms (10:45; 11:42-45; 14:24).[20] The complicated nature of the Old Testament sacrificial tradition is reflected in the complicated appropriation of that tradition. Jesus is presented as the new paschal lamb, especially in the Gospel of John, which begins with John the Baptist identifying Jesus as the Lamb of God (1:35) and ends with Jesus' death at the same moment that the Passover lambs were being slaughtered throughout Jerusalem (19:31).[21] Jesus fulfills Isaiah's prophecy of the Suffering Servant (Isa. 52, 53), the only passage of the Old Testament that presents a person's death as a way of obtaining pardon for the sins of others (Isa. 53:5; Matt. 8:17; Luke 22:37; John 12:38; 1 Pet. 2:21-25).[22] All the different forms of sacrifice recorded in the Old Testament may similarly be seen as fulfilled by Christ in his saving work. He offers himself completely to his Father, as a burnt offering, and yet he also offers himself in a way that leads to a shared meal with his disciples, as a grain offering. The book of Hebrews particularly emphasizes that in Christ we have fulfillment for the Day of Atonement.

In the history of Christian piety, an emphasis on the sacrificial death of Jesus has often been accompanied by a somewhat morbid fascination

---

20. Given the scholarly consensus on the dating of Mark, Markus Barth concludes from these passages: "[I]t seems to be obvious that Paul was not the inventor of a sacrificial sin- or blood-theology. Rather, he continued and unfolded what he heard and found in the churches in and outside Jerusalem and Antioch. Neither can any other among the New Testament authors be credited or blamed for inventing that doctrine. It is spread so widely over the earliest and latest books of the New Testament — whatever books may belong to those two groups — that either an unknown creative genius, or a simultaneous flash of enlightenment coming to all early churches, or Jesus Himself must be considered its originator." Barth, *Was Christ's Death a Sacrifice?*, p. 4.

21. This is why the Gospel of John locates the final discourse "just before the Passover" (John 13:1) and does not include an account of the last supper as a Passover meal; the passion itself is the Passover.

22. These connections are laid out in great detail in J. Ries and G. Mathon, "Sacrifice," in *Catholicisme Hier Aujourd'hui Demain: Encyclopédie publiée sous le patronage de l'Institut catholique de Lille*, ed. G. Mathon and G.-H. Baudry (Paris: Letouzey et Ané, Éditeurs, 1993), pp. 363-426. See Barth, *Was Christ's Death a Sacrifice?*, pp. 9-10, for the sacrificial background to the Isaiah passage.

with his suffering, leading devout believers to focus on his pain in an effort to stir up pity for him as the Man of Sorrows. There is something perverse about such pity. In the Gospel of Luke, Jesus delivers only one rebuke on his way to the cross. He does not rebuke those who mock him, or flay him, or pound nails into him. He rebukes the women who weep for him, telling them that they are wrong to do so, that instead they should be weeping for themselves (23:26-29). It is a gentle rebuke, but still surprising. It would seem that these women are the only people responding appropriately to the events of the passion. But Jesus' rebuke reminds us that in fact the only person in Jerusalem that day who did not need anyone's pity was Jesus himself. He was the only person there — indeed, the only person in the history of the world — not in any trouble, not requiring any rescue, not enslaved by sin, and not deserving of eternal damnation. A few chapters earlier, Jesus had wept over Jerusalem (19:41-44), an appropriate weeping. When the world is seen truly, when we make right distinctions between what is holy and what is not, then pity must always flow from Jesus to us, not the other way around. Again we are brought back to the sacrifice that God most desires — a broken and contrite heart. Our role as fallen humans is to remember our own neediness before God, not to claim the patronizing position of pity over the weak and suffering Jesus.

At the end of the movie *The Fellowship of the Ring*, the first of Peter Jackson's Tolkien films, Frodo, the hobbit, has wandered off alone, and Aragorn (the incognito king) finds him. An army of orcs is approaching, and Aragorn tells Frodo to run, then turns to face the approaching army alone. Freely, bravely, lovingly, he places himself between the small, vulnerable, weak hobbit and the threatening orcs, because he *can;* he is a warrior, and this is something he can do. Viewing that scene, watching him calmly step out to meet his enemies, it would be absurd to pity Aragorn. Even someone who did not know the story, who thought that Aragorn was about to die, would find it absurd to pity him at this moment of power. There is nothing pitiable about him. Frodo is the one to pity, the one who is afraid, and weighed down, and baffled by his burdens. Aragorn is admirable, inspiring, virtuous, maybe even a little frightening, suffering physical pain and facing death, but still not an object of pity. As Jesus walks toward death in the Gospel of Luke, he too is a king and a warrior, placing himself between his weak and vulnerable people and the powers of sin and death, because only he can. It is his moment of power. There is no conflict here between Anselm and Aulén: the cross is both battle and sacrifice.[23] Indeed, sacrifice is Jesus' primary weapon in this battle.

This is not to say that Jesus does not suffer in his sacrifice, but that — precisely because he is without sin and because he is both divine and human — he is able to endure that suffering in ways that one who is only human (let alone a sinful human) cannot. I have often had people, both in the classroom and at church, complain to me that this means Jesus doesn't *really* know how hard our life is, doesn't *really* understand what it is to be fully human, hasn't *really* become one of us. But that is rather like a sick person complaining because her doctor isn't also sick and bedridden. Or, to use C. S. Lewis's example, it is like a drowning person complaining because the person throwing him a lifeline from the shore isn't also drowning. It is like saying to the one who comes to rescue us, "You have an unfair advantage in that you don't need to be rescued yourself." That's rather the point.

This Jesus who is walking to his death is also the eternal Word, the second person of the Trinity, the Son who with his Father and the Spirit spoke the world into being. Here the God who is beyond time and space has entered into time and space. On the cross, God who is pure joy, pure love, pure delight — not potentially or passively, but in pure act — wrestles with the parasitical deprivations of pain, hatred, and death and defeats them once and for all. It is not as if the outcome is still in doubt on the road to the cross, not as if the power of God's goodness and the power of sin are somehow evenly matched. His victory is absolutely certain. When Jesus enters into our world of illusion, his sacrifice brings him all the way into our almost-nothingness as he faces death and the ending of life. He goes to the place of annihilation and there — since he is never separated from his Father or the Spirit, and never ceases to be fully divine — he lets loose the fully actual power of joy and love that is the triune essence, exploding the nothingness of death and sin and flooding all that is connected to him (which is everything, for in him all things hold together) with that fullness of life, fullness of joy. Yes, the cross is painful, and in his human nature Jesus feels all that pain. But even at the most painful moment, there is no doubt that he has won. There is no room for pity here, only for penitence.

The New Testament book that makes the most use of sacrificial imag-

23. See Gustaf Aulén, *Christus Victor: An Historical Study of the Three Main Types of the Idea of the Atonement,* trans. A. G. Herbert (London: Society for Promoting Christian Knowledge, 1931).

ery is the book of Hebrews. The author of Hebrews assumes that his readers (or listeners, since this book was probably first a sermon) understand the great existential problem of the Old Testament: we are made for communion with God, but communion is impossible, both because of our sin and also because of our finitude. Moses begs to see God's face but cannot see him, not because God is unwilling to be seen but because Moses could not bear such glory. The sight of God would kill him. In the Old Testament, sacrifice was an effort to solve this problem, to offer a way of making contact with God — whether for praise, or petition, or penitence — by offering safe access. But even at its best that sacrificial system failed to meet the longing of those who truly thirst for God. Moses, who perfectly embodies the sacrificial system, still begs to see God more directly.

The face of God is only available to us in the incarnate Son. This does not so much establish a superiority of the New Testament over the Old Testament as a superiority of the heavenly sanctuary over any earthly sanctuary (whether tabernacle, temple, or church). Like the worship in the tabernacle, New Testament worship is also symbolic. We are really brought into God's presence in worship only when we leave the earthly sanctuary behind in order to be ushered into the heavenly throne room. Only Jesus, the mediator, is able to blaze a trail into that sanctuary.

Hebrews begins with the clearest statement in Scriptures of the divinity of Jesus, a statement that directly addresses the need to see and know and communicate with God.

> Long ago God spoke to our ancestors in many and various ways by the prophets, but in these last days he has spoken to us by a Son, whom he appointed heir of all things, through whom he also created the worlds. He is the reflection of God's glory and the exact imprint of God's very being, and he sustains all things by his powerful word. When he had made purification for sins, he sat down at the right hand of the Majesty on high. (1:1-3)

Although the passage begins by establishing Jesus as superior to all previous prophets, the author very quickly moves from prophetic to priestly imagery when he credits Jesus with making purification for sin — the work of the high priest on the Day of Atonement. This image dominates the book, which is a sustained exploration of Jesus' high priestly, mediatorial ministry.

In the second chapter, the author of Hebrews moves from a consideration of Jesus' divinity to establish his full humanity, as one who shares a Father with human beings and who "is not ashamed to call them brothers and sisters" (2:11). Jesus' humanity is further established in that he shares the universal human experience of suffering. The author mixes images of sacrifice with images of battle in the following passage, for Jesus is described as "a merciful and faithful high priest in the service of God, to make a sacrifice of atonement for the sins of the people" (2:17b), but also as one who destroys the devil and sets prisoners free (2:14-15). Later the idea of renewing the covenant will be seen as another aspect of this work (9:15-18).

Jesus also embodies the appropriate attitude of sacrifice, the humble heart in the spirit of dependence on the Father. He is faithful to his Father (3:2), appointed by his Father (5:5), and perfected (i.e., completed or consecrated — per Lev. 8:33)[24] by obedience to his Father (5:8). Commenting on this theme of obedience, Gregory Nazianzen explains:

> [I]n His character of the Word He was neither obedient nor disobedient. For such expressions belong to servants, and inferiors, and the one applies to the better sort of them, while the other belongs to those who deserve punishment. But, in the character of "the Form of a Servant" (Philippians 2:7), He condescends to His fellow servants, nay, to His servants, and takes upon Him a strange form, bearing all me and mine in Himself, that in Himself He may exhaust the bad, as fire does wax, or as the sun does the mists of the earth; and that I may partake of His nature by the blending. Thus He honors obedience by His action, and proves it experimentally by His Passion.[25]

This practice of obedience brings his human nature to completion, because he has lived out the life human beings were designed for, a life of obedience to the Father in conformity with the Son in the power of the Spirit. Such a life is lived, not in obedience to an external law, but in con-

---

24. "The LXX used *teleoun* in the technical expression for priestly ordination, 'to fill the hands' (*teleoun tas cheiras,* Exod. 29:9; Lev. 4:5). In Lev. 21:10 LXX, the verb alone has this sense, although it seems unlikely that the verb by itself would have been read as a technical term for ordination in Hebrews." Craig R. Koester, *Hebrews: A New Translation with Introduction and Commentary,* vol. 36, The Anchor Bible (New York: Doubleday, 2001), p. 123, n. 256.

25. Fourth Theological Oration, no. 6. Cited in Dmitri Royster, *The Epistle to the Hebrews: A Commentary* (Crestwood, NY: St. Vladimir's Seminary Press, 2003), p. 78.

formity to a law that has become part of one's own nature and character, because it is now written on the heart (10:15-16). Of course, this means conformity to the person of the Son, since he is the true Law, the Logos, in whom is contained the ordering design of the creation. Therefore it is fitting that he should blaze the path toward such completion for us (4:14; 10:19-20), a path that we are expected to follow in order that we too might come to the perfection (or *telos*) of human life (6:1; 10:22-25).

The central argument of Hebrews, consisting of most of chapters 7 through 10, is that the priesthood of Jesus is superior to the Levitical priesthood, superior because Jesus is a priest who is appointed directly by God for all time, who is sinless and holy with no need to atone for himself, and who makes his sacrifice once-for-all. But most of all Jesus is superior because he makes his sacrifice, not in a temple or tabernacle made with human hands, but in the true temple, the true holy of holies, which is the throne room of God (7:26–8:2). Jesus was killed "outside the city gate" (13:12), but he made the offering of his blood directly to his Father, in the true Holy of Holies that is in heaven (9:11-12).[26] Since Jesus is the Logos, "in whom all things hold together" (Col. 1:17), his offering of blood does not just represent his own life force but all the life of the cosmos (Lev. 17:11).

Human tabernacles and temples are merely sketches or shadows (Heb. 8:5) of the true tabernacle, "the greater and perfect tent" (9:11), which is in God's presence. The Old Testament law "has only a shadow of the good things to come and not the true form of these realities" (10:1). The real world is unseen (11:1), but more real than the world of sight. Earthly sanctuaries are valuable precisely because they reflect, though in a limited way, the glory of the heavenly sanctuary.[27] Ultimately, the unseen will pass away, and only the "kingdom that cannot be shaken" will remain (12:28). "In the end it is clear that Hebrews assumes that Christ's heavenly ministry (*leitourgia;* 8:2, 6) undergirds earthly Christian worship (*latreuein;* 12:28) and that his self-sacrifice gives rise to sacrifices of praise and good works among his followers (13:15-16)."[28] This is true because the heavenly work of

---

26. Richard D. Nelson, "'He Offered Himself': Sacrifice in Hebrews," *Interpretation* 57 (July 2003): 254-56.

27. Koester, *Hebrews,* p. 383. This is in contrast to the Gospel of John, in which the body of Jesus is presented as the new tabernacle (John 1:14; 2:18-21; 14:2) (though Hebrews also uses this imagery in 10:19-20, where the body of Jesus is compared to the ripped veil in the temple).

28. Koester, *Hebrews,* p. 380.

Jesus cleanses us, making true sacrifices of thanksgiving — sacrifices that are internal as well as external — possible.

The mediating work of Jesus does not domesticate or tame God, who is still described as a "consuming fire" (12:29; also 10:31) and who must be approached "with reverence and awe" (12:28). But the mediatorial work of Jesus covers us and makes it safe for us to enter God's presence, to approach the throne of grace boldly with our needs and petitions (4:16). "Instead of downplaying the terrifying aspects of God, Hebrews announces that Christ provides the atonement, cleansing, and sanctification that people need to approach God rightly."[29] Just as the sacrificial rituals of the Old Testament were meant to keep Aaron safe when he approached God (Lev. 16:2), so Jesus' sacrifice keeps us safe, but more effectively and permanently. Our access includes having the privileges of priests ourselves, both the privilege of access into the Holy of Holies and also the priestly privilege of eating that which is sacrificed on the heavenly altar (Heb. 13:10), that is, sharing in the supper of the Lord.

The Efficacy of Sacrifice

Throughout the New Testament, the sacrifice of Jesus is efficacious, not because it allows the Father to mark our debt as paid, but because it effects real change in us. God does not wait for a change in us before he claims us. In that sense, the Reformers were completely right in insisting that we are saved not by our own righteousness but by the imputed righteousness of Jesus. However, such legal and economic language describing our salvation — both of Scripture and of the tradition — must be understood in the fullness of its analogical nature. When God imputes Christ's righteousness to us, his declaration is only analogically related to the actions of a human judge in a human court, for God's declaration is powerful and creative, bringing to pass what he declares. If a human judge were to declare a guilty person innocent, it would be a farcical action, at best a legal fiction. But when God declares us righteous, this is not simply a pretense. There is a reality called into being by that declaration. As already noted, the new law is written not on tablets of stone, but on the heart of believers. That is to say that Christians experience a conforming to the image of Christ, who is the Law/Logos Itself.

29. Koester, *Hebrews*, p. 449.

The Holy Spirit unites us with Christ in our baptism, so that we join both in his sacrificial death and in his resurrection (Rom. 6:3-11). When Jesus descends into hell, we are united with him, and when he releases the power of his joy and life into that abyss, it floods into us (Eph. 4:10). *All* creatures, not just Christian believers, depend absolutely on the Son for knowledge and life and identity, whether or not they realize this, for in him are hidden all the treasures of wisdom and knowledge (Col. 2:3), the fullness of life (John 1:4), and the true name of everything and everyone he has made (Rev. 2:17). When the Spirit unites us to Christ, we stop resisting that dependence, stop taking refuge in illusion, and allow Christ to live in us. It is not that we are made righteous in ourselves when we are so united, but rather that the barriers to Christ's righteousness have been removed, allowing him to take us over, so that it is no longer we who live, but Christ who lives in us (Gal. 2:20).

Calvin begins his teaching on justification with a statement about union with Christ, for union with Christ — union of the most real and ontological sort — is the way in which the justifying work of Christ is applied to us.

> [W]e must understand that as long as Christ remains outside of us, and we are separated from him, all that he has suffered and done for the salvation of the human race remains useless and of no value for us. Therefore, to share with us what he has received from the Father, he had to become ours and to dwell within us. For this reason, he is called "our Head" [Eph. 4:15], and "the first-born among many brethren" [Rom. 8:29]. We also, in turn, are said to be "engrafted into him" [Rom. 11:17], and to "put on Christ" [Gal. 3:27]; for, as I have said, all that he possesses is nothing to us until we grow into one body with him.[30]

The Spirit gives us this union through the gift of faith, but Calvin also suggests that there is a ladder to climb in which our union deepens as we "examine into the secret energy of the Spirit, by which we come to enjoy Christ and all his benefits."[31]

One of the most remarkable stories of sacrifice that I have ever read is *The Deed of Paksenarrion* by Elizabeth Moon. It's a three-volume fantasy

---

30. John Calvin, *Institutes of the Christian Religion,* ed. John T. McNeill, trans. Ford Lewis Battles (Philadelphia: Westminster Press, 1960), 3.1.1, p. 537.

31. Calvin, *Institutes,* 3.1.1, p. 537.

novel, set in a somewhat generically Tolkienesque world, which traces the moral growth of the title character, Paksenarrion. Paks is a young woman who becomes a mercenary soldier largely as a way to enhance her sense of self-determination and control. She wants to be able to fend off all the threats in her life, to keep herself and others safe, and for some time she is able to do this. But eventually she confronts threats that are too much for her, and she is debilitated both physically and spiritually. On her path to healing, Paks comes to admit that she cannot keep herself absolutely safe, that she is not invulnerable, and that the goodness she longs for is only possible if she submits her will to her god. Near the end of the last volume, Paks is called upon to sacrifice herself for the sake of her king, turning herself over to be tortured for five days and nights in exchange for his life and the life of four of their comrades. The suffering that she goes through is real and intense, but with her new spirit of submission she no longer feels a need to deny that suffering, no need to be ashamed of pain or fear. Whereas in her earlier life she had responded to threats with anger, now she "refused the soldier's tactics of defiance, anger, vengeance, and looked into her own fear to find the link to those around her, to find the way to reach those frightened tormentors, the ones not already lost to evil."

> [S]he felt curiously untroubled. Not free of pain, nor free of fear, but free of the need to react to that fear in all the old ways. She had no anger left, no hatred, no desire for vengeance, nothing but pity for those who must find such vile amusements, who had no better hope, or no courage to withdraw. It would all happen to her — all the things she'd feared, every violation of body, everything she'd taken up the sword to prevent — and she consented. Not because it was right: it was never right. Not because she deserved it: no one deserved such violation. But because she could consent, being what she was, and by consenting destroy its power over her and others, proving in her own body that fear's power came from fear, that greater power could from the same dark roots find another way to the light.
>
> This quietness, this consent, formed a still pool in the center of that violent place. At first, only [her torturers] noticed, and flung themselves into a frenzy of violence against it. But it was not brittle steel to break, or crystal to shatter, but a strength fluid and yet immovable, unmarred by the broken rhythm of her breath, or even by her screams. The quietness spread, from gray eyes that held no hatred for those who spat at her face

or tasted her blood, from a voice that could scream in pain yet mouth no curses after, that spoke, between screams, in a steady confirmation of all good.[32]

I know nothing about Elizabeth Moon's religious convictions, but this passage is clearly influenced by the story of Jesus' sacrificial death. Moon appears to be taking an Abelardian approach to the efficacy of suffering, for in this story many of the poor and outcast people who are watching Paks's torture are shamed by her goodness into reconsidering their own moral commitments.

But the death of Jesus is not an event that we experience only as onlookers. In our baptism, we participate in that death. We share in the consent to suffering and the quietness of resting in the Father's care. Only one who is full of life and power and love can take on death and negation without himself being negated. Through our union with Christ, we are also filled with life and power and love — *his* life and power and love, not our own, but we are genuinely participants in his nature. All the promises of God are yes in Christ (2 Cor. 1:20). As we face the no of death we hear the yes of his life. But the no must be absorbed, borne, in order to be defeated. Jesus' sacrifice on the cross is the bearing of that no.

Sharing the Sacrifice

The question remains whether there is any continuing role for sacrifice in the Christian life. Hebrews is very clear that the sacrifice of Jesus on the cross was a one-time event (9:25-26). Does it follow that no sacrifice is expected from us? Paul claims that the sacrifice of Christ continues to work itself out in his life. "I have been crucified with Christ," he says in Galatians 2:19. And again: "I am now rejoicing in my sufferings for your sake, and in my flesh I am completing what is lacking in Christ's afflictions for the sake of his body, that is, the church" (Col. 1:24). This last verse has been used throughout the history of the Christian church to justify practices of extreme asceticism and self-induced suffering. But Paul does not say that he is beating himself or doing himself injury. Rather, he is suffering *on behalf*

---

32. Elizabeth Moon, *The Deed of Paksenarrion* (Riverdale, NY: Baen Publishing, 1992), part III, chapter 27, Microsoft Reader version, pp. 1793-94.

of the church. Throughout the Pauline letters, we have information about the sort of suffering that Paul experienced, and none of it was self-inflicted. Rather, Paul seems to understand his suffering in terms of his union with Christ. Because he is now *in Christ*, the sufferings of Christ overflow into his life, as do the consolations of Christ (2 Cor. 1:3-7).[33] And because he is now *in Christ*, when he suffers — as from his "thorn in the flesh" (2 Cor. 12:7-10) — that suffering may somehow be understood as communion with the grace of Jesus.

People united to Jesus will have cruciform lives, not because they seek out suffering, but because they share in his suffering (Mark 10:40; John 15:18-21) and surrender themselves to him (Mark 8:34-35); not because they inflict suffering on themselves but because they bear the burdens of others (Gal. 6:2) and lay down their lives for others (John 15:13). Near the end of Hebrews, we read a summary of the sort of sacrifice that is still expected of us: "Through him, then, let us continually offer a sacrifice of praise to God, that is, the fruit of lips that confess his name. Do not neglect to do good and to share what you have, for such sacrifices are pleasing to God" (13:15-16). Such sacrifice is not salvific either for the one who sacrifices or for others, but is rather motivated by gratitude and by fellowship with Christ. It is in this spirit that Paul says, "I appeal to you, therefore, brothers and sisters, by the mercies of God, to present your bodies as a living sacrifice, holy and acceptable to God, which is your spiritual worship" (Rom. 12:1).

The primary way in which we share in Christ's sacrifice according to the biblical witness is through the sacraments, for in the sacraments of baptism and the supper the Spirit unites us to Christ, allowing us to participate both in his sacrifice and in his resurrection. The connections between sacrifice and the supper are especially clear. Mary Douglas has drawn some provocative connections between the Levitical cereal offering and Jesus' institution of the supper, connections that she believes the disciples would have seen as a result of their immersion in Jewish sacrificial

---

33. We live in a self-indulgent age, and I myself am a product of that age. I realize that some of my discomfort with extreme asceticism may not be theologically motivated but may rather be a sign of my enmeshment in a consumer culture that sees comfort and health as entitlements. There are certainly many devout believers throughout the history of the church — Francis of Assisi comes to mind — who have found that self-inflicted suffering is spiritually valuable. Still, that does not seem to be the biblical model, and indeed for most people in the world there is enough suffering in life already to challenge us spiritually without adding additional pain of our own making.

ritual.[34] At the institution of the supper, Jesus himself points us toward understanding his sacrifice as a renewal of the covenant. When the people of Israel renewed their covenant with God at Sinai, the ceremony included burnt offerings, peace offerings, and a shared meal in God's presence for the elders who ascended Sinai with Moses (Exod. 24:1-11). Such a breadth of typology does not allow us to understand Christ's sacrifice solely as an interaction between the Father and the Son. In instituting the supper, Jesus deliberately included his disciples as participants in the renewal sealed by his sacrifice.

Hebrews suggests another way in which new covenant people are called to participate in high priestly, sacrificial work under Christ's leadership. The immediate reaction to the mediating work of Christ is prayer. "[W]e have [a high priest] who in every respect has been tested as we are, yet without sin. Let us *therefore* approach the throne of grace with boldness, so that we may receive mercy and find grace to help in time of need" (4:15-16). Prayer is the way in which the daily sacrifice is carried out under the new covenant, serving as a regular recognition of our status as creatures and God's status as the transcendent Creator. Prayers of confession, supplication, and praise all express our helplessness, our dependence, our failure — much as sacrifice in its original design was meant to do. Just as the law is now written on our hearts, so too the work of sacrifice now happens internally, not externally. When we approach the throne of grace, we are approaching the altar at which the blood of Christ has been offered, and we are approaching under the covering of our union with him, a union that makes access to God's presence possible.

Although Christ's sacrificial act was performed once-for-all some two thousand years ago, his priestly work as our mediator continues. Jesus is even now interceding for us before the Father (Heb. 7:25). He has brought our humanity into the throne room of God, and by his continuing incarnation he holds open the door for us to have access to that throne room. Our existential longing to see God face to face is answered in his mediating work, for when someday we see God face to face, it is the face of Jesus that we will see. In his continuing incarnation, he shares our suffering and pain, so that we may find the comfort of knowing that there is one who suffers with us, while also knowing that in God there is a fullness of joy

---

34. Mary Douglas, "The Eucharist: Its Continuity with the Bread Sacrifice of Leviticus," *Modern Theology* 15 (April 1999): 209-24.

that is not vulnerable to suffering, which we will someday share completely. This is the mediating ministry in which we, the priesthood of all believers, are called to share through the work of the Spirit. Through union with Christ, we are also called to a ministry *to* the world in which we are transformed into his likeness so as to reflect his glory and a ministry *on behalf of* the world in which we share in his intercession and compassion.

7 Justification and Ecclesiology

Martien E. Brinkman

This essay concerns the relation of justification and the church. It refers especially to the Lutheran–Roman Catholic international dialogue on this issue, and is meant as a Reformed comment on that dialogue. I will show that there is indeed an important relation between the doctrine of justification and the doctrine of the church. But sometimes in ecumenical discussions the reference to the doctrine of justification has been artificial. Justification is often used only in a metaphorical way, and it would have been sufficient to refer simply to the primacy of the Word of God or the sovereignty of God.

In the end, I will plead for a more precise use of the doctrine of justification in ecclesial discussions. Moreover, we must not forget to reflect on the ecclesiological implications of what for the Reformers was the most important corollary of the doctrine of justification: the Christian idea of freedom.

Justification and Church

A crucial ecumenical document preceding the *Joint Declaration on the Doctrine of Justification* of 1999[1] between Lutherans and Roman Catholics

---

1. Jeffrey Gros, Harding Meyer, and William G. Rusch, eds., *Growth in Agreement II: Reports and Agreed Statements of Ecumenical Conversations on a World Level 1982-1998* (Faith and Order Paper No. 187) (Geneva: WCC Publications and Grand Rapids: Eerdmans, 2000), pp. 566-82.

was *Church and Justification* (1994). *Church and Justification* begins with a summary of previous doctrinal discussions; the Lutheran–Roman Catholic Joint Commission observes that they "relied heavily on the comprehensive American dialogue statement, *Justification by Faith* (1985), and on the justification chapter in the study *The Condemnations of the Reformation Era, Do They Still Divide?* (1986), a product of the German dialogue.[2] The document then elaborates ecclesial aspects of the doctrine of justification.

The Joint Commission strongly supports the idea that the doctrine of justification is foundational for the church, as emphasized in both the American and the German dialogue:

> According to Lutheran tradition the justification of sinners is the article of faith by which the church stands or falls. . . . This is the background against which the Catholic–Lutheran Dialogue has as its theme the relation between justification and the church. A consensus in the doctrine of justification, even if it is nuanced, must prove itself ecclesiologically. Everything that is believed and taught about the nature of the church, the means of salvation and the church's ministry must be founded in the salvation-event itself and must be marked by justification-faith as the way in which the salvation event is received and appropriated. Correspondingly, everything that is believed and taught about the nature and effect of justification must be understood in the overall context of statements about the church, the means of salvation and the church's ministry. This is the necessary precondition by which all the life and activity of the church must constantly be checked.[3]

---

2. Lutheran–Roman Catholic Joint Commission, *Church and Justification: Understanding the Church in the Light of the Doctrine of Justification* (Geneva: Lutheran World Federation, 1994), p. 9. For the American dialogue, see H. George Anderson, T. Austin Murphy, and Joseph A. Burgess, eds., *Justification by Faith* (Lutherans and Roman Catholics in Dialogue 7) (Minneapolis: Augsburg, 1985); and for the German dialogue, Karl Lehmann and Wolfhart Pannenberg, eds., *The Condemnations of the Reformation Era: Do They Still Divide?* (Minneapolis: Fortress, 1990), pp. 30-56.

3. Lutheran–Roman Catholic Joint Commission, *Church and Justification*, p. 13 (No. 2). The Joint Commission points here by way of illustration to Luther's exposition of Psalm 130:4, which for him is the epitome of the doctrine of justification: "for if this article stands, the Church stands; if it falls, the Church falls." See *WA*, 40/III, p. 351, esp. line 35 ("stante enim hac doctrina stat Ecclesia, ruente autem ruit ipsa quoque"); and p. 352, esp. line 3 ("quia isto articulo stante, stat Ecclesia, ruente ruit Ecclesia").

This critical assessment is accepted by both dialogue partners. There can be no fundamental contradiction between the gospel of justification and the church, and if the doctrine of justification is thoroughly relevant to the center of the gospel, it will also be thoroughly relevant to the church. For Lutherans as well as Roman Catholics, the interconnectedness of church and gospel appears in the following three ways: (1) on the one hand, the church lives from the gospel; on the other, the gospel sounds forth in the church and summons people into the church; (2) if we confess in common that the gospel that gathers the church together really is God's creative Word, then we must also confess in common that the church is God's creation and as such is a social reality that unites people; and (3) God, who creates the church through his Word and has promised that it will abide in the truth and will continue to exist, is faithful to his Word and his promise. Until this promise attains its eschatological goal in the consummation of all things, God effects his faithfulness to the church through structures of historical continuity.

Especially to Lutherans, the history of the church appears to be a constant struggle against the dangers of error and apostasy, and finally requires a victory of God's faithfulness over the constantly recurring unfaithfulness of human beings. Lutherans nonetheless are also concerned with the structures that contribute to the church's historical continuity, even if these structures cannot guarantee the church's integrity.[4]

The Joint Commission then goes on to quote approvingly the American Lutheran–Roman Catholic Common Statement on *Justification by Faith:* "Catholics as well as Lutherans can acknowledge the need to test the practices, structures, and theologies of the church by the extent to which they help or hinder 'the proclamation of God's free and merciful promises in Christ Jesus that can be rightly received only through faith.'"[5]

In the Reformed–Roman Catholic dialogue document, "Towards a

---

4. Lutheran–Roman Catholic Joint Commission, *Church and Justification*, pp. 87-88 (Nos. 170-72).

5. Anderson, *Justification by Faith*, p. 69 (§153). The Common Statement refers and quotes here its own §28 where in the description of the "Reformation Doctrine" it states: "They regard it as the heart of the gospel because the gospel message in its specific sense is the proclamation of God's free and merciful promises in Christ Jesus which can be rightly received only through faith. All aspects of Christian life, worship, and preaching should lead to or flow from justifying faith in this gospel, and anything which opposes or substitutes for trust in God's promises alone should be abolished" (p. 25).

Common Understanding of the Church," we also find a paragraph on "The Calling of the Church: Its Role in Justification by Grace through Faith." Here the communal character of the gift of justification is especially underscored: "There is no justification in isolation. All justification takes place in the community of believers or is ordered towards the gathering of such a community."[6] Although the document emphasizes that justification by grace through faith comes to us through the church, it immediately adds: "This is not to say that the church exercises a mediation complementary to that of Christ or that it is clothed with a power independent of the gift of grace. The church is at once the place, the instrument and the minister chosen by God to make heard Christ's word and to celebrate the sacrament in God's name throughout the centuries."[7]

Next to its denial of the independent character of the church, the text points to the sovereign liberty of God to grant grace: "If God chooses to act through the church for the salvation of believers, this does not restrict saving grace to these means. The sovereign freedom of God can always call anyone to salvation independently of such actions. But it is true to say that God's call is always related to the church, in that God's call always has as its purpose the building up of the church, which is the body of Christ (1 Cor. 12:27-28; Eph. 1:22-23)."[8]

It is obvious that the document here tries to avoid the pitfall of every Reformed ecclesiology, namely, that the emphasis on God's sovereign liberty leads to inadequate attention to the importance of the common witness of the church in the world. Time and again a lack of awareness of the necessity of the unity of the church has been evident in the Reformed tradition.[9] In its effort to avoid this problem, the document closes the paragraph on "The Church as *creatura verbi*" with the sentence: "The community of faith is thus not merely the community in which the gospel is preached; by its hearing and responding to the word of grace, the commu-

---

6. Gross, Meyer, Rusch, *Growth in Agreement II*, pp. 780-818, esp. 799 (No. 80).

7. Gross, Meyer, Rusch, *Growth in Agreement II*, p. 800 (No. 86).

8. Gross, Meyer, Rusch, *Growth in Agreement II*, pp. 800-801 (No. 87).

9. See Martien E. Brinkman, "Unity: A Contribution from the Reformed Tradition," in *With a Demonstration of the Spirit and of Power: Seventh International Consultation of United and Uniting Churches* (Faith and Order Paper No. 195), ed. Thomas F. Best (Geneva: WCC Publications, 2004), pp. 19-30, esp. 19. See also Michael Weinrich, "Die Einheit der Kirche aus reformatorischer Perspektive: Ein Beitrag zum protestantischen Ökumeneverständnis," *Evangelische Theologie* 65 (2005): 196-210.

nity itself becomes a medium of confession, its faith a 'sign' or 'token' to the world; it is itself a part of the world transformed by being addressed and renewed by the Word of God."[10] Against the backdrop of this common confession of the church, the Reformed–Roman Catholic dialogue document concludes that the allegation that the Reformed are inclined to separate the church from the work of salvation is a caricature.[11]

Church and Kingdom

Besides the emphasis on the all-pervasive character of the doctrine of justification, the Lutheran–Roman Catholic Joint Commission stresses the ethical implications of this doctrine:

> God accepts the sinful creature in pure mercy and thus cancels out the law of works and achievement as the basis for life. God thus opens up a way of life that most profoundly contradicts that which prevails in the world: the life of love. This love arises out of faith and passes on the boundless mercy that it has received. It suffers from the distress and injustice that others experience and meets it with self-sacrifice and renunciation. And it urges the members of the church to promote justice, peace and the integrity of creation together with all people of good will amid the glaring contrast between poor and rich, and in the conflicts between ideologies and interests, races, nations and sexes. Thus the church is both a contradiction and a challenge in our world, as the place where merciful justification is proclaimed, as the locus for community and love, as a co-shaper of a more just and humane world.[12]

These two points, the relation between justification and church and between justification and ethics, were discussed at great length by the Joint Commission in section 4.5 ("The Significance of the Doctrine of Justification for the Understanding of the Church") and chapter 5 ("The Mission and Consummation of the Church"). What is remarkable in the procedure is that in chapter 5 the concept of justification is virtually absent. Other

---

10. Gross, Meyer, Rusch, *Growth in Agreement II*, p. 803 (No. 101).

11. Gross, Meyer, Rusch, *Growth in Agreement II*, p. 805 (No. 112).

12. Lutheran–Roman Catholic Joint Commission, *Church and Justification*, pp. 16-17 (No. 9).

concepts were apparently regarded to be more adequate for expressing the relation church-world and the relation church-kingdom. The partners in the dialogue may have been aware of the limits of the concept of justification. They also seem to have been looking for more adequate concepts for the church, such as prophetic sign, and wished to emphasize the symbolic character of ministry.

Indeed, "sign" might be one of the best interpretive keys to the relation church-kingdom. It establishes the church's dependence on its Lord. The sign itself is nothing without him who establishes it and points it in the right direction. "Sign" stresses the fact that the church is sent: a sign exists for others; in itself it is worthless. If the adjective "prophetic" is attached to the term "sign," it is in order to recall the dimensions of judgment and salvation, and the eschatological perspective that inheres in the notion of mystery, the "open secret" of God's saving purpose to unite all things and people in Christ. In all this, the church participates in the paradoxes and dynamics of the kingdom within history. It, too, is a net with good and bad fish, a field of wheat and tares. It is a community of sinners and at the same time justified, a beginning not an end, always endangered from within as from without, but preserved at the same time by the grace of God in an unending, renewing process of sanctification.

Taking the sign-character of the church seriously will lead us to ask where the church's practice takes on the character of a sign. Where does the sign become visible in an exemplary way? The calling to be a sign points the churches to modesty and self-criticism on the one hand, and self-esteem and courage on the other hand. The church is no more than a sign that points beyond itself in its proclamation of the kingdom of God.[13] Whenever the church fails to reflect the community of love, justice, freedom, and peace that it is meant to be, it fails in its vocation to be the sign of the kingdom. To be an authentic prophetic sign, the historical and cultural dimension of the church and its pastoral work must be constantly renewed by the Holy Spirit. Despite human sinfulness, the love of God in Christ is mediated to God's people in such a way that, being judged and justified,

---

13. The Dutch Reformed theologian A. A. van Ruler stressed the sign character of the church in relation to the kingdom but did not intend to minimize the role of the church as bearer of the gospel and as such as a peculiar gestalt, a "cathedral of love." On Van Ruler, see Allan J. Janssen, *Kingdom, Office and Church: A Study of A. A. van Ruler's Doctrine of Ecclesiastical Office with Implications for the North American Ecumenical Discussion* (dissertation, Free University of Amsterdam, 2005), pp. 80-122.

they are set free to receive grace, which makes them acceptable for God and initiates the process of sanctification in the world.

What holds true for the church as a whole holds true for ministry as well. It too has a sign (symbolic) character.[14] It is characteristic of the symbol that it evokes something different from what is there at first sight. Something like that is also what church ministry is about. Ministry should be a symbol of something else: a small and modest sign referring to a larger whole of grace and mercy in an often graceless and merciless culture. Every theology of ministry concerns people who for a certain period or even for a whole life stand apart in order to give shape to the content of the gospel. That is what has sometimes been called the "scandal of particularity."[15] There ought not to be a need for ministry-holders. Yet, apparently we cannot do without men and women as pastors who know they are freely called to lead people "in witness and service."[16]

Since they too are human beings in every respect, it is only realistic to regard ministry as both a blessing and a curse for the church. The church has been blessed and punished with ministers, just as the people of Israel were blessed and punished with judges, kings, and prophets. Ministers, like anybody else, are not exempt from the ambiguities of human behavior. A proper theology of ministry, however, tries to clarify as many of those ambiguities as possible.

Without a proper analysis of the function of ministry as a referring

---

14. In this contribution we equate the Latin word "sign" *(signum)* and the Greek word "symbol" *(symbolon)*, although we are fully aware of their different historical backgrounds. Often a sign is more associated with a reference externally given *(signum datum)*, and a symbol with intrinsically given participation. Since, however, both aspects are parts of modern theories of symbolism (interpretation and participation), there is no point in making a sharp distinction.

15. For this expression, see the 1971 report of the World Council of Churches on "Ordained Ministry," published in *Documentary History of Faith and Order: 1963-1993* (Faith and Order Paper No. 159), ed. Günther Gassman (Geneva: WCC Publications, 1993), pp. 116-36, esp. 119.

16. It is by the word "service" that the so-called Lima text of the World Council of Churches summarizes the essence of ministry. See *Baptism, Eucharist and Ministry* (Faith and Order Paper No. 111) (Geneva: WCC Publications, 1982), pp. 20-24 (Nos. 1-18). The churches of the Leuenberg Fellowship prefer to speak of the dual concept of witness and service, thereby underlining more strongly the element of prophetic proclamation. See *The Church of Jesus Christ: The Contribution of the Reformation towards Ecumenical Dialogue on Church Unity* (Leuenberger Texte I) (Frankfurt am Main: Lembeck, 1995), pp. 96-102.

sign (symbol), we cannot adequately account for the character of ministry as witness and service. For we can speak about witness in a meaningful way only when we know with respect to whom and what we make witness. And we can arrive at a meaningful rendering of service only when we are thoroughly aware of the purpose it serves. Only when that which is symbolically represented in the church's ministry is demonstrated to be something that is sadly lacking in our societies — such as trust, amazement, humbleness, forgiveness, reconciliation, and resistance — is it possible not only in the church, but also beyond to speak freely about the *pars pro toto* character of ministry. For in that "one for all" character of ministry lies not only the "scandal of particularity" but also the blessing of the particularity of ministry.

Areas of Remaining Controversy

Despite Roman Catholic–Lutheran consensus, "four areas of controversy" remain in relation to whether the Lutheran doctrine of justification diminishes the reality of the church and whether the Roman Catholic understanding of the church obscures the gospel as it is explicated by the doctrine of justification: (1) the nature of the historical continuity of the church, (2) the divine institution of ordained ministry, (3) the teaching function of ministry, and (4) the jurisdictional function of ministry. Here I shall limit myself to the first two: the continuity of the church and the divine institution of ordained ministry.

Institutional Continuity of the Church

As a creation of the gospel and its proclamation, which is always "external," creative, and sustained by God's faithfulness, the church exists continuously through the ages. It is historical like other creatures, though in a unique way: only the church is promised that it will endure and that the gates of hell will not overcome it. If God creates the church as a historical community with a continuous existence by means of the external gospel, this activity of God has its counterpart in the establishment of structures and institutions. The founding of the church, its institution in the Christ event, and the establishment of structural and institutional forms are indissolubly linked together. At the heart of these forms is the concern to maintain apostolic preaching together with the sacraments of baptism and the Lord's Supper as God-appointed means and signs of the continuity of the church.[17] Preaching and sacraments have taken different forms over the course of history and have given rise to other structures and institutions that have contributed to the continuity of the church and have therefore also proven themselves to be enduring.

Having arrived at this point, *Church and Justification* then identifies a remaining controversy:

> Our two churches give in part different and indeed controversial responses to the question of how far and to what degree these ecclesiastical realities that have arisen in history share in the enduring quality of the realities established when the church was founded. However, in the midst of this controversy, they did not dispute that these realities arose in the history of the church and were not directly and explicitly established when it was founded; that they can certainly give expression to the continuity of the church and be of service to it; and that they nevertheless remain capable of renewal and in need of renewal.[18]

Their effectiveness as signs and means of the continuity of the church is limited and called in question when and for as long as their relatedness to and transparency for the gospel are diminished or obscured. This is, so the document states, true for how the church deals with the realities that are integral to its foundation and are indispensable to it, such as the Word of God available in the canon of Holy Scripture and the sacraments of baptism and the Lord's Supper. But this is, so it continues, especially true of the signs and means of continuity that have emerged in history:

> Here the idea of the indispensable nature of these signs and instruments of institutional continuity for the church, as advocated not only but especially on the Catholic side, may itself invoke the concern, and indeed reproach, that the gospel of the radical gratuitousness of the gift of salvation and unconditional nature of the reception of salvation is

---

17. Lutheran–Roman Catholic Joint Commission, *Church and Justification*, p. 90 (No. 178).

18. Lutheran–Roman Catholic Joint Commission, *Church and Justification*, pp. 89-91, esp. p. 91 (No. 179).

being obscured. Consequently, special care is needed to see to it that these instruments and signs of institutional continuity in the church do not cease to function as servants of the gospel, not even when one seems obligated to grant them an ecclesially indispensable and binding character.[19]

Of great help here might be the insights developed in the Reformed–Roman Catholic dialogue on the sacramental character of the church. The document "Towards a Common Understanding of the Church" underlines that the reference to the church as sacrament or sign designates the church at once as the place of presence and the place of distance, of visibility and invisibility. The church is instrument and minister of the unique mediation of Christ. The church is always the servant of this unique mediation, never its source or its master.[20] The church is an instrument in Christ's hands because it carries out, through the preaching of the Word, the administration of the sacraments, and the oversight of communities, "a ministry entirely dependent on the Lord, just like a tool in the hand of a worker."[21]

These formulations attempt on the one hand to emphasize the communion of the church with Christ, and on the other hand to maintain that Christ is "over against" his church. The interconnectedness of communion and distance is derived from the Francophone ecumenical Groupe des Dombes: "A sacrament holds two extremes together: plenitude and vacuousness, glory and humiliation. . . . Speaking about the living sign in relation to the Church, is describing it as the simultaneous place of presence and absence."[22]

This veiling and unveiling character of the symbol — its "transparency" and "hiddenness," "fullness" and "emptiness"[23] — evokes the views of the French Protestant philosopher Paul Ricoeur and the French Roman

19. Lutheran–Roman Catholic Joint Commission, *Church and Justification*, p. 91 (No. 181).

20. Gross, Meyer, Rusch, *Growth in Agreement II*, p. 804 (No. 106).

21. Gross, Meyer, Rusch, *Growth in Agreement II*, p. 804 (No. 108).

22. Groupe des Dombes, *L'Esprit, l'Église et les Sacrements* (Taizé: Les Presses de Taizé, 1979) pp. 36 (No. 42) and 57 (No. 85): "Un Sacrement tient ensemble deux extrêmes: La plénitude et l'apparente vacuité, la gloire et le dépouillement," and "Parler de signe vivant à propos de l'Église, c'est la décrire à la fois comme le lieu de la *présence* et celui de la *distance*."

23. See also Groupes des Dombes, *L'Esprit, l'Église et les Sacrements*, pp. 22-23 (No. 22), 25 (No. 25), and 78 (No. 131).

Catholic theologian Louis-Marie Chauvet. Ricoeur speaks of the symbol as characterized by the movement of disclosure and disguise. It hides what it expresses.[24] For Chauvet, symbolic representation lies between commemoration (anamnesis) of the past that is lost ("objet perdu") and the promised future that is not yet. So the Christian symbols signify an absence, yet simultaneously evoke a presence. The signified always remains at a distance, and the difference is never overcome. The divine reality in one and the same movement shows itself and recedes, just as Jesus at the moment he is recognized, disappears (Luke 24:31).[25] The nature of symbolism does not allow a petrification of the divine presence.

In Chauvet's work, the story of the men on their way to Emmaus is the key to his doctrine of the sacraments.[26] His approach to the sacraments takes as its starting point the resurrection, and not the incarnation. Consequently, his concept of the church as a sacrament necessarily rejects the idea that the church is a *Christus prolongatus* — and thus rejects employment of the incarnation as a formal category in ecclesiology. Calling the church a symbolic, sacramental reality, however, by no means prejudices the irreplaceable work of Christ.[27]

Ordained Ministry as Divinely Instituted in the Church

Human beings, including believers, cannot say to themselves what God has to say to them and cannot bring themselves the salvation that God alone has prepared for them. This structural movement "outside us and for us" is constitutive of the saving revelation of God in Christ. It continues in the proclamation of the gospel and must continue there if the gospel is not to

24. See Paul Ricoeur, *Symbolism of Evil* (New York: Harper & Row, 1967), p. 17.

25. See Louis-Marie Chauvet, *Du symbolisme au symbole: Essai sur les sacrements* (Paris: Cerf, 1979), pp. 77-79 and 91-93. On the enriching contribution of Chauvet's theology of the symbols to an ecumenical ecclesiology, see Louis-Marie Chauvet, *Symbole et sacrement: Une relecture sacramentelle de l'existence chrétienne* (Paris: Cerf, 1987), pp. 85-115. See also A. H. C. van Eijk, "The Church as Sacrament: A Contribution to Ecumenical Understanding," *Bijdragen* 48 (1987): 234-58; and A. H. C. van Eijk, "The Church: Mystery, Sacrament, Sign, Instrument, Symbolic Reality," *Bijdragen* 50 (1989): 178-202.

26. See Chauvet, *Du symbolisme au symbole,* pp. 87-97; and Chauvet, *Symbole et sacrement,* pp. 172-76.

27. Van Eijk, "The Church as Sacrament," p. 247.

be obscured. For this purpose, God established the ordained ministry.[28] The Lutheran–Roman Catholic dialogue on the church's ministry had drawn attention to this in the so-called Accra document and, later, in the Lima text on *Baptism, Eucharist and Ministry* — both texts of the World Council of Churches. According to these documents, the presence of the ministry in the community signifies the priority of divine initiative and authority in the church's existence.[29]

Hence, the Joint Commission asserted that the doctrine of justification must be the criterion for ordained ministers' self-understanding and actions. Reference to the New Testament roots of the ministry of the church is as such no guarantee against abuse and false doctrine. Nevertheless, from the Lutheran side too, it was entirely possible to acknowledge that the historical development of an episcopate into a historic succession was not something purely within the sphere of history, set in motion only by sociological and political factors, but rather had taken place with the help of the Holy Spirit and constituted something essential for the church.[30]

Here the Joint Commission mentions a second area of controversy. Lutherans could not agree that there was something necessary in these historical developments of the ministry. They were concerned that putting episcopacy on such a level endangered the unconditional nature of the gift of salvation and its reception. And that was precisely at stake in the Reformation doctrine of justification. Only that may be considered necessary for the church to be church that was already given by Jesus Christ himself as means of salvation. If ecclesial structures that emerged in history are elevated to that level, they become preconditions for receiving salvation and so, in the Lutheran view, are put illegitimately on the

---

28. Lutheran–Roman Catholic Joint Commission, *Church and Justification*, pp. 93-94 (No. 188).

29. Lutheran–Roman Catholic Joint Commission, *Church and Justification*, p. 94 (No. 189). For the text of the Lutheran–Roman Catholic Dialogue on ministry, see Harding Meyer and Lukas Vischer, eds., *Growth in Agreement: Reports and Agreed Statements of Ecumenical Conversations on a World Level* (Faith and Order Paper No. 108) (New York and Geneva: WCC, 1984), pp. 248-74, esp. 253 ("The Ministry in the Church" [1981], No. 20). In turn, this document quotes the so-called Accra document, *One Baptism, One Eucharist and a Mutually Recognized Ministry: Three Agreed Statements* (Faith and Order Paper No. 73) (Geneva: WCC, 1978), p. 33 (No. 14).

30. Lutheran–Roman Catholic Joint Commission, *Church and Justification*, p. 95 (No. 191) (quoting "The Ministry in the Church," No. 49).

same level with the gospel proclaimed in Word and sacrament that alone is necessary for salvation.[31]

In contrast, Roman Catholics see a "divine institution" of the ministry as it developed in history.[32] They regard it as a development led, willed, and testified to by divine providence. Under the operation of the Holy Spirit within the apostolic tradition, episcopacy and apostolic succession have developed as the expression, means, and criterion of the continuity of the tradition. The episcopate and apostolic succession are in the Roman Catholic view essential for the church as church, and so are necessary and indispensable.[33]

Nevertheless, for Roman Catholics too, Word and sacrament are the two pillars of the church. The episcopate and apostolic tradition support the church's ministry of salvation, so that the Word will be authentically preached and the sacraments rightly celebrated. The Spirit of God uses the episcopate to root the church of every time and place in its apostolic origin, to integrate the faithful in the one universal faith of the church, and so through the episcopate to make faith's liberating force effective. In this sense, the episcopate is in the Roman Catholic view necessary for the gospel, which is itself necessary for salvation.[34]

For the Joint Commission, the emphasis on ministry as service to the gospel demonstrated that the differences between Roman Catholics and Lutherans on the episcopate were not radically contradictory. It was not the case that a Lutheran rejection of, or even indifference toward, this ministry found itself in opposition to a Catholic assertion of its ecclesial indispensability. The question was rather one of gradation in evaluating this ministry, which has been described on the Roman Catholic side as "necessary" or "indispensable" and on the Lutheran side as "important," "mean-

31. Lutheran–Roman Catholic Joint Commission, *Church and Justification*, pp. 95-96 (No. 192).

32. For the ecumenical discussion of the historical interpretation of the expression "divine institution" (ordinatio divina) at the Council of Trent and at Vatican II, as distinguished from the expression "jus divinum," see Carl J. Peter, "The Office of Bishop and Jus Divinum. Trent and the Lutheran Confessions: A Rereading with Ecumenical Possibilities," *Canonical Studies* 8 (1987): 93-113; and Avery Robert Dulles, "Ius Divinum as an Ecumenical Problem," *Theological Studies* 38 (1977): 681-708.

33. Lutheran–Roman Catholic Joint Commission, *Church and Justification*, pp. 96-97 (Nos. 195, 196).

34. Lutheran–Roman Catholic Joint Commission, *Church and Justification*, p. 97 (No. 196).

ingful," and even "desirable."[35] Yet, behind these differences in the evaluation of ministry, so the Joint Commission concluded, one can nevertheless recognize two different ways of correlating salvation and church.

According to the Lutheran doctrine of justification and of the church, it is only through the proclamation of the gospel in Word and sacraments, to which ordained ministers are called, that the Holy Spirit effects justifying faith and the church is created and preserved. Following this ecclesiological line, nothing besides the gospel proclaimed in Word and sacraments may be considered ecclesially necessary, in the strict sense of the word, lest the one thing necessary for salvation, the gospel, be endangered.

The Lutheran and Reformed churches that have signed or are participating in the Leuenberg Agreement (1974) concur — so they stress in their so-called Tampere Theses (1986) — that the ordained ministry belongs to the being of the church. They emphasize, however, that the whole community and not just the ordained ministry has responsibility for the proclamation of the Word and for the right use of the sacraments. Therefore, the ordained ministry by itself does not guarantee the true being of the church but rather remains subordinate to the Word of God.[36] The ordained ministry rests upon a particular commission of Christ, but stands together with the whole congregation in serving the Word of God.[37] The Lutheran churches, especially in Scandinavia, put more stress on continuity with the historical office of the bishop, whereas the Reformed churches are committed in principle to a presbyterial-synodal church order. Reciprocal acknowl-

---

35. Lutheran–Roman Catholic Joint Commission, *Church and Justification*, pp. 97-98 (No. 197). Compare "The Ministry in the Church," Nos. 65 and 66, in Gross, Meyer, Rusch, *Growth in Agreement*, p. 268: "Thus, despite diverse historical developments, the Lutheran Reformation affirmed and intended to preserve the historical continuity of church order as an expression of the unity of the apostolic church among all peoples and throughout all centuries, presupposing, of course, that the gospel is rightly proclaimed. This intention must be maintained even in the face of contrary historical developments for the sake of the faith that the church abides" (No. 65). "These considerations provide the basis for a Lutheran evaluation of the historic succession as a sign of unity. The Lutheran conviction is that acceptance of communion with the episcopal office in the historic succession is meaningful not as an isolated act, but only as it contributes to the unity of the church in faith and witnesses to the universality of the gospel of reconciliation" (No. 66).

36. For the Tampere Theses, see *Leuenberger Kirchengemeinschaft — Gemeinschaft Reformatorischer Kirchen in Europa: Sakramente, Amt, Ordination* (Texte 2) (Frankfurt am Main: Lembeck, 1995) pp. 96-101, esp. 97 (Thesis 1).

37. *Leuenberger Kirchengemeinschaft*, p. 98 (Thesis 2).

edgment of ordained ministry is not impeded as long as the question of church leadership remains subordinate to the sovereignty of the Word.

Critical Remarks

Although the Joint Commission, in line with Luther, related the doctrine of justification to the church, the results sometimes seem artificial. The point at issue is always the primacy of the gospel over the church, and the service of the church to the gospel. In short, the issue is the relation of gospel and church. The doctrine of justification, understood as the content of the gospel, is often understood in highly general terms, such as the priority of God's initiative, or the freedom, sovereignty, and ultimate binding nature of the gospel as God's Word of grace. Referring to the doctrine of justification as such adds little to what the reference to the gospel already implies.[38]

The significance of *Church and Justification* lies more in what is said about the relation church-gospel rather than in what is said about the doctrine of justification. This was to be expected, because the doctrine of justification deals with the question of the relation between the individual believer and God, and can be applied to institutions, structures, and organizations only by way of metaphor. The same objection may be raised when justification is understood as meaning, liberation, or creation. These are strongly metaphorical uses of a concept that has first of all a strongly individual-existential, even judicial meaning, with its climax in acquittal.

By no means does this focus imply an individualistic understanding of justification and the church. Just the opposite is the case, as Eberhard Jüngel underscored in his address to the European Protestant Assembly at Budapest in 1992:

> [The churches] have the priceless advantage over all secular institutions not only of being able to say what should and should not be, but also of having the authority to *forgive* guilt and sin in God's name, if what should not be nevertheless happens. When forgiveness is experienced, it sharpens the conscience and creates much more awareness of responsibility than any moral imperative can do. . . . For this reason, the church

38. See, for example, *Leuenberger Kirchengemeinschaft*, p. 103 (No. 211): "The issue is, first and foremost, the primacy of the gospel over the church — the freedom, sovereignty and ultimate binding nature of the gospel as God's word of grace."

. . . can really call guilt by its proper name without lapsing into the role of the moralist, who as a rule has the effect rather of hardening the heart than of helping.[39]

The judicial meaning of justification does not limit the doctrine's significance to personal relations, but rather frees people for their proper roles in society.

The French Lutheran ecumenist André Birmelé sees rich ecumenical possibilities in relating justification and church to one another. He nevertheless turns very quickly to concepts that are not characteristic of the doctrine of justification. For example, he argues for an ecclesiology that accepts the doctrine of justification as a decisive criterion whereby "every action of the Church [is] totally transparent for the sole action of Christ." Yet, one might well arrive at the same insight from differently composed ecclesiologies.[40]

Hence, Birmelé's former colleague at the Lutheran ecumenical institute in Strasbourg (France), the German ecumenist Harding Meyer, remarked that we must be careful not to frame all the debated problems too one-sidedly in terms of the doctrine of justification:

Quite apart from the danger of reaching only a sterile schematism, even some sort of theological game, it should not be forgotten that we are talking about a specifically Lutheran perspective on the problem, and that this should not be imposed on the Catholic partner, not simply out of esteem and friendship for this partner, but in the last analysis because of the New Testament witness and the Christian message, which we do not treat fairly if we always and everywhere try to interpret and proclaim them as the witness and message of justification.

39. Eberhard Jüngel, "The Gospel and the Protestant Churches of Europe: A Protestant View of Christian Responsibility in Europe," *EPD-Dokumentation* 17 (1992): 55-72, esp. 70-71. See for a similar, positive emphasis on the judicial focus of the doctrine of justification, Wolf-Rüdiger Schmidt, "Christianity minus Grace: Justification from a Philosophical Perspective — A Conversation with Odo Marquard," in *Justification in the World's Context* (Documentation 45), ed. Wolfgang Greive (Geneva: Lutheran World Federation, 2000), pp. 169-76; and Martien E. Brinkman, *Justification in Ecumenical Dialogue: Central Aspects of Soteriology in Debate* (IIMO Research Publications 45) (Utrecht: IIMO, 1996), pp. 206-12 ("Individual Conscience and Experience of Guilt").

40. André Birmelé, *Le Salut en Jésus Christ dans les Dialogues Oecuméniques* (Paris: Cerf, 1986), pp. 311 and 472.

Even if we can commonly acknowledge that the doctrine of justification touches all spheres of the doctrine of the church and of Christian faith, "this does not rule out other important interpretations of the salvation event that can express certain essential aspects of the divine action, of the gospel message, of the ecclesiological reality and of Christian responsibility more adequately and contribute more effectively to their safekeeping than can an interpretation of the gospel directed solely towards justification."[41] It is in accordance with Meyer's analysis to keep in mind here especially the idea of Christian freedom.

Justification and Freedom

The emphasis on the relation of justification and the church has at least three important consequences: In the first place, it confronts us clearly with the relation of the gospel and the church. Every historical development of the sacraments and ministry has to be measured according to this more fundamental relation. Although no church tradition can find a blueprint of its own church order exactly in the New Testament, each church order needs biblical legitimation. Every church has to stand in the apostolic tradition, i.e., according to the definition of apostolicity as given in the Lima text:

> continuity in the permanent characteristics of the Church of the apostles: the witness to the apostolic faith, proclamation and fresh interpretation of the Gospel, celebration of baptism and the eucharist, the transmission of ministerial responsibilities, communion in prayer, love, joy and suffering, service to the sick and needy, unity among the local churches and sharing the gifts which the Lord has given to each.[42]

No church can ignore these criteria of apostolicity. In a certain sense, we could say: Time and again the doctrine of justification has pointed the church to these characteristics of apostolicity and serves as the basis for purifying historical or contextual developments of the church.

Second, and as its main role, the doctrine of justification points to the

---

41. Harding Meyer, "The Doctrine of Justification in the Lutheran Dialogue with Other Churches," *One in Christ* 17 (1981): 86-116, esp. 116.

42. *Baptism, Eucharist and Ministry*, p. 29 (M-34).

salvific function of the ministry of reconciliation, exercised by the church on behalf on her Lord. Justification presupposes an authority that calls us to account and that transcends our existence, an awareness on our part that we are not able to justify ourselves before this authority, and a conviction that the authority that calls us to account is the same authority that is able to acquit us. It is this theocentric accountability — call it theonomy — which most fundamentally defines human autonomy and which has everything to do with one's personal accountability before God and one's fellow human beings, such as expressed in the "eternal" questions from the book of Genesis: "Where are you?" (Gen. 3:10) and "What have you done?" (Gen. 4:10). Paradoxically it is exactly this theocentric, God-imposed accountability that makes our own decisions absolutely serious to the very end.

Third, it is only on the basis of this ministry of reconciliation that the church can proclaim the "freedom of the children of God" (Rom. 8:21). To Luther and Calvin the essence of the doctrine of justification was preeminently the experience of liberation. Attention has recently been drawn in numerous official dialogues to this element of freedom in the doctrine of justification. Thus, the *Joint Declaration on Justification* of Lutherans and Roman Catholics speaks of justification as forgiveness of sins and liberation from the prevailing power of sin and death and from the yoke of the law (no. 11).[43] And the Protestant churches in Europe united in the Leuenberg Church Fellowship point out that the biblical message calls freedom an essential feature of human existence.[44]

It would not be difficult to show by means of numerous other examples from ecumenical discussions just how much the churches of the Reformation see freedom as a fruit of the doctrine of justification. This liberating aspect of the doctrine of justification is expressed especially in humans' realistic self-acceptance. The recognition that one is capable of justifying oneself only to a very limited degree implies the recognition that one has to rely on "acquittal" from "elsewhere." Acknowledging this limit to self-justification may be characterized as one of the most radical forms of self-acceptance. Becoming aware of this "deficit" clears the way for the

---

43. Gross, Meyer, Rusch, *Growth in Agreement II*, p. 568 (No. 11).

44. See Wilhelm Hüffmeier and Christine-Ruth Müller, eds., *Wachsende Gemeinschaft in Zeugnis und Dienst Reformatorischer Kirchen in Europa: Texte der vierten Vollversammlung der Leuenberger Kirchengemeinschaft in Wien, 3. bis 10. Mai 1994* (Frankfurt am Main: Lembeck, 1995), pp. 93-126 ("Das christliche Zeugnis von der Freiheit") and 133-49.

acceptance of a divine "credit," the merciful gift of forgiveness as a constitutive factor of human freedom. It is only where humans have been freed from the need to construct their self-image, with often relentless cycles of adding and subtracting their good and bad actions, that susceptibility to a "merciful" acceptance of oneself arises. In that case nobody has to appear better or feel worse than he or she is in the eyes of God — and that means: in reality.

It is only on the basis of such a realistic self-image that the concept of human freedom can be discussed without exaggerated optimism or pessimism. The human experience of freedom is always linked to the experience of a gift — in this case, the gift of acquittal. Whereas in litigation between human beings, under certain conditions defined by the law, we can speak of the "right" to an acquittal, the doctrine of justification speaks of the "gift" of acquittal. Consequently the desire to live by this gift is the most essential characteristic of the Christian idea of freedom, splendidly expressed by Paul in a few rhetorical questions: "What do you have that was not given to you? And if it was given, how can you boast as though it were not?" (1 Cor. 4:7). Being truly free implies the acceptance of this merciful gift and therefore the willingness to eat the bread of grace.

Freedom as Baptismal Rebirth

The churches of the Leuenberg Fellowship are thoroughly aware that freedom is never exercised in a vacuum. Even Christians freed by the gospel will have to face the ambiguities of human history and individual human existence. In reaction to the twentieth century's bloody wars of liberation, international politics now seems to have lost the pathos of freedom. An echo of this is also heard in church documents. "Freedom, freedom, how many crimes have been committed in your name!" is what we read in the "Christian Witness of Freedom" ("Christliche Zeugnis von der Freiheit") of the Leuenberg churches.[45]

---

45. See Hüffmeier and Müller, *Wachsende Gemeinschaft,* p. 101: "'Freiheit, Freiheit, wieviel Verbrechen sind in deinem Namen begangen worden!' So seufzt, wer von den alltäglichen Problemen aufsieht und einen Blick nach rückwärts auf die Geschichte der Freiheit wirft. Wieviele Gefangene, wieviele Kriege und wieviele Tote im Namen der Freiheit! Wieviel Zensur, welche Lügen, wieviel Folter!" ("'Freedom, freedom, how many crimes have been committed in your name!' So one sighs who looks up from his everyday problems and

Nevertheless, the willingness to begin anew is anchored in the gospel and expressed in the church's theology of baptism. Baptism points to repentance and rebirth. At first sight, repentance and rebirth appear to refer mainly to human decisions and thus to fit closely with what is the general view of baptism today, i.e., that people, parents or candidates for baptism, decide to have their children baptized or to be baptized. The whole emphasis is on human decision. However, the words "repentance" and "rebirth" clearly express more. They presuppose that one turns and converts to something that one has not oneself created, and becomes a different, reborn person through a power that comes from elsewhere. Just as humans do not bring about their own birth, they do not effect their own rebirth. They are actively and totally involved, but it is a process that is initiated elsewhere, "from above," as Jesus says in his conversation with Nicodemus.[46]

The doctrine of justification — forgiveness *sola gratia* — is at the core of both baptism and the Lord's Supper. However, these two sacraments also demonstrate that this divine gift of grace requires a human answer. That is why the Lima text discusses baptism's character both as a gift and as an answer.[47]

Baptism and the Kingdom of God

The New Testament gives a clear indication of what kind of answer God expects by relating baptism to the expectation of the kingdom of God. Humility is a central characteristic of those who expect the kingdom of God, as Jesus tells his audience when asked how they could ever inherit this kingdom (Matt. 25:31-46). This humility also has a social dimension, namely, the way in which they mortify themselves not only before God but

---

takes a look back at the history of freedom! How many prisoners, how many wars, and how many dead in the name of freedom! How much censorship, what lies, how much torture!" [editors' translation])

46. In the Greek text of John 3:3, Jesus' remark about the necessity of rebirth is rendered by means of the word *anothen*, meaning "from above" in the sense of "from heaven, from God." For the emphasis on the gift and liberation character of freedom, see Michael Weinrich, "Zur Freiheit befreit," in *Freiheit verantworten: Festschrift für Wolfgang Huber zum 60. Geburtstag*, ed. Hans-Richard Reuter et al. (Gütersloh: Gütersloher Verlagshaus, 2002), pp. 90-101.

47. *Baptism, Eucharist and Ministry*, p. 3 (B-8).

also before one another. It is only because of this solidarity in humility that the Lima text can speak of baptism as a "sign of the kingdom." Baptism marks the initiation of the reality of the new life given in the midst of the present world. The baptized participate in the community of the Holy Spirit. Baptism is a sign of the kingdom of God and of the life of the world to come. Through the gifts of faith, hope, and love, baptism has a dynamic that embraces the whole of life.[48]

The central place that penance has traditionally occupied in the ritual of baptism precludes any confusion with those social utopias that, especially in the twentieth century, have left a trail of corpses behind them.[49] Any Promethean tint is alien to good baptismal theology. Rather, in baptism Christians expresses their awareness that one is not in the world without a sinful past, and that one therefore has a sinful ancestry. We are never a *tabula rasa*. Although such a sense of realism does not diminish the desire for another, better world, it does remove any naïveté that we might have about it. It makes us realize that evil does not lurk only in others but also in ourselves. Over recent decades some philosophers have not tired of pointing out to Christians the humanizing effect of the doctrine of (original) sin, so wrongly maligned by so many Christians.[50] This sense of realism need not have a fatalistic effect. Two thousand years of Christianity show that its greatest social influence has not been in stimulating social utopias, secularized or not, but in building up the care of the sick, the elderly, and the poor; the development of agriculture; and the founding of schools and universities. All these activities would not have been possible without the expectation of the "new," without the notion of another world.

48. *Baptism, Eucharist and Ministry*, p. 3 (B-7). For the development of criteria for "an adequate theology of baptism" as fundamental Christian theory of human freedom, see Martien E. Brinkman, *The Tragedy of Human Freedom: The Failure and Promise of the Christian Concept of Freedom in Western Culture* (Currents of Encounter, vol. 20) (Amsterdam and New York: Rodopi, 2003), pp. 61-83 ("The Reborn Person").

49. For a Protestant approach to the role of penance in baptism, see Martien E. Brinkman, "Penance as an Indispensable Existential Sacramental Moment," in *Tibi Soli Peccavi: Thomas Aquinas on Guilt and Forgiveness*, ed. J. M. Schoot (Leuven: Peeters, 1996), pp. 97-122.

50. See Keith Ward, *Religion and Human Nature* (Oxford: Oxford University Press, 1998), p. 185. Ward points to the twofold, salutary effect of the doctrine of original sin, keeping us from both overconfidence and despair: "The doctrine of original sin prevents us from being Utopian about human dreams of a perfect society. . . . It prevents one from falling into despair over the evident moral failures of individuals and societies."

The radical break with the past to which baptism bears witness is totally different from the one that was propagated in many, sometimes realized, "concrete" utopias. The break with the past in the French, Russian, and Chinese (Cultural) Revolutions did not rest on the kind of confession of guilt with which this break is traditionally associated in the Christian liturgy of baptism. The latter is a repentant acceptance of one's own life history, and the former always a form of settling scores with the sinful past of others.

Even as Christians have professed to break with their past through baptism, they have been aware of the fact that baptized persons are not saints. The references to the *simul iustus et peccator* and the phenomenon of penance, understood as a continuous existential return to one's baptismal experience of submersion and resurrection, bear witness to this.

Conclusion

The central aspects of the doctrine of justification — guilt-acquittal-rebirth-freedom — belong to an adequate ecclesiology, including a sound theology of the sacraments of baptism and the Lord's Supper. We therefore need a more explicit and detailed analysis of all the rich aspects of this doctrine than has been given so far in the topical bilateral dialogues. This doctrine cannot be limited only to the primacy of the Word of God. Even the meaning of the very core of this doctrine — acquittal — might inform the church's witness more directly and frankly. Our societies need such a witness, including the proclamation of the freedom of the children of God.

8 Justification and Eschatology

Christiaan Mostert

1. Introduction[1]

In the churches of the Reformation and in their theologies, the doctrine of justification by faith — more completely expressed in the formulation *justification by grace through faith* — has played a decisive role. To claim, as Alister McGrath does, that "there never was, and there never can be, any true Christian church without the doctrine of justification,"[2] is to claim too much. Karl Barth regarded this doctrine, though of very great importance, as "only one aspect of the Christian message of reconciliation."[3] It is not the *unum necessarium* of Christian doctrine, and Barth allowed that the "objective truth" of the gospel could be stated in other terms.[4] However, its importance lies particularly in its accentuation of the objectivity of the good news of salvation, its givenness, before any consideration of the subjective aspect. People — indeed, the world itself — are justified because *God* justifies. Therefore, "faith lives by the certainty and actuality of the reconciliation of the world with God accomplished in Jesus Christ."[5]

---

1. Between the first and second drafts of this chapter I had the benefit of important conversations with Beverly Gaventa and Douglas Harink, each of whom directed me to significant new resources.

2. Alister E. McGrath, *Iustitia Dei: A History of the Christian Doctrine of Justification* (Cambridge: Cambridge University Press, 1986), p. 1.

3. Karl Barth, *Church Dogmatics*, IV/1, trans. G. W. Bromiley (Edinburgh: T. & T. Clark, 1956), p. 523.

4. Barth, *Church Dogmatics*, IV/1, p. 524.

5. Barth, *Church Dogmatics*, IV/1, p. 518.

To speak of justification is to speak of the ground of salvation *extra nos*, in a salvific event that expresses the righteousness of God — especially the "right-setting" act of God in Jesus Christ — without regard to any claim of our own, not even our faith. Justification is fundamentally about how God deals with humans and the broken, sinful world in which they live.[6] It is above all about grace.

The interpretation of the term "justification" is not without its problems. In its long history it has been taken to mean different things. In fact, it has become such a "loaded" term, not to mention its intrinsic ambiguity and its disputed meaning even in Paul's own usage, that alternative words might well be preferable.[7] Broadly speaking, justification has been understood as the whole of salvation or as a particular aspect of God's putting things right with and for people. In the latter usage, attention is focused on particular metaphors drawn from the law-courts, which have to do with a verdict of acquittal or release from a charge. The precise meaning of the word "justification" has long been a contentious matter, and was so especially at the time of the Protestant Reformation. In the Lutheran and Reformed confessional traditions, "justification" has taken on the character of a technical term, even a banner, under which to accentuate major theological points about the nature of salvation.[8]

The broader and less technical usage of "justification" is more or less equivalent to, perhaps even interchangeable with, "salvation." Justification is only one way of speaking about salvation. New Testament writers other than Paul write about salvation without using this term, and their accounts of salvation are not deficient on that account. The Eastern church has never given prominence to "justification," preferring other metaphors

---

6. Gerhard Sauter begins the introduction to his study of justification with the three questions that take us directly into the doctrine of justification: How do we stand before God? How does God deal with us? What may we expect from God? Gerhard Sauter, *Rechtfertigung als Grundbegriff evangelischer Theologie* (München: Chr. Kaiser Verlag, 1989), p. 9.

7. J. Louis Martyn uses the term "rectification" to emphasize "God's making right what has gone wrong." *Galatians*, The Anchor Bible (New York: Doubleday, 1997), pp. 249-55, 263-75. See Martyn, *Theological Issues in the Letters of Paul* (Nashville: Abingdon Press, 1997), ch. 9.

8. One should not overlook the long history of the doctrine of justification before the Reformation, notably the emphasis given to it by Augustine; see McGrath, *Iustitia Dei*. Recently the typical Protestant understanding of justification has been strongly challenged; see Douglas Harink, *Paul among the Postliberals: Pauline Theology beyond Christendom and Modernity* (Grand Rapids: Brazos Press, 2003), ch. 1.

of salvation, notably that of *theosis,* ambiguously translated as "divinization."[9] Each term can be seen as putting the multifaceted reality of salvation in a particular light, without the implication that any term, including "justification," is indispensable. T. F. Torrance, commenting on the Scots Confession of 1560, observes that this confession has no separate article on justification, but justification, as "the cutting edge" of the gospel, belongs to its very texture; it does not fail to make clear "the very essence of the Gospel of salvation by Grace."[10] This is not to deny the rich and distinctive content of the metaphor of justification, but to suggest that this is not the only (and not necessarily the preeminent) way to speak of salvation. Salvation is too rich a gift of God to be controlled by any one metaphor, least of all to be reduced to one. The theology of justification by faith deserves accentuation, however, because it makes clear that salvation is the work of God and that people, though far short of the glory of God, "can already be sure of their participation in eschatological salvation."[11]

To speak of *eschatological* salvation is to bring to the fore the other part of the title of this chapter: eschatology. On the basis of a broader, less narrowly Protestant, understanding of "justification," the question with which this chapter is concerned is the relation between salvation and eschatology. This is not to try to effect an artificial connection between two terms that are only extrinsically related. On the contrary, it is not possible to understand salvation (and therefore justification) except in an eschatological framework. Moltmann argued decades ago that eschatology (or "the eschatological") is "the medium of Christian faith as such, the key in which everything in it is set, the glow that suffuses everything [in it] in the dawn of an expected new day."[12] Nowhere is this truer than in questions of soteriology. In the theology of Paul, in keeping with its whole tenor, salva-

---

9. The Finnish school of Luther-study has not only proposed a new reading of Luther's own theology, especially on the subject of justification, but argues that justification and deification should not be set over against each other. The motif they have in common is that of "union with God." See Veli-Matti Kärkkäinen, *One with God: Salvation as Deification and Justification* (Collegeville, MN: Liturgical Press, 2004).

10. T. F. Torrance, "Justification: Its Radical Nature and Place in Reformed Doctrine and Life," *Scottish Journal of Theology* 13 (1960): 225.

11. Wolfhart Pannenberg, *Systematic Theology,* vol. 3, trans. G. W. Bromiley (Edinburgh: T. & T. Clark and Grand Rapids: Eerdmans, 1998), p. 236.

12. Jürgen Moltmann, *Theology of Hope,* trans. J. W. Leitch (London: SCM Press, 1967), p. 16.

tion is through and through eschatological.[13] Salvation and eschatology are thus integrally and organically connected.

2. Justification and Salvation in Paul

The doctrine of justification is entirely "funded" by the language and theology of the apostle Paul; it is essentially a Pauline doctrine.[14] Clearly, it is of immense importance in Paul's own theology; there are scores of instances of *dikaios, dikaiosynē,* and *dikaioun* in Romans and Galatians alone. It is a major point at which Paul polemicizes against the "Teachers," the Christian-Jewish evangelists who came into the churches of Galatia after Paul moved on, those who are "confusing" his readers and "perverting the gospel of Christ" (Gal. 1:7).[15] What is at stake in this (his fiercest) rhetoric is how God has made and will make things right in the world. There is nothing in Paul's other writings to compare with the hostility of his letter to the Galatians, and the passages about justification are key elements in this. However, what God has done through the cross of Christ, the faithful obedience of Christ, is not exhaustively described in the language of justification. James Dunn writes, "There was something so rich and real in the various experiences of conversion which Paul's gospel brought about that Paul had to ransack the language available to him to find ways of describing them. The vitality of the experience made new metaphors necessary if the experience was to be expressed in words . . . and to be communicated to others."[16] So we find metaphors drawn from the law, from commerce, from war and battle, from the institution of slavery, from conflict and estrangement, and from citizenship, as well as other areas of everyday life. The word

13. J. Louis Martyn endorses the view of Ernst Käsemann and J. Christiaan Beker that "Paul's theology is thoroughly apocalyptic, and is different from the theology of early Christian enthusiasm primarily in its insistence (a) that the world is not yet fully subject to God, even though (b) the eschatological subjection of the world has already begun, causing its end to be in sight." See Martyn, *Theological Issues,* p. 113.

14. The converse is also true; as Harink says, "When Protestants think of Paul, they think of the doctrine of justification by faith in Jesus Christ." *Paul among the Postliberals,* p. 25.

15. Martyn, *Galatians,* pp. 18, 117-26, 588.

16. James D. G. Dunn, *The Theology of Paul the Apostle* (London: T. & T. Clark, 1998), p. 332.

soteria (salvation) itself comes from the world of health and well-being, rescue and safety. In addition, there are images from the major events of life: birth and adoption, marriage and death. The language is rich and varied because it has to express the richness of the new life given *in* and *through* Christ and the radical difference that the cross has made, not just to humankind — Gentile as well as Jew — but to the entire created world.

There is a more important point, however, than the richness of the language required for expressing the inexhaustible gift of salvation. "Justification," like any significant term, has its own distinctive metaphorical force, as do other terms that later assumed particular theological importance. But our concern with *what* Paul is saying must not be obscured by observations about *how* he says it, though, of course, content and form are inseparable. In Paul's gospel everything hinges on the fact that the death and resurrection of Jesus Christ have changed the world so radically that it is now possible to speak of an old world (or age) and a new one; the cross marks the boundary between them. Two points should be made about this: the first about *what* Paul is opposing here and the second about *whom* he is opposing. First, the great antithesis in Paul, especially as seen in the letter to the Galatians, is not between justification by faith and justification by works, though nearly five hundred years of Protestant preaching have solidified such a view. It is between justification by "the works of the Law" and justification through Christ crucified and risen. That a person is not justified by observing the Law is the negative form of Paul's gospel, which he boldly claims to have been revealed to him by Christ, not some human source (Gal. 1:11f.). The positive form of the gospel is "the faith *of* Jesus Christ" (*pistis Christou Iēsou*), which we usually see translated as "faith *in* Jesus Christ."[17] By "the faith *of* Christ" is meant not Christ's faith (in the narrower sense of the word) but Christ's faithful obedience and death. The decisive point is what Christ has done or, rather, what God has done through the death of Christ. Paul thus opposes the view of those who insist that Gentiles who wished to become Christians must not only have faith in Christ but also observe the requirements of the Law; this amounts to teaching a different gospel (Gal. 1:6), if indeed it can be called a "gospel" at all.

---

17. The point has been much discussed and is controversial. Which translation is adopted — both being grammatically possible — has enormous theological implications. See Martyn, *Galatians,* comment #28, pp. 263-75 (also Martyn, *Theological Issues,* pp. 141-56); and Harink, *Paul among the Postliberals,* pp. 40-45.

This is already to touch on the second point, about his antagonists. The Jewish Christians who have come to exercise such an influence over the Galatian churches have replaced Paul's *either/or* with a *both/and*. They hold both the death of Christ as a sacrifice for sin and the continuing force of the Law to be at the heart of the faith. Paul sees this as a complete nullification of the gospel: if justification comes through the Law, then Christ died for nothing! (Gal. 2:20). Not an inch of ground is to be conceded to those who have come with a message as spurious as this. The reason that Gentiles can be equally acceptable to God as Jews is that Christ died for them also. Even if Jewish Christians continue to observe the requirements of the Law, it cannot be required of Gentiles; this is not the way God has made things right with and for the world. The conflict at the center of the letter to the Galatians is not between Christians and Jews, but between Paul, whose theology of the "rectifying" death of Christ made Law-observance redundant, and his critics and opponents, who taught that the Law retained its force and that the conditions for crossing the boundary between Jew and Gentile had not changed.[18] In itself, the matter of the believers' faith *(fides qua creditur)* was not at issue.[19] The point for Paul was *what* they believed *(fides quae creditur)*; and what he believed and taught was far more radical than what his opponents taught. What he proclaimed as the gospel was, of course, to be received in *faith*, for through faith (and by baptism) we become participants in the death and resurrection of Christ. Through baptism (which presupposes faith) we become one with Christ (Rom. 6:3-5); rising from the water of baptism, we are clothed with Christ (Gal. 3:27).

Paul pushes his argument relentlessly as he writes on. He cannot understand how the Galatian churches have let themselves be talked out of the faith that he taught them. He appeals to their experience of the Spirit: "Did you receive the Spirit by doing the works of the Law or by believing what you heard?" (Gal 3:2), meaning the gospel of what God had done through the crucified, risen Christ. To be *in* Christ is also to live in the power of the Spirit. On this point Paul did not have to argue with his

18. Dunn sees Paul "fiercely resisting his own earlier pre-Christian assumption that God's righteousness was only for Israel, and only for Gentiles if they became Jews and took on the distinctive obligations of God's covenant with Israel." Dunn, *Theology of Paul*, p. 371.

19. Harink argues that Paul paid little or no attention to faith, either as directed to its object, Jesus Christ, or as a basic dynamic in human existence. Harink, *Paul among the Postliberals*, pp. 30-38.

Galatian readers; he had only to insist that if they *lived* by the Spirit they had also to *walk* (be guided) by the Spirit (5:25). For the Spirit is both the source and power of the new life and its norm. The theology of the Spirit is no less major a part of Paul's theology of salvation than is his Christology. Life in and from the Spirit is, for Paul, "the eschatological existence into which the believer is placed by having appropriated the salvation deed that occurred in Christ," as Bultmann expresses it.[20] "The drought of the Spirit had ended," says Dunn, and the experience of the Spirit was no less decisive for the way believers understood themselves than Jesus' resurrection. The last days were upon them, for the resurrection of the dead had begun.[21] The Spirit sealed all this on their hearts and empowered them for the battle into which their baptism had unavoidably launched them.

Before considering more explicitly the eschatological character of salvation, Paul's argument in Galatians must be taken one step further. In the second justification/rectification passage in Galatians (3:6–4:7) the same antithesis of reliance on fulfilling the requirements of the Law and reliance on the faithful death of Christ is reinforced. There is, to be sure, a discussion of faith, but not such as to make it one of the elements in the antithesis. Faith is about trust in God; its model is Abraham, who trusted in God before there was any Law. To rely on doing what the Law requires, regardless of failure or success in this, is to remain under the curse from which Christ redeemed us (3:10-14). For Paul, faith is trusting acceptance of the message of the crucified and risen Christ, who has become "the fully trustworthy Lord of the cosmos."[22] Most important in this second passage, however, is the further light it sheds on the meaning of justification/rectification. Paul brings the sharp antithesis already described "into the perspective of cosmic apocalyptic, in which God has set things right by acting against real enemies," the "elemental spirits of the world" which enslave humankind (4:3).[23] The law *curses*, but in the death of Christ on the cross God *blesses*, by doing battle with all the powers that oppose God and keep us captive to the power of sin (3:22). Justification is then about putting the

---

20. Rudolf Bultmann, *Theology of the New Testament*, vol. 1, trans. Kendrick Grobel (London: SCM Press, 1952), p. 335.

21. Dunn, *Theology of Paul*, p. 418.

22. Martyn, *Galatians*, p. 275.

23. Martyn, *Theological Issues*, p. 155. For a discussion of the question whether Paul's theology in Galatians can or cannot be described as "apocalyptic," see Martyn, "Apocalyptic Antinomies," *Theological Issues*, pp. 111-23.

whole cosmos aright through the death and resurrection of Christ. The frame of the discussion is decisively expanded. With the death of Christ, in which alone Paul will boast (6:14), the world has been "crucified" to Paul, just as he has been "crucified" to it. The cross is "the watershed event for the whole of the cosmos, affecting everything after it."[24] The demise of the world's enslaving powers has begun; a new world is coming into being, though not without a fight! What has begun is "God's liberating invasion of the territory of tyranny."[25] The goal of this invasion includes the forgiveness of sin, but is as much about disempowering the powers and setting its captives free. This is the full scope of the doctrine of justification, and it is set in an unmistakably eschatological key.

3. Salvation as Eschatological

It appears, then, that the doctrine of justification in Paul, once he articulated it in the letter to the Galatians, is as comprehensive in character as it is central in importance. The more its universal, cosmic scope is understood — better expressed in a term like "rectification" than "justification," despite the doctrinal weight of the latter — the more persuasive is the view that "justification" and "salvation" are more or less synonymous, at least for Paul.[26] Nevertheless, even in the letters of Paul the weight falls on the justification of the human person as sinner, whose sin is forgiven and whose reconciliation is effected on the cross. We live in hope of the liberation of the cosmos "from its bondage to decay" and its receiving "the freedom of the glory of the children of God" (Rom. 8:20); but what Paul emphasizes is the way the world is changed for humankind, first in its relation to God and then in the structures of its sociality (and therefore also its politics). It cannot be wrong, therefore, when Barth discusses justification within the larger framework of the doctrine of reconciliation, which accentuates the relational and personal aspect. That this in no way turns justification into an *anthropological* doctrine is made clear in the opening statement of Barth's discussion. Reconciliation is directed to "the lost

---

24. Martyn, *Galatians*, p. 564.

25. Martyn, *Galatians*, p. 273; Martyn, *Theological Issues*, p. 154.

26. Even the term "redemption" can be used in this comprehensive sense. See Hans Küng, *Justification: The Doctrine of Karl Barth and a Catholic Reflection* (40th anniversary ed.) (Louisville: Westminster John Knox Press, 2004), p. 227.

cause of man, who has denied [God] as Creator and in so doing ruined himself as creature," but God "makes [this cause] His own in Jesus Christ"; it is therefore an utterly *Christocentric* doctrine. But even this is not yet to say enough; Barth speaks here also of "the free act of the faithfulness of God" and concludes this concentrated programmatic statement by describing this work of God as God's "maintaining and manifesting His own glory in the world."[27] It is thus, in the sharpest sense, a *theological* doctrine.

The strength of the post-Reformation theology of justification, notwithstanding intra-Lutheran and Lutheran-Reformed differences over the question whether justification precedes or includes the renewal of the justified, is its strong emphasis on the objectivity of justification. This is, as it were, the first word to be said about it, though it is incomplete without the second word, namely that this divine work, decisively centered on the cross and resurrection of Jesus Christ, is effective in and for the world, for the human being whom God has "elected" to be a covenant-partner and who is reconciled to God on account of this event and nothing else. Hans Küng summarizes: "In the death and resurrection of Christ, justification is established with final validity."[28] Whenever the question is asked, "When were you saved?", the first answer must always be in terms of the death and resurrection of Jesus. It would not, of course, be the only answer; salvation requires articulation as a past, a present, and a future reality. George Hunsinger describes Luther's view of justification as "an eschatological event," but "an event that had three tenses."[29] Paul himself leaves his churches in no doubt that they *have been* justified, but he also uses *dikaioun* in the present and future tenses.[30] In the preaching of the gospel in the present time — any present — justification takes place as a gift in the experience of new believers, without in any sense modifying the decisiveness of what took place "once for all."

27. Barth, *Church Dogmatics*, IV/1, p. 3.

28. Küng, *Justification*, p. 231. Küng does not see Catholic teaching on justification as opposed to this, but rather that different things are accentuated.

29. "As an eschatological event, justification was at once completed on the cross, yet to be fulfilled at the Last Day, and received continuously by faith here and now." George Hunsinger, *Disruptive Grace: Studies in the Theology of Karl Barth* (Grand Rapids: Eerdmans, 2000), p. 296.

30. It is not suggested that the location in time of justification hangs on the tense of a few verbs. The heart of the matter is its grounding in a particular event, which, for all Christians, lies in the past.

The same must be said in respect of this experience in the future. Every Christian, no matter how certain of his or her justification as a given reality, knows that something is still outstanding. Unless justification is understood narrowly in forensic terms or in terms of imputed righteousness, it continues in our reception of it and submission to it. Certainly this is not to imply that, after the initial gift, the rest is our own contribution: that would be self-justification. But that which was begun in the event of the death and resurrection of Christ, God will bring to an eschatological completion in the future. As long as justification as objectively grounded in Christ crucified and risen and as subjectively received as the determining center of one's life are not confused (but also not separated), the description of justification in three tenses is unproblematic.

This does not mean that justification is a process, as if Christians become more and more justified as they continue in their faith. Commenting on Barth's debt to Luther, Hunsinger notes the opposition of both to any kind of "soteriological gradualism," whether in terms of justification or sanctification. To quote Luther, God's grace "does not come in portions and pieces, separately, like so many gifts; rather it takes us up completely into its embrace for the sake of Christ our mediator and intercessor, and in order that the gifts may take root in us."[31] Commitment to the objective givenness of justification is characteristic of both. Barth regards progress in sanctification as about as significant as "different levels on the surface of the earth when seen from the standpoint of the sun."[32] Such a statement certainly has rhetorical force, but it leaves little room for the effect of justification in a person's life, for its renewal in communion with Christ. Strictly speaking, such renewal of life may be distinguished from justification but not separated from it, as Lutherans acknowledge in the *Joint Declaration on the Doctrine of Justification* of 1999.[33] Catholic tradition speaks of both "uncreated" and "created" grace: grace as utterly gratuitous love and mercy on God's part and grace as effective in the lives of believers. This is not far removed from what Protestant theology knows as "forensic" and "effective" justification.[34] Be

31. Hunsinger, *Disruptive Grace*, p. 296, quoting from *Luther's Works*, American ed., vol. 35 (St Louis: Concordia and Philadelphia: Fortress), p. 370.

32. Hunsinger, *Disruptive Grace*, p. 298, quoting from Barth, *Ethics* (New York: Seabury Press, 1981), p. 410.

33. The Lutheran World Federation and the Roman Catholic Church, *Joint Declaration on the Doctrine of Justification* (Grand Rapids: Eerdmans, 2000), §26, p. 19.

this as it may, the Joint Ecumenical Commission in Germany, in its discussion of justification, stated, "Protestant theology does not overlook what Catholic doctrine stresses: the creative and renewing character of God's love; nor does it maintain what Catholic theology is afraid of: God's impotence toward a sin which is 'merely' forgiven in justification but which is not truly abolished in its power to divide the sinner from God."[35] The justifying action of God, grounded in the cross, is effective and transforming in the present, and it is important, as Reformed theology has recognized more strongly, to connect with this a doctrine of sanctification. Barth, especially, has a subtle view of their relation.[36] But at every point we are confronted with the one action of God, grounded in Jesus Christ, which embraces us in every moment of our lives.

In what sense can justification be regarded as an eschatological event, as was suggested above? The only answer can be along the lines that all Christian experience of salvation is subject to the eschatological proviso: what we have received here and now is truly the reality of salvation, God's gift to us in the conditions of our time and space, but it is not yet that experience of it that awaits us when "Christ has destroyed every ruler, every authority and power" and God is "all in all" (1 Cor. 15:24, 28). When for various reasons the accent falls overwhelmingly on the former, it is very easy for the latter to be obscured. However, neither the tension between them nor their essential identity must be lost sight of; what is already experienced and what still remains a matter of promise and hope are connected *and* differentiated. Wolfhart Pannenberg has investigated this relation with the help of the con-

34. Karl Lehmann and Wolfhart Pannenberg, eds., *The Condemnations of the Reformation Era: Do They Still Divide?*, trans. Margaret Kohl (Minneapolis: Fortress Press, 1990), p. 48.

35. Lehmann and Pannenberg, *Condemnations*, p. 49. Long before the *Joint Declaration on the Doctrine of Justification*, Hans Küng in 1999 wrote: "Protestants speak of a declaration of justice and Catholics of a making just. But Protestants speak of a declaring just which includes a making just; and Catholics of a making just which presupposes a declaring just." Küng, *Justification*, p. 221. This is not to suggest, as Küng does, that the differences are unreal but that in the last half-century discontinuities in thought can more easily be held together with continuities.

36. Barth speaks of the one reconciling action of God (and the one grace of God) with different moments or aspects. These are "different 'moments' of the one redemptive occurrence coming to man in the *simul* of the one event." They are not identical. However, neither are they temporally successive, nor are they related as superior and subordinate. *Church Dogmatics*, IV/2, pp. 502-8.

cept of "anticipation" and sees it as "a fundamental structural element both of cognition and of language, and of the being of beings in their temporality."[37] It is clear that for Paul (as well as for very many theologians who have not made this eschatological proviso a matter for explicit thematization), statements about salvation as a reality already received and statements about salvation as a matter of hope are equally important. There is no doubt, as Paul sees it, that we have been justified *(dikaiōthentes)* through Christ (Rom. 5:1). Having been justified, we now have peace with God. This in turn becomes the ground for hope, the hope of sharing the glory of God, the hope of salvation (5:2, 5). Having been justified by Christ, how much more shall we be saved by him from the wrath (5:9); having been reconciled to God by the death of his Son, how much more shall we be saved by his life (5:10). The focus is on the salvation which lies ahead, but God's saving action, grounded in a past event, "is now being realized in Christ."[38] It is already experienced as a present reality; and it remains a future hope.

Lest it be thought that this construal of the matter is possible only on the basis of a confusion of different terms used by Paul, it is noteworthy that he actually makes the same point in terms of justification. In the first letter in which he uses the idea of justification, the Galatian letter, he emphasizes that God has justified the Galatian Christians, not through the Law but through the death of Christ. In Galatians 5:5, however, he says that, "having the Spirit in our hearts, and having the confidence that comes from faith, we eagerly await the hope of rectification."[39] In the context of the message of this letter, Paul affirms that "God's deed of rectification in Christ is accomplished." But it is also susceptible to attack, especially if the Galatians accept the spurious gospel of the false teachers. The Galatians have lost hold of the true gospel of God's justifying grace. For those who have not succumbed to the false teaching the matter stands differently: eagerly and with confidence they await the hope of justification. Concluding his comments

37. Wolfhart Pannenberg, "Response to the Discussion," in *Theology as History* (New Frontiers in Theology), vol. 3, ed. James M. Robinson and John B. Cobb (New York: Harper & Row, 1967), p. 260. For a discussion of Pannenberg's concept of anticipation, see Christiaan Mostert, *God and the Future: Wolfhart Pannenberg's Eschatological Doctrine of God* (London: T. & T. Clark, 2002), pp. 112-26.

38. Brendan Byrne, *Romans* (Collegeville, MN: Liturgical Press, 1996), p. 165.

39. This is J. Louis Martyn's translation. See *Galatians*, pp. 8, 472, 478-79. The usual translation, as in the NRSV, is "the hope of righteousness." However, there is no reason whatsoever to prefer "righteousness" over "justification" or "rectification" to translate *dikaiosyne*.

on this passage, Martyn quotes Käsemann: rectification is "to be had on earth only as a pledged gift, always subject to attack, always to be authenticated in practice — a matter of promise and expectation."[40] It has to be remembered, however, that the justification hoped for in the future is of a piece with the justifying act of God in the death and resurrection of Jesus Christ. This eschatological tension is not confined to soteriological passages; it is paralleled in the discussion of the gift of the Spirit. In many of his letters Paul takes for granted the fact that the members of his churches have received the Spirit. But it is quite clear that the Spirit is also to be received and understood as a first installment of what is still to come in its fullness, a guarantee of the redemption that lies in the future (Rom. 8:23; 2 Cor. 1:22; 5:5). Not that the future was thought to be far away. Oscar Cullmann wrote decades ago (about "time" in the New Testament): "It is already the time of the end, and yet it is not *the* end. This tension finds expression in the entire theology of Primitive Christianity."[41] In a recent comment on biblical eschatology, Brendan Byrne writes, "In a way unforeseen in the traditional eschatology, believers live in a curious time of 'overlap' between the old age and the new."[42] Despite the world-changing event of the death of Christ, their justification has not made them immune to the powers of the old age; they are still subject to sin and death. But in the Spirit the reality of the new age has begun to be realized, if brokenly; and because of the gift of the same Spirit, who is the guarantee of the eschatological fullness of salvation, their hope is justified and remains strong.

4. Living in the Eschatological Present

Living as Christian believers in the eschatological present is living in the overlap of the two ages, the old and the new. Such life is shaped first of all by our having received baptism. To be baptized is to be formed for discipleship, a formation that has a number of complementary aspects:

40. Martyn, *Galatians,* p. 479, quoting Ernst Käsemann, *New Testament Questions of Today* (London: SCM, 1969), p. 170.

41. Oscar Cullmann, *Christ and Time: The Primitive Christian Conception of Time and History,* trans. Floyd V. Filson (London: SCM Press, 1951), p. 145.

42. Byrne, *Romans,* p. 23. Dunn writes that "the distinctive feature of Paul's theology at this point is *not* the eschatology, but the *tension* which his revised eschatology sets up." *Theology of Paul,* p. 465.

Christological, pneumatological, eschatological, ecclesial, and ethical.[43] Baptism, though we receive it only once in our life, is not just one event at the beginning of our lives as Christians. It defines our identity as Christians throughout our lives.[44] We never leave it behind us; it is "there all our lives."[45] Living eschatologically also has a eucharistic quality, most obviously because it is a form of thanksgiving, gratitude for the good news of an already effective justification. In the eucharistic prayer of the worshiping community, all the "mighty acts" of God in the history of salvation are gratefully brought into the present, culminating in the cross and resurrection of Jesus Christ. But the eucharist also has a strong eschatological content: as a meal, it anticipates the feasting of the kingdom of God; its celebration of the presence of Christ anticipates our seeing him face to face in the kingdom; and everything about eucharist that is incomplete and imperfect will find its completion and perfection in the final reign of God.[46] To live baptismally and eucharistically is also to live in hope, the hope that the kingdom of God will come, the hope that we will not "make shipwreck" of our faith.[47] Living in hope also means living prayerfully, with not only praise and thanksgiving but also confession and intercession constantly on our lips (1 Thess. 5:17f.). Indeed, life in the eschatological present without worship is unthinkable. Apart from the praise of God, its central and constitutive element, worship, as Gordon Lathrop suggests, is "a continual reminding, continual reinsertion in baptismal faith."[48]

43. This roughly follows the categories under which the meaning of baptism is discussed in *Baptism, Eucharist and Ministry,* Faith and Order Paper No. 111 (Geneva: World Council of Churches, 1982), §§3-7.

44. See Rowan Williams, "Sacramental Living: Living Baptismally," *Australian Journal of Liturgy* 1 (2003): 3-18.

45. Wolfhart Pannenberg, *Systematic Theology,* vol. 3, p. 273. William Willimon sees baptism as "the norm, the model, the pattern, the beginning and end of the Christian life." *Remember Who You Are: Baptism, A Model for Christian Life* (Nashville: The Upper Room, 1980), p. 108.

46. See Geoffrey Wainwright, *Eucharist and Eschatology,* 3rd ed. (Akron, OH: OSL Publications, 2002), pp. 182-83.

47. I owe this phrase to Rodney Horsfield, *Baptism: An Evangelical Sacrament* (Melbourne: Uniting Church Press, 1984), p. 41.

48. Gordon Lathrop, "The Water That Speaks: The *Ordo* of Baptism and Its Ecumenical Implications," in *Becoming a Christian: The Ecumenical Implications of Our Common Baptism,* Faith & Order Paper No. 184, ed. Thomas Best and Dagmar Heller (Geneva: WCC Publications, 1999), p. 20.

Life in the overlap of the two ages — between an already effective justification and an experience of salvation that is as anticipatory as it is real — raises for Christians the question of assurance. In faith we receive the good news of our justification, and we are called to live in this faith. But we are faithful one day and unfaithful the next; our faith is strong today and weak tomorrow. There is little assurance in our faith *(fides qua creditur)*. If it is a terrible (fearful) thing to fall into the hands of the living God (Heb. 10:31), it is "a more terrible thing to fall out of them."[49] Can we be certain that, despite everything, these hands will hold us? The Reformers taught us that "believers should not look to themselves but look solely to Christ."[50] In a sense, nothing more need be said than this. For Barth the "right of God" is the "backbone" of the event of justification.[51] It is the sovereign right of God to be gracious and to act for the salvation of the world in accordance with God's own being. The key to it, in a summary phrase, is "the grace of Jesus Christ," of which Barth, making more than one pertinent point, says:

> The grace of Jesus Christ deserves and demands faith and obedience and all confidence and all sacrifice and its relentless proclamation on the right hand and the left, both to Jews and Gentiles; its revelation and promulgation is the irruption of the last day, and the free word of its proclamation can anticipate the end of the last day and be pronounced as the final word even in a present which is still characterized by the flesh and sin and death, just because the grace of God as such is the out-working and fulfillment of the right of God, his righteous judgment.[52]

That said, there is not much left to say in protest. There is no other basis than this, and no other ground for assurance. Barth spells it out in other wonderful passages, such as his account of the confrontation of Jesus' *Yes* with Judas's *No*.[53] Barth will not say that Judas is an example of *apokatastasis* (universal salvation), but neither will he proclaim a divine grace and faithfulness that cannot stand against the force of human evil. The church

---

49. This line is attributed to D. H. Lawrence, but I do not know its exact source.

50. The Lutheran World Federation and the Roman Catholic Church, *Joint Declaration on Justification*, §35.

51. Barth, *Church Dogmatics*, IV/I, p. 531.

52. Barth, *Church Dogmatics*, IV/I, p. 531.

53. Barth, *Church Dogmatics*, II/2, pp. 475-506, esp. 475-80.

will not preach an *apokatastasis*, but neither will it preach "a powerless grace of Jesus Christ or a wickedness of men which is too powerful for it. But without any weakening of the contrast . . . it will preach the overwhelming power of grace and the weakness of human wickedness in face of it. For this is how the 'for' of Jesus and the 'against' of Judas undoubtedly confront one another."[54]

For Barth too, the present time is a time of overlap, a time of double determination. It is a time determined by the resurrection of Jesus Christ, but it is also determined by the fact that the final word has not yet been spoken. However, because the Christological *not yet* and the Christological *already* cannot stand in contradiction, Barth speaks about hope. "Grounded in God, namely, in the God who acts in Jesus Christ, and orientated on him, Christian hope is an uninterrupted and unequivocally positive expectation of the future."[55] To believe in Christ and to love him is also to hope in him. The one who justifies (and sanctifies) us is also our hope. What God has done in Christ cannot be other than what God will do in him. What this means is hidden from us; it exceeds what we can imagine. Gerhard Sauter speaks of "a hope that claims nothing for itself, that does not even know what it desires but can desire only what God desires."[56] Such a hope will focus on the divine promise, which has already been fulfilled, is even now being fulfilled, and will, in the fullness of time, be fulfilled unreservedly. With such a promise, it is possible to live hopefully in the present time, rather than despair about the state of the world, the weakness and disunity of the church, the brokenness of our lives, and the fragility of our faith.

Living in the eschatological present is to live in the tension of a declaration of justification that is worthy of acceptance, indeed already effective, and a rectification of all things in the world, which still lies in the hiddenness of the future. Expressed in different terms, it is to live in the tension of the kingdom of God, which *has* come and which *will* come. The life of the church, notably the regular worshiping assembly, exemplifies both sides of the tension; it celebrates the gospel and it ignores, even betrays, the gospel. Nothing is yet what we hope it will be. This gives rise to a

---

54. Barth, *Church Dogmatics*, II/2, p. 477.

55. Barth, *Church Dogmatics*, IV/3.2, p. 910.

56. Gerhard Sauter, *Eschatological Rationality: Theological Issues in Focus* (Grand Rapids: Baker Books, 1996), p. 176.

simultaneously positive and negative assessment of the present in relation to the future, without either neutralizing the other. Seen in positive terms, the present is already the enjoyment of what Jesus Christ, in whom true humanity has been actualized, has made of us and is making of us. Already we are justified in and through him; already, in him and because of him, our humanity is a new humanity, in which the human vocation to be God's covenant-partner is being actualized. At issue here, as Bruce McCormack points out, is a theological ontology implied in the doctrine of justification.[57] What we are *essentially* is not best described in metaphysical terms, but in terms of what God has chosen us to be in entering into covenant with us. Our *nature* (what we make of ourselves as self-determining agents) does not (or not continuously) coincide with our *essence*. In McCormack's words, "We are what we truly are (and what we will be in the eschaton) in those moments when our humanity is conformed on the level of lived existence to the humanity inaugurated in time by Christ's life of obedience."[58]

McCormack's proposal of a covenantal ontology does enable us to see the *already* in a very positive way, even as it views salvation eschatologically. Another way of doing so, famously associated with Wolfhart Pannenberg, is to accentuate the futurity of salvation and its anticipation in the present. Living in the eschatological present is not so much a matter of living from the past *toward* the future but *from* the reality of the future. Just as the resurrection of Jesus is to be seen as the appearance, ahead of its time, of the eschatological resurrection of the dead, so the justification of sinful people is their assurance of participation *already now* in the eschatological reality of salvation, even though that participation is partial and fragmented. In this proposal the present is seen more strongly in its rela-

57. Bruce McCormack, interpreting Barth, speaks of a "covenantal ontology," a new way of being human, implied in the realization of true human personhood in the humanity of Jesus Christ. See his "Grace and Being: The Role of God's Gracious Election in Karl Barth's Theological Ontology," in *The Cambridge Companion to Karl Barth*, ed. John Webster (Cambridge: Cambridge University Press, 2000), p. 107. In a later essay, McCormack develops this idea of covenant ontology further. See "What's at Stake in Current Debates over Justification," in *Justification: What's at Stake in the Current Debates*, ed. Mark Husbands and Daniel J. Treier (Downers Grove, IL: InterVarsity Press, 2004), pp. 81-117, esp. 113-17. I owe these references to Douglas Harink.

58. McCormack, "What's at Stake in Current Debates over Justification," p. 115. This schema "works" only on the condition that "nature" and "essence," terms with their own metaphysical baggage, can be persuasively distinguished.

tion to the eschatological future than to the past. What something is at any given time is an anticipation of what the future will determine it to be. Pannenberg has articulated this in terms of an ontology in which the future has priority.[59] The transformation of our existence that is the Spirit's eschatological work is experienced proleptically already now, a first install-ment of what will finally be given in its eschatological fullness (2 Cor. 1:22), a beginning, but "of a piece" with what is awaited from the future. Pannenberg emphasizes the continuity between them, without losing sight of the difference. To see the relation between present and future in this way gives clarity about human projects. The *already* of the eschatological ten-sion prevents the fall into cynicism or despair, while its *not yet* keeps our feet on the ground and prevents us from overvaluing progress or absolutizing present political and social institutions.[60]

However, when the *discontinuity* between the experienced present and the hoped-for future is more heavily accentuated, a very different theology will take shape. Jürgen Moltmann's theology of hope quickly turned into a political theology, followed by North and South American theologies of liberation.[61] In his *Theology of Hope* Moltmann saw hope's "passion for the possible" in connection with the suffering of the poor, the hungry, and the neglected of the world. "Hope finds in Christ not only a consolation *in* suffering, but also the protest of the divine promise *against* suffering."[62] Suffering has therefore to be contradicted; "the goad of the promised future stabs inexorably into the flesh of every unfulfilled present." The promise of a new future for the world creates hope, and hope makes the church "a constant disturbance in human society, seeking as the latter does to stabilize itself into a 'continuing city.'"[63] For Moltmann, justification is not only an event in the past; it "begins with

59. See note 37 above. See also Wolfhart Pannenberg, *Metaphysics and the Idea of God*, trans. Philip Clayton (Edinburgh: T. & T. Clark, 1990), p. 96.

60. Pannenberg, *Systematic Theology*, vol. 3, p. 181.

61. Gerhard Sauter describes the theology of Pannenberg and Moltmann as sharply dif-ferent. Moltmann sees history as "stamped by contradictions, antagonisms, and clashes" that could easily lead to the abyss. Pannenberg sees history as "a context which constitutes a unity which progressively sublates . . . all individual moments, all differences and opposites." See Sauter, *What Dare We Hope?: Reconsidering Eschatology* (Harrisburg, PA: Trinity Press International, 1999), p. 134.

62. Moltmann, *Theology of Hope*, trans. James W. Leitch (Minneapolis: Fortress, 1993), p. 21.

63. Moltmann, *Theology of Hope*, p. 22.

the forgiveness of sins and ends with the wiping away of all tears."[64] In between, theology must be explicitly political (it can in any case not avoid being at least implicitly so), a theological commitment he shares with Johann Baptist Metz.[65] Those whom God has justified have no option but to protest against the injustice of the world. Divine justification and divine justice have to be spoken of in the same breath, for those who have been set in a right relation to God may not be indifferent to God's promise to make all things in creation right. The movement from justification to glorification — both creation's glorifying God and God's glorying in creation — is one of "exuberant intensification."[66] It raises sharply the question how the glory of God should shape the structures and institutions of life in the present. Justification, eschatology, and the strenuous pursuit of justice are inextricably connected.

Those who have heard the good news of justification through grace and the promise of the eschatological rectification of all things cannot live in the present time without prayer, both thanksgiving for the economy of creation and redemption, and intercession for the world, which in many respects remains unreconciled and unjust. Prayer for the coming of the reign of God and hopeful action to give it anticipatory expression in the structures and dynamics of the world belong together; that has always been the experience of Christians. It belongs to the *raison d'être* of the church that it should glorify God and voice the thanks of all creatures for the wonder of creation and salvation. But intercession is also "a fundamental vocation of the church."[67] In a broken, suffering world, in which the gap between the promise of God for human life and the conditions in which very many of the world's people actually live is inexcusably wide, the church cries out for the promises of God and the hope they generate to be fulfilled. We long *now* for the transformation of life for all, especially the most disadvantaged and marginalized.[68] Intercession has added urgency

64. Moltmann, *The Way of Jesus Christ*, trans. Margaret Kohl (San Francisco: Harper, 1990), p. 183.

65. See Johann Baptist Metz, *Theology of the World* (New York: Crossroad, 1969) and *Faith in History and Society: Toward a Practical Fundamental Theology* (New York: Seabury Press, 1980).

66. Moltmann, *The Way of Jesus Christ*, p. 186.

67. See Don Saliers, *Worship as Theology: Foretaste of Divine Glory* (Nashville: Abingdon, 1994), p. 126.

68. See Christiaan Mostert, "Intercession — a Theological Account," in *Prayer and*

in the overlap of the ages, between God's decisive act of justification and the promised justice and peace of the whole creation. The desire that all people, far and near, should receive a share in the blessing of creation and the rectifying work of God in the world is expressed in both action and prayer, both of which God uses in the establishment of God's reign in all things. Given the limited nature of every human act, prayer, as Pannenberg suggests, is "the highest form of our participation in bringing in the kingdom of God,"[69] though this remains God's own act. In prayer we bring the world and its needs into our participation in Christ, who ever intercedes for us (Heb. 7:25) and thus brings both us and the world into his communion with the Father.

5. The Justification of God

This chapter has been concerned with God's justifying, rectifying work in the world, understood as grounded in the definitive and unsurpassable event of the cross and resurrection of Jesus Christ and as anticipating an eschatological completion in the consummation of all things. To speak of the "justification of God" in this context is to employ a subjective genitive; it is humankind that receives the divine action and gift of justification. However, it should at least be asked whether the concept of justification in its Christian usage has room for a question about the "justification of God," understood now as an objective genitive. In this case, whose action would the justification be? One of the lessons of the book of Job is that God does not have to render account to the creation: "I will question you and you shall declare to me" (38:3). Only God can justify God, just as only God can reveal God; there can be no question of a role-reversal here! What is ultimately at stake, as Barth makes clear in a passage quoted earlier, is "God's maintaining and manifesting His own glory in the world."[70] This glory includes the justice and goodness of God in the justification and redemption of the world. What it is about, suggests Hans Küng, is "not primarily the justification of man, whereby man receives justice, but the *self-*

Thanksgiving, ed. W. W. Emilsen and J. T. Squires (Sydney: UTC Publications, 2003), pp. 43-57, esp. 49-50.

69. Pannenberg, *Systematic Theology,* vol. 3, p. 210.

70. See note 27 above. Barth, *Church Dogmatics,* IV/1, p. 3.

justification of God, whereby God, willing from eternity salvation and creation, is proven just."[71] This has to be remembered if we enter the fraught area of theodicy.

All proposals for a theodicy, a justification of God, can only be attempted with the utmost humility and only as an attempted anticipatory echo of God's own final self-justification. Even then, they take us only so far, and they will have to have an eschatological character.[72] As long as life in this world is broken and, particularly for some, involves constant suffering and grief, the cry, "How long, O Lord?," cannot be silenced. The answer, of course, will not be in the form of a good explanatory account but can only be in the form of a decisive act of justice, vindication, and compensation. Precisely such an action of God is the subject of Christian hope, responding to the promise of a new heaven and a new earth, in which tears and grief and death will be no more (Rev. 21:1-4). With the new creation of the earth, God is justified, says Moltmann.[73] When evil is overcome and suffering is ended, the praise of God can be universal and God's glory sung by all. The coherence of the divine economy in the midst of all contingency and freedom will become apparent, as will the character and nature of all God's works. The same Spirit who is the source and power of the new life in the overlap of the two ages will also, in the fullness of time, make the creation new, and thus effect the justification of God.[74] The justification of God is nothing other than the demonstration of God's deity in the final coming of God's reign. As the world is reconciled to God and perfected for its participation in the glory of God, the love of God will be unambiguously clear and the folly of unbelief incontrovertibly established.[75]

Throughout this chapter, what has been under discussion is the priceless gift of salvation, in particular as brought to speech in the influential metaphor of justification, which eventually crystallized into a major and divisive doctrine. What this doctrine articulates is at the core of the gospel, though it has never been the only way to say it. Precisely because it does not, so to speak, "say it all," I have necessarily located it in a larger linguistic

---

71. Küng, *Justification,* p. 231 (emphasis Küng's).

72. See Christiaan Mostert, "Theodicy and Eschatology," in *Theodicy and Eschatology,* ed. B. Barber and D. Neville (Adelaide: AFT Press, 2005), pp. 97-120.

73. Moltmann, *The Way of Jesus Christ,* p. 187.

74. The last section of Pannenberg's *Systematic Theology,* vol. 3, ch. 15, §5, pp. 630-46, is entitled "The Justification of God by the Spirit."

75. Pannenberg, *Systematic Theology,* vol. 3, p. 632.

framework. The juxtaposition of "justification" and "eschatology" is necessary because the more encompassing concept of salvation is an eschatological reality; it includes the decisive "justifying" event of Jesus' death and resurrection, as well as the continuation of life, already transformed and made new, in fellowship with Christ and in the power of the Spirit. But it awaits and anticipates a decisive consummation, the final eschatological renewal of all things, also the work of the Spirit. We who live now, live our lives in the overlap of two ages. We live after Easter and Pentecost, but the parousia lies ahead of us; we look backward and forward; we remember and we hope. Neither is separable from the other, for we have been justified and we live in hope of the "making right" of all things. As God has done a new thing "in the fullness of time," so God will "make all things new" in the fullness of time. This nourishes our hope and sends us in the ongoing mission of God into a world still broken. It helps us to recognize the eschatological future in its many and varied anticipations in the present, not least in the worship of the community of faith and hope. There, above all, we are taught again and again to "look to Jesus," who has come and who will come, to reconcile all things to God.

9 Justification and Justice: Toward an Evangelical Social Ethic

George Hunsinger

The theme of "justification and justice" was not directly addressed by the classic confessional writings of the Reformed tradition. Indeed it would not seem to have emerged as an explicit topic until Karl Barth's 1938 essay on "Rechtfertigung und Recht" ("Justification and Justice"). Since then, though it has been taken up from time to time by various theologians, how justice might well be grounded in justification is still not entirely clear.

One way to think about how justification could be related to social justice would be to start by considering how justification is related to ethics more generally. In the Reformed tradition, however, as for example in Calvin, ethical questions were more likely to be considered on the basis of expressions of the law, like the Ten Commandments or the Golden Rule. Unlike Luther, who thought about the Ten Commandments entirely from a center in the doctrine of justification, Calvin dealt with them more straightforwardly from the standpoint of creation and covenant.

This essay centers on how Luther drew ethical implications from the doctrine of justification. By using the Golden Rule as a foil against which Luther can be understood, I contrast Luther's method, indirectly, to the one more usually favored by Calvin and the Reformed tradition. It is Luther's approach, however, rather than Calvin's, that provides the most useful bridge to the theme of justification and justice — especially as developed by Karl Barth. Insofar as this inquiry proves fruitful, the old adage is validated that to be a good Calvinist one must first be a good Lutheran.

Barth's Essay Reconsidered

The odd thing about Barth's essay "Justification and Justice"[1] was that it had so little to say about justification and justice. It addressed other matters, which explains why "Church and State" was chosen as the title of the English translation. The essay presented church and state as having distinctive tasks. The church was to preach justification by faith, while the state would ensure justice in society. Barth wanted to establish a bond of unity between these two tasks while still maintaining their distinction.

In the midst of the German church struggle, Barth hoped to counteract the crippling effects of the traditional "two-kingdoms" doctrine. Because the state was not autonomous, he argued, but belonged in principle to the Christological sphere, securing justice in the secular realm was an object of Christian responsibility. The state did not have merely the negative role of using coercion to prevent disorder. It also had a positive duty, under the Lordship of Christ, to pursue a larger social welfare. The church was called to participate in this duty actively and responsibly. It could not restrict social responsibility to passive and subordinate obedience.

With respect to religious truth, the state's task was to remain neutral. Religious neutrality meant allowing the church to proclaim the gospel. The church expected no other benefit from the state. Barth was emphatic, however, that it did expect this benefit: "All that can be said from the standpoint of divine justification on the question . . . of human law is summed up in this one statement: the church *must have freedom to proclaim divine justification*" (p. 147, italics original). Why the church's freedom to proclaim the gospel should depend so heavily on state permission, however, was not explained.[2]

Barth presented freedom of proclamation as a test case. The church had a right to liberty, a right that undergirded the rule of law. "Wherever

1. Karl Barth, "Church and State," in *Community, State and Church*, ed. Will Herberg (Garden City, NY: Doubleday/Anchor Books, 1960), pp. 101-48. Hereafter references to this essay will be cited in the text.

2. For a rather different view, see Dietrich Bonhoeffer: "The freedom of the church is not where it has possibilities, but only where the Gospel really and in its own power makes room for itself on earth, even and precisely when no such possibilities are offered to it. The essential freedom of the church is not a gift of the world to the church, but the freedom of the Word of God itself to gain a hearing." Bonhoeffer, *No Rusty Swords* (New York: Harper & Row, 1965), p. 104.

this right is recognized," he stated, ". . . there we shall find a legitimate human authority and an equally legitimate human independence" (p. 147). Where liberty existed for the church, legitimacy would exist for the state. Tyranny and anarchy would be dethroned; the true order of human affairs — justice, freedom and peace — would be secured (p. 148). Why civil liberties should depend so heavily on liberty for the church, however, rather than the other way around, was again not explained. Yet Barth's intention was clear. He wanted to encourage the church — and especially the confessing church — to fight for its own liberty against very real encroachments by the state, and not for that alone, but also for the liberty of others at a time of increasing brutality and injustice.

Working for justice, however, was not the church's primary concern. The church best served the state by being the church. It thereby made an indirect, though essential, contribution to society. Two tasks in particular were lifted up: proclamation and intercession.

Proclamation expressed the ultimate basis of earthly justice. "By proclaiming divine justification," stated Barth, "[the church] offers the best possible service to the establishment and maintenance of human justice" (p. 146 rev.). Barth's whole argument depended on this important claim. How the cause of justice was served by the proclamation of divine justification, however, was again not made clear.

Intercession, for its part, disclosed the limits of the state. By interceding in prayer for those with secular authority, the church showed that the state was not the object of worship, and that its authority was restricted. "In principle and speaking comprehensively," wrote Barth, "[intercessory prayer] is the essential service which the church owes the state. It is the form of service that includes all others within itself" (p. 136 rev.). The more unjust or even brutal the state might become, the more the church was responsible to work for a better society through prayer — followed by the corresponding action.

Barth argued that secular injustice always ran up against a divinely imposed limit. Injustice was finally forced in spite of itself to serve a higher good. The paradigmatic case was the trial of Jesus before Pilate. Despite the way injustice ran its course, Pilate was finally an instrument through which the justification of sinful humanity took place once for all. No earthly power, Barth concluded, stood outside the mysterious governance of God. "The state, even in this 'demonic' form, cannot help rendering the service it is meant to render" (p. 111). No illegitimate state would finally achieve what it desired. All demonic forces would at last be pressed "into the service and glorification of Christ, and, through him, of God" (pp. 116-17). God was secretly at work, even in the political order, to make good come out of evil. This was the word of hope that Barth extended to the beleaguered confessing church.

In short, although Barth set out to show that justification was related to justice through "an inward and vital connection" (p. 101), the goal was not well met. His essay was more illuminating on how the church was related to the state than on his announced, more technical theme. Focusing on the Christian community more than on justification by faith — on the proclaimer, so to speak, more than on the message it proclaimed — Barth found it difficult to develop his intuition that justification and justice were inwardly linked. Only a more direct focus on the doctrine of justification could succeed in showing how the two were related.

The Evangelical "As"

A clue resides in what might be called the evangelical "as." It was Martin Luther who, in principle, first grasped this point. Evangelical ethics, for him, was a matter of acting toward others *as* God had acted in justifying us. This pattern of ethics — which moved by analogy from the indicative to the imperative — was already incipient in the New Testament. It should not be confused, however, with a similar pattern that the New Testament also sets forth. This second pattern, which I will call the dominical "as," starts from the optative mood rather than the indicative.

Consider these two verses:

Do to others as you would have them do to you. (Luke 6:31)

Live in love, as Christ loved us and gave himself up for us. (Eph. 5:2)

In the familiar Golden Rule as taught by Jesus, the standard of moral behavior derives from how we ourselves would like to be treated.[3] Just as we

---

3. For an account of Calvin's ethics that focuses on the Golden Rule, see Guenther H. Haas, *The Concept of Equity in Calvin's Ethics* (Waterloo, Ontario, Canada: Wilfrid Laurier University Press, 1997). For a survey of Calvin's positive use of the law, with remarks on how it proceeds without reference to the doctrine of justification, see I. John Hesselink, *Calvin's Concept of the Law* (Allison Park, PA: Pickwick Publications, 1992).

do not wish to be treated unfairly by others, so we ought not to treat others unfairly.[4] It is a matter of simple consistency. No one is entitled to an exemption from the duty to deal fairly with others,[5] and everyone has some idea of fairness, since we routinely invoke it in our own case. The Golden Rule makes explicit what is implicit in our ordinary judgments. It takes up the standard we use to judge how we ought to be treated and makes it universal for the sake of consistency. It derives the imperative (how we ought to treat others) from the optative (how we wish to be treated ourselves). The dominical "as" links fairness, universality, and consistency on the basis of ordinary self-regard. *Do to others as you would have them do to you.*[6]

When we turn to the evangelical "as," the frame of reference shifts. The standard of moral behavior derives not from how we would wish to be treated but from how we were actually treated. It arises not from ordinary self-regard but from God's unexpected regard of us. *While we were yet sinners, Christ died for us* (Rom. 5:8). According to the gospel, we are sinners who are not only met with undeserved grace, but are spared from deserved condemnation. The condemnation was borne by another, who died that we might live. We were absolved by an act of unfathomable love.

From this indicative, there arises an ethical imperative. If possible, the evangelical obligation is even greater than the duty arising from simple fairness. It is no longer only a matter of living consistently with our ordinary wish for fair treatment (as binding as that is). It is now a matter of living consistently with how we have in fact been treated by Christ. A new and higher norm confronts us. It is a norm defined by severe mercy and costly grace, by what Dostoevsky once called a harsh and dreadful love.

This love obligates us because it delivered us at great cost from the

---

4. I must assume here without argument that the negative form of the Golden Rule — *What (or as) you do not wish to be done to yourself, do not do to others* — is in agreement with the positive form. I agree with Marcus G. Singer that the two forms are equivalent. See Singer, "The Golden Rule," *Philosophy* 38 (1963): 293-314.

5. For example, one may not grant preferential treatment to oneself without good reason.

6. The Golden Rule, of course, pertains to more than just a desire for fair treatment. When I am in need, for example, I might desire to be helped. As a person, I might desire to be treated with respect and not be humiliated. The salient point for our purposes here, however, is the role played by desire (or self-regard) in deriving an ethical norm. That role remains the same regardless of what the desire is for (as long as it can pass the tests of universalizability, impartiality, and role-reversal, in ways that cannot be explored here). The desire not to be treated unfairly, or not to be humiliated, or not to be denied needed help (without good reason) is representative.

peril of eternal death. We have ourselves been spared from a condemnation that would otherwise have been ours. From now on there is nothing for us but to live a life of gratitude. Correspondence to Christ in thanks and praise is the only fitting response. The standard of behavior is not set by our wishes but by another's act of love. We would fall into contradiction with Christ if we failed to live in accord with his mercy toward us. The evangelical "as" links deliverance, gratitude, and conformity to Christ on the basis of Christ's self-giving love. *Live in love, as Christ loved us and gave himself up for us.*[7]

These moral standards — the dominical "as" and the evangelical "as" — are self-involving, since they both rest on already existing practices. The standard of universal fairness derives from our ordinary practice of judging how we would have others treat us. The standard of conforming to Christ's love — severe and costly for himself, merciful and gracious toward others — derives from his personal work of intercession for us. In the one case we are involved, so to speak, by nature; in the other by grace. In either case we are fully implicated as moral agents in a way that determines our outlook on the world. Just as we cannot fail to treat others fairly without lapsing into self-contradiction, so we cannot fail to act kindly toward others without entering into contradiction with Christ.

We might say that whereas self-contradiction violates the law, contradicting Christ violates the gospel. To that extent, the dominical "as" operates within the realm of necessity, while the evangelical "as" operates within the realm of freedom. The dominical "as" is necessarily self-involving, for it requires the consistent application of a standard we already employ. But beyond all strict necessity, the evangelical "as" is maximally and spontaneously self-involving, for it invites a fitting response to a wondrous gift of love. *Love so amazing, so divine,/Demands my soul, my life, my all* (Isaac Watts).

Finally, it may be noted that the two standards, each in its own way, seek to inculcate an ethics of empathy. The dominical "as" arguably seeks

7. Here is a passage where Luther connected the dominical "as" with the evangelical "as." He asked how the Christian should relate to another who is weak in faith and defective in conduct. He answered that the Christian should treat such a person "as he would himself be treated, and as Christ has indeed treated him in similar and more important matters." See *Sermons of Martin Luther,* ed. John N. Lenker, vol. 6 (Grand Rapids: Baker Book House, 1989), p. 49. Luther rightly saw that though the two norms are compatible, they stand in a certain order of significance.

to enlarge our already existing feelings of self-regard so as to include comparable feelings of regard for others. We are to put ourselves, by way of empathy, in their place. The evangelical "as," in turn, seeks to expand our feelings of gratitude toward Christ so as to include feelings of benevolence toward others akin to his mercy toward us. Moreover, insofar as *imitatio Christi* rests on *participatio Christi,* the action of conforming to the mercy of Christ *(conformitas Christi)* (with whom we are united into one body by faith) serves an evangelical function, for it at once attests to his mercy in its uniqueness, while also mediating it in some form to others. We are so to empathize with the plight of others as to be moved by the same compassion as was Christ's in his identification with us.[8]

It was Luther who first interpreted the evangelical "as" in terms of an ethic of freedom. In evangelical ethics, as he saw it, gratitude was the only proper motivation, benevolence was the decisive content, and freedom was the essential form.[9] Gratitude to Christ meant conforming to him through acts of kindness that were freed from all thought of benefit for oneself.

Luther based his evangelical ethics on the indicative of grace. He could affirm this indicative with exuberance:

> Well now! My God has given to me, unworthy and lost human being, absolutely for nothing and out of pure mercy, through Christ, the fullness of all godliness and blessedness, so that I henceforth need nothing more than to believe that it is so.[10]

The gift of salvation to lost sinners was a complex event. It occurred in Christ alone, by grace alone, through faith alone. Accomplished by Christ in his saving obedience there and then *(solus Christus),* complete salvation in all its fullness *(tota salutis)* was given — absolutely for nothing and out of pure mercy *(sola gratia)* — to unworthy and lost human beings here and now *(totus peccatores),* on the sole condition that they receive it by

---

8. A good discussion of *conformitas Christi* in Luther and his sources can be found in Dietmar Lage, *Martin Luther's Christology and Ethics* (Lewiston, NY: Edwin Mellen Press, 1990).

9. Although I speak of benevolence, I assume throughout this essay that beneficence is implicit within it.

10. Quoted in Anders Nygren, *Agape and Eros* (Philadelphia: Westminster Press, 1953), p. 727 n. 2. The passage cited is from WA 7, p. 35, the German-text version of Luther's "The Freedom of a Christian." I owe this reference to Robert McAfee Brown, *The Spirit of Protestantism* (New York: Oxford University Press, 1961), pp. 65-66.

faith *(sola fide)*. As seen from salvation's originating side, divine mercy was the inner motivation, steadfast love was the enacted content, and sovereign freedom was the essential form of this gift.

Ethics was then a matter of deriving the human imperative from the divine indicative. The indicative established the model (the *analogans*) to which our lives were meant to conform (the *analogate*). Conformity to Christ (with due respect to his unrepeatable uniqueness) emerged as the guiding norm. In response to his self-giving love, our lives were to be distinguished by gratitude, benevolence, and freedom. Luther continued:

> Well, then, for such a Father, who has so prodigally lavished upon me his blessings, I will in return freely, joyously and for nothing do what is well-pleasing to him, and also be a Christian toward my neighbor, as Christ has been toward to me; and I will do nothing except only what I see to be needful, useful and blessed for him, because I indeed through my faith have enough of everything in Christ. See, thus there flows from faith love and delight in God, and from love a free, willing, joyous life to serve our neighbor for nothing. For just as our neighbor suffers want and is in need of our superabundance, so have we suffered want before God and been in need of his grace.[11]

The evangelical "as" found expression here at two points:

> *As our neighbor suffers want, so we have suffered want before God.*
> *I will be toward my neighbor as Christ has been toward me.*

An analogy of neediness called forth an analogy of benevolence. It was a pattern that moved from the greater to the lesser. Since God had delivered us so lavishly from the greater need of sin, death, and the devil (as Luther might put it), how could we fail to reach out to our neighbors when we saw them in temporal need? Since God had so abundantly blessed us, we would gladly do in return what was pleasing to God. That meant acting toward others as God in Christ had acted, and continued to act, toward us. We would undertake whatever was "needful, useful and blessed" for them. In accord with the grace we had received, we would serve them "freely, joyously and for nothing." We could not love God and take delight in him without reaching out in kindness to our neighbor.

---

11. Quoted in Nygren, *Agape and Eros*, p. 727 n. 2 (WA 7, p. 35).

The ethical analogy thus moved from the indicative to the imperative. It moved from divine grace to human gratitude, from divine benevolence to human kindness, and from divine freedom to human liberty. Gratitude meant doing what was pleasing to God, kindness meant being charitable in our judgments, and liberty meant having no secondary or ulterior motives of our own. Together they meant treating our neighbor as an end in him- or herself rather than as a mere means. In particular, our neighbor was not to be helped in order that we might obtain some benefit, "whether temporal or eternal."[12] Otherwise we would be seeking our own profit, supposing, for example, that through good works our sins would be purged or that in them we might find salvation. "In this way," observed Luther, "Christian liberty perishes altogether" (p. 370).

Christian liberty was either gratuitous, seeking nothing in return, or else it was not Christian liberty. Christian liberty meant living not in ourselves, but in Christ and in our neighbor. It meant living in Christ through faith and in our neighbor through love (p. 371). Because in receiving Christ himself *(solus Christus)* believers had already received the fullness of salvation gratuitously *(tota salutis gratis)* — having obtained it solely by faith *(sola fide),* and as a gift that could neither be merited nor repaid *(sola gratia)* — they were to perform works of kindness gratuitously in response.[13]

The ethics of justification not only required gratuitous kindness, but also mercy in particular toward the unworthy.

> Why should we be unwilling to do for others what has been done for us by God, of whose blessings we are far less worthy than anyone can be of our help? Since God has been friendly and kindly disposed toward us in bestowing upon us his loving kindness, let us conduct ourselves similarly toward our neighbors, even if they are unworthy, for we too are unworthy. (p. 142)

Charitable judgments were, for Luther, the core of the evangelical "as."

> Though our neighbors may be blind, erring and wicked, yet we should be charitable in our judgment and cheerfully endeavor to please them,

---

12. Luther, "The Freedom of a Christian," in *Luther's Works,* vol. 31 (Philadelphia: Fortress Press, 1957), p. 370. Hereafter page numbers cited in the text. Other references to this volume cited hereafter as *LW* 31.

13. *Sermons of Martin Luther,* vol. 6, p. 239 (see n. 5 above). Hereafter page numbers cited in the text.

remembering God's similar attitude toward us when we were as they. (p. 143)

Others were to be regarded with charity despite their guilt and shame, for that was how Christ had regarded us. Since we all shared a solidarity in sin, we could not deny them a measure of the kindness that Christ had shown to us.

Benevolence should not be withheld even from our enemies, for we were once enemies of God (Rom. 5:8, 10).

> Regard your enemies with the utmost charity. Act kindly, ever remembering you yourself were once as they are in the sight of God. Faith and love certainly can do it. Note this: the truly Christian life is that which does for others as God has done for itself. . . . God did not appear to us, or save us, because of our righteousness. . . . If we, though unworthy, were received through mercy, to receive the favors of God in spite of our great demerits and the enormity of our sins, why should we withhold our favors from others? . . . Let us not withhold; no, let us rather be children of God, doing good even to our enemies and to evil-doers: for so God has done, and still does, to us, evil-doers and his enemies. (p. 148)

Justification meant that God loved us not because we were righteous, but while we were still unrighteous. God loved us to make us righteous. We were not loved because we were loveable; we became loveable because we were loved.[14] We should so love our neighbors in return.

When we acted with gratuitous kindness, and judged our poor neighbors with charity, our lives became parables of grace. Such conduct proclaimed the gospel.

> When such Christian conduct is manifest before sinners and the spiritually weak, their hearts are attracted to God and forced to exclaim: "Truly, he must be a great and gracious God, a righteous Father, whose people are these; for he desires them not to judge, condemn nor reject us poor, sinful and imperfect ones, but rather to receive us, to give us aid and to treat us as if our sins and imperfections were their own. Should we not love and exalt such a God?" (p. 55)

---

14. Luther, "Heidelberg Disputation," *LW* 31, p. 57.

By approaching others non-judgmentally and in a spirit of charity, we praised God and attested him.[15]

Mercy versus Justice?

An objection to this ethics, as presented so far, may now be considered. We might well wonder how the sinfulness of sin can simply be overlooked. Shouldn't sin be condemned, wrongdoing censured, and injustice punished? Isn't this ethics of justification in danger of accepting the unacceptable and condoning evil? Doesn't it seem to value mercy over justice, and forgiveness over accountability? Is there no relevant analogy to the severity evident in God's mercy, the costliness in God's grace, and the harshness in God's dreadful love? Hasn't the law been eviscerated by an ethics that offers grace without judgment?

In response to this objection Luther had at least two moves. One was to distinguish between one's own case as a Christian and that of one's neighbor. If one's own well-being came under attack, the proper response, Luther thought, was to endure suffering rather than to inflict it. In this way one responded to others as God in Christ had responded to us. For even when our sinfulness had meant enmity toward God, it led Christ to suffer for our sakes. Whether this line of reasoning was sufficient for all cases, even at the interpersonal level, however, was not greatly considered. In one's personal affairs as a Christian, might one never have a justified claim to self-protection or self-defense? Could an ethics based on justification allow for a more complex and open-ended view?

If one's neighbor was threatened, on the other hand, then defensive or protective measures were in order. The defense or protection of one's neighbor was not to be undertaken by private persons, however, but only by those with the proper authority. A strong line between the private and the public domain was drawn.

Luther's second move (distinguishing between private and public) thus merged with the first (distinguishing between oneself and one's

---

15. Luther made an important exception to this standard. When the truth of the gospel was at stake, above all in public teaching, the faithful had no choice but to expose the false teaching and to attack the authority of the false teachers. The graver the threat, the more vehement the attack.

neighbor). He held that the secular authority in society had been appointed with the means of coercion for the purpose of protecting and defending one's neighbors (and to some extent oneself) from harm. Whereas one's personal well-being as a Christian was relegated to the private domain, that of one's neighbor required public means of protection.

Without going into the ramifications of this position, which are many, a basic tendency was clear. By distinguishing one's case from that of one's neighbor, and by defining one's own case as "private" while viewing one's neighbor's case as "public," a split seemed hard to avoid. The claims of mercy were in danger of divorce from those of justice.

Unrestricted mercy seemed to govern the private affairs of the Christian. The Christian was to refrain from self-assertion even if it meant suffering injustice. Meanwhile, rough justice seemed to govern the public affairs of society (composed of one's Christian and non-Christian neighbors). Society was entitled to use coercion for self-defense and self-protection, even if it meant ruthlessly forgoing mercy. How to forestall a tragic split between "mercy without justice" in private and "justice without mercy" in public has been an ongoing dilemma for Reformation ethics.

In discussing the commandment that prohibits false witness against one's neighbor, Luther addressed this dilemma while also illustrating it. The public/private distinction governed his line of reasoning. In private or interpersonal affairs, not only should we prefer to hear good rather than evil about our neighbor, but we should always speak well of our neighbor even if we know him to be guilty. "God desires to keep us from speaking evil of another, guilty though he may be, and to our certain knowledge."[16] In the private realm a person's honor and reputation were always to be protected.

The rationale again seemed to derive from Luther's doctrine of justification. Because we ourselves were offenders before God, circumspection was in order regarding what we might say about another. As our sins had been covered by Christ's righteousness, so also should our neighbor's failings be covered by us. "We are to use our tongues to speak only good of everyone, to cover the sins and infirmities of our neighbor, to overlook them and to adorn him with due honor" (pp. 65-66). Luther continued:

---

16. *Luther's Large Catechism*, tr. J. N. Lenker (Minneapolis: Augsburg, 1967), p. 63. Hereafter page numbers cited in the text.

In our conduct one toward another, we are to adorn what is dishonorable and uncomely in our neighbor's character and do our utmost to help and serve him and to promote his honor. On the other hand, we are to prevent anything that tends to his dishonor. (p. 66)

In the realm of personal affairs, we were not to harm anyone — whether guilty or innocent, friend or foe — by speaking ill of him. The tendency of justification was to err on the side of generosity and to hide a multitude of sins.

On the other hand, wrongdoing should by no means be condoned. "The commandment must not be understood," wrote Luther, "as permitting evil to go unreproved" (p. 63). Much of his concern about not speaking evil of another, even if that person were guilty, was directed against excesses in private conversation. If one had evidence of serious wrongdoing, the proper recourse was to inform the duly constituted authorities, not one's gossipy neighbors. "It is necessary that evil be charged, that investigation and testimony be employed" (p. 64). In the public domain it was essential that justice be administered with equity, especially because the poor were often unjustly defeated in court by the wealthy and powerful (pp. 60-61). "Here is presented the end to which jurists should strive to attain — perfect justice in every case. Right is to be always right, not perverted, concealed or silenced for the sake of gain, honor or power" (p. 61). Luther placed his hopes for judicial equity not in social structures but in godly magistrates.

In the end, however, a perennial problem remained. While it was clear why harmful gossip should be prohibited, it was not clear why someone known to be guilty of wrongdoing should be always be protected in private affairs. Nor was it clear why those convicted in public should always be bereft of the possibility of mercy. Could a Reformation ethics of justification find appropriate ways to temper mercy with justice in private affairs, while moderating justice with mercy in the public sphere? Could it sometimes allow for tough-minded forms of private self-defense, on the one hand, and principled forms of public vulnerability, on the other? Could such possibilities be grounded in the doctrine of justification? We will return to this question below.[17]

17. See Barth, "Justification and Justice," part II.

Socializing the Evangelical "As"

In working out his ethics of justification, Luther restricted the evangelical "as" to the private sphere. For him, the injunction to show kindness toward others with their moral weaknesses and failings, as Christ had done toward us, pertained only to private or interpersonal relations, or to the spiritual realm of faith and Christian community. It did not directly carry over into secular government or political affairs. A different calculus was in order there — one less generous, more limited, and more severe. Social ideals inspired by the gospel, like forgiveness, equality, and non-retaliation, did not apply in the public domain, where the attempt to realize them could only go awry. Luther's famous opposition between the law and the gospel (with its obvious Augustinian roots) led him to posit a dichotomy between the secular and the spiritual realms.

When the secular realm was redefined by Barth as falling under the lordship of Christ, it became possible for him to socialize the evangelical "as." While he did not make that move in his 1938 essay, he went on to make it elsewhere. He followed the exact logic of Luther's ethics while extending it into the sphere of social and political responsibility. He reasoned by analogy from justification to justice. In his hands, the doctrine of justification led to a Reformation version of what Latin American theologians would later call "God's preferential option for the poor."

Like Luther, Barth argued that for lost sinners the righteousness of God meant both mercy and judgment. Insofar as the sinner was condemned and put to death, God's righteousness meant the awfulness of judgment. But insofar as the sinner was justified by grace and endowed with the blessing of faith, God's righteousness meant the primacy of mercy.

Righteousness was a predicate that defined who God was, both in himself and for us. Barth wrote:

> God is righteous in himself, always doing what befits him and is worthy of himself, defending and glorying in his divine being. He does this also when he makes himself to be our righteousness. He procures right for those who in themselves have no righteousness, indeed for those whose righteousness he discloses as unrighteousness. He does not leave them to themselves. On the contrary, he gives himself to them in his own divine righteousness. Against their merit and worth, and solely by his own

merit and worth, he makes himself to be the ground on which . . . they can truly stand and live. (II/1, 387 rev.)

God's righteousness, according to Barth, embraced both retributive and restorative aspects. It slayed in order to make alive, and it made alive by slaying. The selfsame sinner who was abolished in Christ was restored with him from the grave. In his death Christ was made one with the condemned, while in his resurrection he triumphed as their hope. His union with them was at once vicarious and yet real. In an unparalleled, apocalyptic transaction, retribution had been justly carried out even as the sinner was restored to new life. God had not compromised his righteousness one whit while still causing his mercy to prevail. For Barth there was no *iustitia restitutiva* that was not retributive, and no *iustitia retributiva* that was not restorative. In the judgment of divine grace, the condemned sinner became a new creature who had been done away with in order to be made new.

From this astonishing affirmation of God's righteousness in the service of his mercy — the divine indicative — there followed, Barth believed, a social imperative. God's work of mercy implied "a very definite political problem and task" (II/1, 386). God had intervened on behalf of lost sinners despite the end they deserved. From one standpoint, the forgiven sinner simply represented human misery as seen in all who were weak and defenseless, all who were helpless and in distress (cf. Rom. 5:6). God's mercy toward sinners had consequences for all other, if lesser, needs. Barth noted that God's concern for the harassed and oppressed people of Israel — and in Israel "especially the poor, the widows and orphans, the weak and defenseless" (II/1, 396) — had foreshadowed God's intervention on the cross.

The God of the Bible was a God of righteous mercy who took human misery to heart, entered into it himself, and overcame it from within (II/1, 369). Reasoning from the greater to the lesser, Barth concluded:

To establish justice for the innocent who are threatened and the poor, the widows, the orphans and the strangers who are oppressed . . . God stands at every time unconditionally and passionately on this and only on this side: always against the exalted and for the lowly, always against those who already have rights and for those from whom they are robbed and taken away. (II/1, 386 rev.)

God's concern for those in distress could not be taken seriously, Barth wrote, "without feeling a sense of responsibility in the direction indicated" (II/1, p. 386). A definite political attitude was established by God's work of mercy. The believer "justified by Christ's blood" (Rom. 5:9) was made responsible "to all those who are poor and wretched." The believer was summoned to show mercy as he or she had received mercy, and therefore "to espouse the cause of those who suffer wrong" (II/1, 387). Why? Because in them it was made manifest what he or she was in the sight of God — a person in need of mercy that rectified wrong (II/1, 387). A solidarity in need connected believers to the poor and oppressed.[18]

The justified sinner therefore

> knows that justice — every rightful claim which one human being has against another or others — enjoys the special protection of the God of grace. As surely as [the believer] lives by the grace of God, he cannot avoid this claim. He cannot avoid the problem of human rights. He can only will and affirm a state which is based on justice. By any other attitude he rejects the divine justification. (II/1, 387 rev.)

Divine justification meant mercy toward those in need. It meant that God had not only dealt with our sin, but had looked from our sin to our suffering, from our guilt to our bondage, and from our arrogance to our folly (II/1, 371). It meant that our negation of God's affirmation had been negated by grace so that our liberation and restoration prevailed. Justification meant the removal of injustice, the prevailing of mercy, the restitution of the sinner, and the imperative of justice for the oppressed.

The judgment scene in Matthew 25:31-46 pointed in the same direction. Especially important was v. 40: *As you did it to one of the least of these my brothers and sisters, you did it to me* (ESV mar.). "This is the Magna Carta of all Christian humanitarianism and Christian politics," noted Barth (III/2, 508). It indicated where Jesus could be found on earth. He was present, though hidden,

> in all who are now hungry, thirsty, strangers, naked, sick and in prison. Wherever in the present time between the resurrection and the *parousia*

---

18. See Barth's interpretation of the parable of the Good Samaritan: "The lawyer's first need was to see that he himself is the man fallen among thieves and lying helpless by the wayside. . . . He has to be found and treated with compassion by the Samaritan, the foreigner, whom he believes he should hate . . ." (*Church Dogmatics* I/2, 418).

one of these is waiting for help (for food, drink, lodging, clothes, a visit, assistance), Jesus himself is waiting. Wherever help is granted or denied, it is granted or denied to Jesus himself. For these are the least of his brothers and sisters. They represent the world for which he died and rose again, with which he has made himself supremely one, and declared himself in solidarity. (III/2, 507-8 rev.)

When Christ died for our sins, he had made the sufferings of the world his own. He had personally identified himself with all who were suffering and in need, so that in them he was now at hand. Those who received Christ by faith were called into conformity with his compassion. They were "to be affected by the concrete miseries of the world" (III/2, 508). Through their union with Christ, they were given a certain share in his work. They were not to pass by on the other side. They were called to be "simply and directly human" (III/2, 508). How could they love Christ without being devoted to the poor and needy whom he loved? In serving them, they served him, even as they themselves were served by him.

Barth wrote:

It is to be noted that those who are righteous and therefore justified at the last judgment do not know with whom they really have to do when they act with simple humanity (vv. 37f.). . . . They had helped the least of his brothers and sisters, they had helped the world in its misery for its own sake. They had no ulterior motive. As the true community of Jesus, they saw the need and did what they could without any further design or after-thoughts. They could not do their duty or fulfill their mission without realizing their solidarity with those in affliction and standing at their side. . . . They were simply concerned with human beings as human beings, and therefore treated them as brothers and sisters. If they had not done so, they could not have claimed Jesus as their Brother or God as their Father. (III/2, 508 rev.)

At least two points in Barth's interpretation of Matthew 25:31-46 require comment. (1) Who are "the least" in this parable? (2) In the Last Judgment how are works related to faith? (1) In much traditional interpretation (including Luther and Calvin) as well as in some contemporary interpretation, the "least" in this parable are seen as members of Christ's community. The reason why help is offered to Christ when it is offered to them is because they are united to Christ by faith. Barth need not object to this interpretation unless it is meant to be restrictive. He has already established that there is a pattern of distinction-in-unity and unity-in-distinction between believers and the wretched of the earth. Just as Christ died not for our sins only but for the sins of the whole world (1 John 2:2), so he has made himself one not with believers only, but with all those in distress. (2) Barth takes Matthew 25:31-46 as it stands. According to the passage, and in Barth's interpretation, works of mercy play a decisive role in the Last Judgment. He of course presupposes, but does not here state, the standard Reformation position (usually worked out in connection with Rom. 2:6-10) that persons are saved by faith not by works, but that saving faith is not without works, so that the works in question here have the status of being signs of saving faith. Faith is logically prior to kindness but cannot exist without it. Where there is no kindness there is no faith, even though kindness does not belong to the definition of saving faith.

In spelling out the ethics of justification, it is noteworthy how closely Barth followed Luther.

- Like Luther, Barth urged that love for Christ meant loving those whom Christ loved. Conformity to Christ was the ground of benevolence toward those in need.
- Like Luther, he believed that this conformity made love's scope universal. No one was outside the bounds of Christ's love.
- Like Luther (though perhaps more pointedly), he saw that conformity to Christ involved a certain bias. The poor and needy were commended as the primary recipients of benevolence. Moreover, in some sense benevolence always aimed toward the rectification of injustice.[19]
- Like Luther (though perhaps less pointedly), he stressed that neediness took precedence over merit. The justified were called to alleviate suffering without regard to the deserts of those in need.
- Like Luther, he noted that believers were called to act gratuitously.

---

19. An asymmetry exists here, which Barth took for granted. God's act of mercy had rectified injustice by doing away with the offending sinner for the sake of restoring him to new life. Rectification of the sinner by death and resurrection, being Christocentric and apocalyptic in its execution, was obviously incomparable and unrepeatable. By contrast, human acts of mercy could only imperfectly rectify injustice (and remove misery) by intervening on behalf of the sufferers. Such rectifying human acts were imperative regardless of their limitations, and were similar to the divine mercy despite their great dissimilarity. Whether divine or human, and however variously, mercy involved the rectification of injustice.

They were to have no ulterior motives, whether for temporal or eternal gain.

- Like Luther, he saw benevolence as both an end in itself and a means to the end of witness. Benevolence was intrinsically valuable in itself even as it pointed to something greater, namely, God's incomparable grace to lost sinners.

- Finally, like Luther, he saw that the evangelical "as" established a principle of solidarity between believers and those in need. No superiority was implied of believers, or inferiority of the needy, when help was extended and received.

In short, with respect to the ethics of justification, Barth and Luther were in basic agreement on the imperative of benevolence. They agreed about its ground, its scope, its bias, its priorities, its motivation, and its purpose. They also agreed about the moral status of its agents and recipients.[20]

They differed, however, on the question of wide applicability. Where Luther set the spiritual and the secular realms in basic opposition, Barth placed them in a pattern of distinction-in-unity and unity-in-distinction. He radically reconfigured Luther's two-realms idea without abandoning it completely.

For Luther the two realms were like two circles sitting side by side with no overlap. The one was centered in Christ; the other, in human self-seeking. The one was governed by mutuality, the other by coercion. The primary threat to secular society was anarchy rooted in self-seeking. Therefore, the primary purpose of secular government was to maintain order by means of the sword. The best hope for mitigating the harshness of the secular realm, with its stubborn inequalities and injustices, lay in the existence of godly princes, magistrates, and citizens. Fairness in the dispensation of secular justice was more nearly a matter of persons than of institutions.

For Barth, by contrast, the two realms were like two concentric circles,

---

20. This status was always categorical before it was a matter of gradations or distinctions. Categorically, whether as agents or recipients, all were somehow variously sinners who were nonetheless the objects of divine mercy. Their dignity was conferred on them from without by grace (justification). Within this egalitarian category there could then be various distinctions. Different agents might have differing obligations; for example, different recipients might have differing claims to beneficence, and some persons (whether agents or recipients) might have more moral integrity than others (sanctification).

whose common center was Christ. The inner circle was the community of Christians, the outer circle the community of citizens. While neither was immune to the corruptions of self-seeking, both were under the sway of Christ's lordship, though in different ways. The purpose of secular government was not merely negative but positive, not merely to prevent anarchy by means of coercion but also to establish a measure of liberty, equality, and justice. The public good did not depend only on persons but also on institutions, which could be fashioned into parables, however distant, of God's kingdom. Because Christ was secretly the Lord of the secular realm, possibilities were constantly to be sought even now, regardless of how dire the situation, for making institutional arrangements less harsh and more human.

In secular society, Barth maintained, the church should stand for social values consistent with the gospel. The needs of concrete human beings should be placed over abstract causes. The rule of law and constitutionality should be upheld. The socially and economically disadvantaged should be given priority. Freedom of conscience, speech, and religion should be protected. The right to vote for all adult citizens, regardless of race, creed, sex, or class, should be established by law. Separation of powers (legislative, executive, judicial) should be institutionalized. The larger social good should take precedence over narrow parochial interests (in particular, over those of the wealthy and powerful). War and political violence should be legitimate only as a last resort.

In his 1946 essay "The Christian Community and the Civil Community," Barth argued that the "church must stand for social justice in the political sphere."[21] Echoing his previous move from justification to justice, he began by noting that the church's primary concern was to bear witness to the Son of Man who came to seek and to save the lost (the indicative). Conformity to Christ meant concentrating on the needs of those at the bottom of society (the imperative). The poor, the socially and economically outcast, and those most at risk required special attention. The church was called to speak out for the weaker members of society (p. 173).

A church concerned about the poor needed a healthy hermeneutic of suspicion. The community should not be taken in by slogans. "Equality be-

---

21. Karl Barth, "The Christian Community and the Civil Community," in *Community, State and Church: Three Essays* (Garden City, NY: Doubleday & Company, 1960), p. 173. (Hereafter cited by page number in the text.)

fore the law," for example, might be a façade behind which the weak were exploited by the strong, the poor by the rich, or employees by employers. It was clear to Barth that the church had to stand on the democratic left. Progressive politics represented the fixed side of his social ethics as grounded in justification by faith. From there a measure of flexibility was called for:

> And in choosing between the various socialist possibilities — social-liberalism? co-operativism? syndicalism? free trade? moderate or radical Marxism? — [the church] will always choose the movement from which it can expect the greatest measure of social justice (leaving all other considerations to one side). (p. 173 rev.)

Barth took a dim view of capitalism. Parliamentary democracy, he believed, did not work very well without economic democracy. Economic liberalism (or capitalism) was a system that concentrated wealth and power in the hands of the few. By contrast, economic democracy (or democratic socialism) promised to distribute power more equitably. It would eliminate extreme disparities in wealth by subjecting the market to social control. Without economic democracy, parliamentary democracy was hampered. When power was in the grip of the wealthy few, democracy was bent toward elitist ends. Social needs went unmet. Necessities were denied to the many while luxuries were delivered to the few. Without regulation, antisocial phenomena — like huge armaments industries, imperialistic wars of aggression, and nationalistic diversions at home — were the rule.[22] Capitalism went hand in hand with the suppression of democratic change and with large quotients of social misery. Barth opposed the depredations of capitalism, and favored a practical, non-authoritarian socialism, because he believed in democracy and social justice.

---

22. Although it is a forbidden thought that capitalism might have something to do with imperialism and wars of aggression, it is an idea that has standing in serious discussion. "As capitalism spreads," writes John Gray of the London School of Economics, ". . . it has been accompanied by major conflicts and social upheavals. The expansion of European capitalism in the nineteenth century involved the Opium Wars, genocide in the Belgian Congo, the Great Game in Central Asia, and many other forms of imperial conquest and rivalry. The seeming triumph of global capitalism at the end of the twentieth century followed two world wars, the cold war, and savage neocolonial conflicts. Over the past two hundred years, the spread of capitalism and industrialization has gone hand in hand with war and revolution." See Gray, "The World Is Round," *New York Review of Books* 52, no. 13 (August 11, 2005), p. 13, col. 4.

The Christian community, he urged, should not allow itself to be tricked by the "great self-deception" of capitalism (III/4, 541). The purported efficiencies, practicalities, and benefits of this economic system were not easily compatible with the ethics of justification. The myth should not be accepted, for example, that although the wealth under capitalism is inequitably distributed, each person's income reflects how hard or valuably that person has worked. The command of God, Barth wrote, "is self-evidently and in all circumstances a call for counter-movements on behalf of humanity and against its denial in any form, and therefore a call for the championing of the weak against every kind of encroachment on the part of the strong" (III/4, 544). Writing in the postwar era, Barth insisted that the Christian community was wrong to be so preoccupied with communism. It had better concentrate on "the disorder in the decisive form still current in the West [capitalism], to remember and to assert the command of God in face of this form, and to keep to the 'Left' in opposition to its champions, i.e., to confess that it [the Christian community] is fundamentally on the side of the victims of this disorder and to espouse their cause" (III/4, 544 rev.). The ethics of justification meant solidarity with the victims of disorder and therefore opposition to systems of social and economic injustice.[23]

Conclusion

As developed by Luther and expanded by Barth, justification by faith did not lead to ethical quietism or withdrawal from the world. Ethical passivity can be attributed to Luther only when his profound insistence on the evangelical "as" is overlooked. Yet this factor in his ethical teaching has not received the attention it deserves.[24] More common is a judgment like this:

23. For a recent critique from a theologically informed point of view, see *Economic Justice for All* (Washington, DC: United States Catholic Conference, 1986). For reasons similar to Barth's, this pastoral letter by the U.S. Catholic bishops sees the U.S. economic system as structurally "unjust."

24. Kathryn Tanner is one of the few to remark on this aspect of Luther's ethics, but it does not seem greatly to interest her, perhaps because her idea of justification depends more on the divine covenant than on Christ. See Tanner, "Justification and Justice in a Theology of Grace," *Theology Today* 55 (1999): 522. Commentators — they do not, of course, ascribe mere passivity to Luther — who have little or nothing to say about it include: Paul Althaus,

"At times he makes it sound as if grace accomplishes nothing substantive in the Christian life."[25] At times, perhaps this is so. But if due regard is given to what he wrote in "The Freedom of a Christian," what he preached in his sermons, and what he developed in "The Large Catechism" when expounding the Ten Commandments (among other writings), then it can scarcely be denied that for Luther the doctrine of justification led inexorably to an ethics of benevolence.

Whether intuitively or by direct influence, Barth carried this aspect of Luther's thought forward into an obligation to struggle for social justice. He did so by reconfiguring the "two-kingdoms" doctrine and socializing the evangelical "as." Elements of the chronology, as presented here, can be summarized as follows:

- 1938. In his essay on "Justification and Justice," Barth set an agenda that he did not quite meet but that he would later go on to fulfill.
- 1940. Barth's account of God's merciful righteousness (perhaps unsurpassed in the theological literature), with its direct appeal to justification by faith, was an important stage along the way. It explicitly set forth the implications of justification for social justice. Barth in effect politicized the ethic of benevolence that Luther had derived from divine justification (*Church Dogmatics* II/1).
- 1946. The discussion of God's mercy and righteousness stood in the background for what Barth then wrote in "The Christian Community and the Civil Community." It pertained especially to the social implications involved in bearing witness to the Son of Man who came to seek and save the lost. How could this Son of Man be venerated if the church did not stand for social justice?

The Ethics of Martin Luther (Philadelphia: Fortress Press, 1972); George W. Forell, *Faith Active in Love: An Investigation of the Principles Underlying Luther's Social Ethics* (Minneapolis: Augsburg, 1954); Reinhard Hütter, "The Twofold Center in Lutheran Ethics," in *The Promise of Lutheran Ethics*, ed. Karen Bloomquist and John Stumme (Minneapolis: Fortress Press, 1998); Dietmar Lage, *Martin Luther's Christology and Ethics* (Lewiston, NY: Edwin Mellen Press, 1990); William H. Lazareth, *Christians in Society: Luther, the Bible, and Social Ethics* (Minneapolis: Augsburg Fortress Publishers, 2001); Anders Nygren, *Agape and Eros* (Philadelphia: Westminster Press, 1953); Helmut Thielicke, *Theological Ethics*, 2 vols. (Grand Rapids: Eerdmans, 1959, 1979).

25. Jesse Couenhoven, "Grace as Pardon and Power: Pictures of the Christian Life in Luther, Calvin, and Barth," *Journal of Religious Ethics* 28 (2000): 73.

- 1948. In interpreting the parable of the Last Judgment (Matt. 25:31-46), Barth described it as the Magna Carta of Christian humanitarianism and Christian politics. He again asked: How could Jesus be attested, and even politically served, if the church failed to show simple humanity toward the least of those brothers and sisters with whom he had made himself one? (*Church Dogmatics* III/2).

- 1951. Finally, if, as Barth had suggested, justification established a rectifying bias toward the poor and the oppressed, then a confrontation with unjust social arrangements and dysfunctional economic systems could not be avoided. Capitalism, Barth believed, was the great disorder in the West. As an engine of social misery, imperialistic wars, and communal disintegration, it was extraordinarily successful in camouflaging the havoc it wreaked. Insofar as it was unregulated by social constraints, Barth judged it to be "almost unequivocally demonic" (*Church Dogmatics* III/4, 541).

In short, as Barth saw it, the doctrine of justification established an ethics of benevolence (as Luther had explained), which in turn implied a social ethic inclined toward the poor and oppressed. Divine justification, which had rectified human unrighteousness through an incomparable work of mercy, called forth parables of itself not only in private relations, but also in the political realm.

10 Justification and Reconciliation: Considerations from the Churches in Eastern and Central Europe

Sándor Fazakas

The relevance of the message of the justifying act of God is not limited to its religious proclamation in liturgical services, but extends to concrete human social life. One sometimes gets the impression that the relationship of the free grace of God to righteousness through works is viewed today either as a matter for ecumenical dialogues and agreements (in the hope of reconciling different confessional traditions with each other), or as a topic of theoretical theological education, with no connection to the life and faith of ordinary people. But the doctrine of justification is meaningless if it is not connected with human life. When Luther praises the *articulus iustificationes* as "teacher and prince, lord, captain and judge of all forms of doctrine,"[1] he simply expresses the fundamental truth that the message of the incarnated mercy of God affects all areas of life and church praxis: proclamation, pastoral care, ethics, and the shape of life in the church. The situation of the countries of Eastern and Central Europe offers a special horizon of experience *(Erfahrungshorizont)*[2] against which to discuss the biblical message of justification, as these countries struggle with issues of historical guilt and reconciliation since the end of communist domination.

The continent that had been divided for such a long time can once again be considered in terms of its unity. But it is becoming increasingly clear that the unification of Europe is dependent on more than political and economic measures. Beyond the economic is another dimension of

---

1. Martin Luther, WA 39/1, p. 205.
2. Michael Beintker, *Rechtfertigung in der neuzeitlichen Lebenswelt* (Tübingen: Mohr Siebeck, 1998), pp. 33-34.

Europe: the yearning for spiritual and cultural unity. The church is especially relevant in this respect. But what is the task of the church here — prophetic pronouncements on social conditions, concrete social and cultural diaconal work, or something else? In this essay, I investigate how the Protestant concept of "reconciliation" can make a special contribution. How can the doctrine of justification play a role in the process of social reconciliation in which the churches should actively participate? How can this doctrine reframe the way in which we view the guilt of the past and the criteria for the renewal of society? For the guilt of the past continues to manifest itself in people's guilty consciences today, and in a mentality of sacrifice, hate, silence, mistrust, and the inability to make decisions — both in society and in the church — more than fifteen years since the great political changes.

Under communism, the churches of the East Bloc developed different strategies for negotiating the difficult path between accommodation and resistance. As a rule, they sought to legitimize their accommodation theologically and to cover up the sinful failures of ecclesiastical leaders. The doctrine of justification, which connects confession of sin and forgiveness, remained hidden from view. How from our viewpoint today should we appraise the actions of these churches?

Immediately after the revolution in Hungary in 1989, István Török pointed to the complexity of "coming to terms with the past":

> [It was] as if lack of interest descended like a cloud over the decades behind us, although all of us personally were representatives of this theology of yesterday, active representatives of certain gradations of positive or negative relation to it. . . . For a proper assessment, however, a careful analysis of the theological thinking of that time is essential. Its mistakes and its good intentions must be investigated. Otherwise we may overlook the fact that there may be at times only a verbal difference between the theology of yesterday and today. We may find that we are continuing under a different banner — perhaps under a different name — along the same road that we traveled before.[3]

---

3. István Török, "A megújulás teológiai feltétele" (The Theological Preconditions of Renewal), *Confessio* 1 (1990): 122-24.

1. The Message of Justification in the Context of Eastern and Central Europe

Coming to terms with the past is a challenge for an entire society. The church can deal with this problem only by being closely connected to its society. The social and political upheavals of the last decades have led worldwide to the organization of various symposia, commissions, and research projects under the key terms of "justice" and "reconciliation." Experience and research projects confirm that — in addition to penal law and politics — dealing with the past, as well as working for reconciliation, are significantly influenced by religious, cultural traditions. The following considerations are related to the European, particularly the Hungarian, experience.

1.1. A New Beginning or Continuity?

In distinction from South Africa and the former German Democratic Republic, efforts to come to terms with the past in Hungary did not take a political or judicial form. No commissions — along the lines of the South African Truth and Reconciliation Commission[4] — were established to contribute publicly to reconciliation between the perpetrators and the victims of the former regime. No public institutions intentionally concerned themselves with the victims and their fates. Already at the beginning of the 1990s, attempts at judicial reevaluation of the past as well as establishment of a parliamentary committee (along the lines of the German Commission of Inquiry)[5] met with failure.[6]

There are several reasons for the complete absence of public encounter, discussion, and exchange between those who enacted or carried out

4. Truth and Reconciliation Commission Website, www.doj.gov.za/trc; see *Truth and Reconciliation Commission of South Africa Report* (Cape Town, October 1998).

5. See *Materialien der Enquete-Kommission: "Aufarbeitung der Geschichte und Folgen der SED-Diktatur in Deutschland,"* vols. 1-9, ed. Deutschen Bundestag (12. Wahlperiode des deutschen Bundestages) (Baden-Baden: Nomos Verlagsgesellschaft, 1995).

6. See "Az igazságtétel nehézségei: Az ELTE Bölcsészettudományi Karának Társadalom-tudományiés Etika Tanszékeáltal rendezett szimpózium anyaga" (The Difficulties of Maintaining Justice: Texts of a Symposium Organized by the Chair of Ethics and Social Sciences of the Humanities Faculty of the Eötvös Loránd University in Budapest), *Világosság* 8-9 (1990): 661-77. Also, see Sándor Fazakas, *Erinnerung und Versöhnung* (Budapest: Kálvin Kiadó, 2004).

the policies of the earlier regime and its victims. As Joachim Gauck in looking at the German Democratic Republic perceptively remarked, the secular state does not feel competent to adjudicate questions of the "moral" or "metaphysical" dimensions of guilt. The state does not view it as its task to make space for the spiritual and religious dimensions of reconciliation.[7] Guilt and forgiveness are supposed to be resolved in the personal sphere rather than being politically institutionalized. In addition, *political* and *socio-psychological* factors have impeded both disclosure of the truth about past injustices and the nurturing of reconciliation.

Without providing a detailed political analysis of social developments in Hungary and surrounding countries, we can simply state that many people have regarded the absence of a comprehensive reevaluation of the past to be an "intended byproduct"[8] of the peaceful political transition, by which the old political elite handed its power over to the new elite.[9] Political efforts to deal with the past have had to steer between Scylla and Charybdis, between making a clean break with the past on the one hand and politically investigating the earlier elite on the other. Calls to forget the past or, alternatively, to disqualify political opponents by associating them with the past, have inevitably served particular political interests.[10] But

---

7. "Gespräch mit Joachim Gauck, 2.6.1997, BStU Berlin," quoted in R.-K. Wüstenberg, "Versöhnung durch Wahrheit: Die politische Dimension der Versöhnung in Südafrika und Deutschland," in *Wahrheit, Recht und Versöhnung: Auseinandersetzung mit der Vergangenheit nach den politischen Umbrüchen in Südafrika und Deutschland,* ed. R.-K. Wüstenberg (Frankfurt am Main: Peter Lang Verlag, 1998), p. 117.

8. Rudolf Tőkés, "Az új magyar politikai elit," *Valóság* 12 (1990): 10; and M. János Rainer, "Múltunk kritikus kérdései — 1956," *Életés Irodalom* (June 16, 2000): 9-10.

9. Samuel Huntington distinguishes three categories — "revolution," "replacement," and "exchanging places" — for the social upheavals in Latin America and Southern and Eastern Europe. By "revolution," he understands the process of democratization initiated by the reform communists; by "replacement," the total overthrow of the old regime and the taking of power by the opposition; by "exchanging places," a unified undertaking by the reigning party and the opposition. For the Hungarian revolution, in my view, all three categories complement each other. See Samuel P. Huntington, "Democratization and Security in Eastern Europe," in *Uncertain Futures: Eastern Europe and Democracy,* ed. Peter Volten (New York: Institute for East-West Security Studies, 1990), p. 41.

10. This is worked out more precisely in Dagmar Unverhau, ed., *Lustration, Aktenöffnung, demokratischer Umbruch in Polen, Tschechien, der Slowakei und Ungarn: Referate der Tagung der BstU und der Akademie für Politische Bildung Tutzing vom 26-28.10.1998* (Münster: Lit Verlag, 1999). Also, see Gary Smith and Avishai Margalit, eds., *Amnestie oder die Politik der Erinnerung in der Demokratie* (Frankfurt am Main: Suhrkamp, 1997).

where political will or interest is lacking, legal measures to deal with the past also remain problematic. It is very difficult to make judicial judgments about crimes that occurred in a different political context from the present. It is very difficult to use the present system of justice in relation to the old system without causing new forms of injustice.

1.2. Fear and the Identity Crisis

Although no political force or social group has gone to either extreme of condemning the past completely or arguing for total social change, different fears have nevertheless emerged with respect to how to deal with the past objectively. From a socio-psychological point of view, there is nothing remarkable about the fact that left to themselves people avoid examining their past as a history of guilt. They prefer to deny it rather than to look at it self-critically. When people, however, play down their guilt and zealously try instead to justify and defend themselves, new crises arise: new injustices, untruths, lies, and thus further guilt.

In addition to the fear of retribution, a "lesser fear" affects individuals. Collective remembering and repentance are hindered by people's desire to maintain a sense of continuity with their former way of life, by the loss of their earlier identity, and by the fact that values that were once in force are no longer valid. Whenever the guilt of the past is reduced to a personal matter and the individual is not allowed to move beyond his or her past, there can be no breakthrough to accepting guilt and repenting. Rather, fear becomes the starting point for new forms of servility, dependence, and compromise. Whenever in addition fear is politicized, one hears talk of the "scapegoat syndrome" and the "martyr complex." This twofold tendency was present from the beginning of the 1990s in Hungarian society. As Ferenc Pataki correctly points out, the assessment of history became the occasion for hostile judgments lacking all objectivity, on the one hand; on the other, the martyrdom that some had suffered led to the social phenomenon that they were regarded as eminently suited for special societal roles, offices, and privileges, regardless of their personal abilities.[11]

A fundamental reevaluation of this history can eliminate political misuse of such fears, and can assist us in critiquing self-styled autobiogra-

---

11. Ferenc Pataki, "Társadalomlélektani tényezők a magyar rendszerváltásban," *Valóság* 6 (1990): 1-16, esp. 15.

phies and new myths of identity. But precisely for that reason, it is also the case that the events of 1989-90 in Hungary and most of Eastern and Central Europe do not meet with an unambiguously positive echo in the collective memory of the population.

This social context shapes the particular situation in which the church finds itself. The Catholic theologian István Máté-Tóth uses the results of psychoanalysis to assess the church. He refers to Sigmund Freud's concept of "the inhibited mourner" and to Yorick Spiegel's categories of different phases of grief.[12] Máté-Tóth writes, "If the process of grieving is interrupted and not completed, the patient then remains in a pathological connection to the deceased and can easily and hastily enter into a (second) marriage."[13] This image applies to the Hungarian churches in the period 1948-89 as well as after the democratic revolution of 1989. The sudden death of the traditional social role of the church in 1948-50 hit Christians like a shock. Systematic discrimination against Christians, dissolution of church institutions, and selective replacement of church leaders by puppet figures loyal to the state prevented the church from making sense of its new situation. The church was not in the position to respond to these radical changes or to reflect on them theologically. Rather, it continued pathologically to stand beside the deathbed of "the feudal-clerical role of the church,"[14] and thus was never able to get beyond the shock. Today we need to remember and reevaluate this grieving process.

This pathology also explains why the churches in Hungary reacted so slowly to the events of 1989. They remained pathologically attached to their old ways of thinking and unconsciously sought to reconstruct old and familiar forms of church identity.[15] In addition, they were ambivalent about coming to terms with the past. On the one hand, they saw the importance of interpreting the past and confronting the churches' compromises, and did not simply want to forget everything. To find a way into the future and to avoid past mistakes, they knew that the past had to become

12. András Máté-Tóth, *Theologie in Ost (Mittel) Europa: Ansätze und Traditionen* (Vienna: Schwabenverlag, 2002), pp. 173-76. Also, see Yorick Spiegel, *Der Prozess des Trauerns: Analyse und Beratung* (Munich: Kaiser-Taschenbücher, 1981), and Sigmund Freud, "Erinnern, Wiederholen und Durcharbeiten," in Sigmund Freud, *Gesammelte Werke*, vol. 10 (Frankfurt am Main: Fischer-Verlag, 1967).

13. András Máté-Tóth, *Theologie in Ost (Mittel) Europa*, p. 174.

14. András Máté-Tóth, *Theologie in Ost (Mittel) Europa*, p. 174.

15. Pataki, "Társadalomlélektani," pp. 14-15.

transparent. So, the churches began to sponsor careful historical research. On the other hand, the churches wanted to come to terms with the past in a *pastoral theological* way and to make important distinctions: Who suffered *what*, under *what* pressures, and with *what* modus vivendi? Who made *what* compromises in order — more or less successfully — to create space for the church?

In each case, it is essential to judge matters of guilt and confession of guilt in terms of both the earlier political context and the relationship of reconciliation and forgiveness. The General Synod of the Reformed Church in Hungary has not been satisfied with the practice of voluntary self-examination. It has asserted that the church must also reflect on these matters theologically — not only to avoid the instrumentalization of the question of guilt by political or church interests but also, above all, to serve the church's self-knowledge and renewal.[16]

1.3. The Interpretation of History as Self-Justification

Another problem of coming to terms with the past is the temptation to identify the acts of God with the events of history, a temptation that characterized the theological worldview of the "Church in Socialism." After the loss of the Second World War people spoke of the judgment of God, but the fact that the church continued to exist during socialism was understood — in spite of the sins of the past — as a sign of God's grace. Thus socialism became the period of grace. This "message" was called "prophetic," because it appealed to Old Testament prophecy and oriented itself to the destiny of the people of God in history. The order of the day was seen as God's command, and historical events as a manifestation of the will of God. Resistance to tyranny (for example, the 1956 popular uprising, after whose bloody suppression the old order was strengthened) was branded as "rebellion against the Word of God." This view had the result of bringing the churches into line politically and justifying their accommodation to the state.

It has been Vályi Nagy who has most consistently applied Barth's "No!" to a theological view of history. He argues that the theme of history

---

16. *A Magyarországi Református Egyház XI: Zsinatának jegyzőkönyve* (Minutes, 11th synod of Hungarian Reformed Church), 12.ülésszak, 154/2001, sz. határozat. 2001, május 10.

is one of the basic unexplored problems of modern theology.[17] Drawing on Barth's polemical work "Theologische Existenz Heute" (1933) and the Barmen Declaration (1934), Nagy attempts to expose the untenable premises of the theological thinking on history that characterized the Hungarian church leadership. As early as 1955, that is, at a time in which the communist regime had already forced the church to cooperate, he wrote that the "mission of the church does not consist in recognizing so-called historical necessities and cooperating with 'historical forces,' and also not in infusing these necessities with Christian ideas and morality. The mission of the church refers to the 'one thing needful' (cf. Luke 10:42), thus to the salvation event — and only in that way to secular history."[18] The source of revelation is not the structure of states, peoples, or societies but rather God's Word alone. Knowledge of God does not emerge from the church's option for particular political interests. The foundation of the church — theoretically and practically, internally and externally — does not consist in a philosophy of history but in the message of the Crucified and Resurrected Lord.

In searching for theological criteria for church renewal after the 1989 revolution, István Török similarly moves Christology to the center of the church's proclamation. Jesus Christ is the "one Word of God" and thus the only head of the church. In a seminal lecture he argues: "Characteristic of heresy is that, next to Jesus Christ as the center, heresy wants to make something else a secondary center. This secondary center then begins to grow and turns the primary center into its servant. Such secondary aspects can . . . be nationalism built on a racist basis or dictatorial socialism."[19]

Both Nagy and Török look skeptically at the political revolutions of 1989-90 in Hungary and Central and Eastern Europe. They fear that misguided theological interpretations of history could again become fashionable, with the effect of limiting the chances for objective investigation of the past. At issue is the not superfluous question of whether Christian theology and faith should either unconditionally confirm secular politics and economics, or critically assess them. Neither "confirmation" nor "transforma-

---

17. Ervin Vályi Nagy, "Wahrheit und Geschichte," in *Geschichtserfahrung und die Suche nach Gott*, ed. Ágnes Vályi-Nagy (Stuttgart, Berlin, and Cologne: Kohlhammer, 2000), p. 97.

18. Ervin Vályi Nagy, "Gott oder Geschichte? Über die Prämissen der heutigen reformierten Kirchenführung in Ungarn (1955)," in *Geschichtserfahrung und die Suche nach Gott*, p. 32.

19. István Török, "A megújulás teológiai feltétele," pp. 122-24.

tion" should be the reality, goal, or task of theology and church.[20] It is more important to ask: What role do we accord the biblical message of the justifying act of God in the theological evaluation of historical reality today?

The question of the relationship of God's will to history is still significant today: the necessary distinction between historical truths and God's revelation means that there can be no retreat into "theological abstraction" — as Gerhard Sauter states[21] — or refuge in an understanding of salvation as something internal and private without political relevance. On the contrary, we need increased critical theological reflection on both the past and the present of the church in Eastern Europe.

2. Justification and Reconciliation in Concrete Experiential Contexts

Critical theological reflection on guilt and forgiveness in order to come to terms with the past would be in the interest of the churches' very mission — not only to preserve peace or to do justice to social expectations but also to highlight the social relevance of justification in a world in which politico-economic structures always produce victims. In the following observations I will refer to several problems that are of particular interest in this connection.

2.1. The Problem of Collective Guilt and God's Justifying Grace

Church history demonstrates that confession of corporate guilt has always been an essential element of Christian community. Today, the historical experiences of the twentieth century — world wars, millions of victims of concentration camps and the Gulag, suffering and human rights violations under communist dictators — have also led secular societies to recognize the collective dimensions of guilt, and the need for social reconciliation.

---

20. Jan Milič Lochman, "Ökumenische Theologie der Revolution," *Evangelische Theologie* 27 (1967): 644; also, see Ervin Vályi Nagy, "Theologie als Bestätigung und als Öffnung: Wirkliche Wandlung oder Variation des Gleichen?," in *Geschichtserfahrung und die Suche nach Gott*, p. 66.

21. Gerhard Sauter, "Theologische Kriterien für kirchliches Handeln nach dem Ende des Ost-West-Konfliktes," *Evangelische Theologie* 3 (1995): 260-77, esp. 272.

Nevertheless, one might question whether societies can deal with the supra-personal dimensions of guilt. Can one really speak of the collective involvement of a people in guilt? While the answer of the victim is a self-evident "yes," there is considerable evidence that contemporary societies still resist acknowledging collective guilt. In some European countries, laws that once served to justify expulsion of, or other forms of retribution against, particular ethnic groups have not been removed from the books. Peoples of different cultural, religious, and national backgrounds remain strangely silent about the crimes that they have committed against each other. This collective blindness suggests the impossibility of acknowledging collective responsibility, and may even give rise to new dictatorships. We seem left with the passive acceptance of the injustices committed both before and after the 1989-90 revolutions. In response, Zsolt Kozma, the prominent Reformed theologian from Klausenburg (Cluj), states: "I believe that God never confronts us with the question of why we never passionately and openly took action against those in power, but he cannot close his eyes to our compliance, our omissions, and our self-ghettoization."[22]

Here we cannot trace the philosophical and theological discussion of the question of collective guilt after World War II further. We can only point out that assertions of collective guilt have covered a wide spectrum, from the *culpability in corporate guilt* in the Old Testament,[23] through the view that the *collective* entity can also be treated *as an ethical subject,*[24] to the conviction that collective guilt arises from the *interaction of individual failures and social systems.*[25] Examples of collective guilt have included enterprises that act criminally, peoples as national collectives that engage in ethnic and martial conflicts, and churches that develop strategies of social conformity.

In the latter case, the issue is not only the personal failures of church

---

22. Zsolt Kozma, *Önazonosságés küldetés* (Identity and Mission) (Kolozsvár: n.p., 2001), p. 10.

23. See Christof Gestrich, *Die Wiederkehr des Glanzes in der Welt: Die christliche Lehre von der Sünde und ihrer Vergebung, in gegenwärtiger Verantwortung* (Tübingen: Mohr Siebeck, 1989), pp. 284-93.

24. See Martin Honecker, "Individuelle Schuld und kollektive Verantwortung: Können Kollektive sündigen?," *Zeitschrift für Theologie und Kirche* 90 (1993): 213-30.

25. Michael Beintker, *Die Eigendynamik der Sünde in sozialen Systemen* (unpublished manuscript), pp. 9-10.

officers or employees (which was certainly the case)[26] but also the subsequent institutional crisis. What Martin Honecker has stated of the church in the former GDR is true of what occurred in other Eastern Bloc countries as well: "In a totalitarian state, churches' ways and forms of behavior are adapted to the political structure."[27] The churches were shaped by their historical context. The fact that church leaders cooperated with the state bureaucracy shows that they trusted more in church diplomacy than in the power of God.[28] The aim of church leaders was to preserve the churches. But their actions become problematic if they do not later confess or acknowledge them as sinful but instead legitimate and glorify them as inevitable compromises. Such a stance is more than a personal failure, for it contributes to the church's loss of credibility in the public eye and to a deep crisis of trust among church members in relation to the church.

Historically, failure in office (whether ecclesiastical or nonecclesiastical) has consequences for the whole social system.[29] Omissions and irresponsibility among leaders result in collective guilt. In light of the historical experiences of the most recent past, it is no wonder that no one in the political sphere has confessed to such "position-specific guilt." But Christian faith cannot stop simply at the establishment of collective guilt. As long as the failures and injustices that church leaders committed are generalized and hidden within the collective or, conversely, collective guilt is personalized according to the scapegoat principle,[30] Christian faith must

---

26. Churches were in no way natural allies for the communist dictatorship but were, rather, viewed as the last pillars of the imperialistic enemy. The situation in the beginning was as follows: pastors, professors of theology, and church leaders were arrested, deported, and tortured, and forced, asked, or invited to cooperate with the police. The question was: What should they do "sub poena non existentiae," and what should be seen as going beyond that in the sense of eager and voluntary cooperation? On this matter, see János Antal, ed., "Coping with the Past," in *Life in Fullness: Global Vision, Local Action* (Proceedings of the European Area Council of the World Alliance of Reformed Churches in Oradea, Romania, August 18-23, 2002) (Geneva: World Alliance of Reformed Churches, 2004), pp. 44-64; and Frigyes Kahler, *III/III-as történelmi olvasókönyv: Adalékok az emberi jogok magyarországi helyzetéhez az 1960-asévekben* (Documents from the III/III Division), vols. 1-3 (Budapest: Kairosz Kiadó, 2001, 2002, 2005).

27. Honecker, *Individuelle Schuld*, p. 224.

28. Honecker, *Individuelle Schuld*, p. 225.

29. See Eilert Herms, "Schuld in der Geschichte: Zum 'Historikerstreit,'" in Eilert Herms, *Gesellschaft gestalten* (Tübingen: J. C. B. Mohr, 1991), pp. 1-24, esp. 15-16.

30. István Török also fears that the greatest hindrance in the search for suitable criteria

continue to inquire into the origins and dynamics of this guilt. Christian faith is authorized to do so by the reference to the One who has taken all guilt upon himself — both individual as well as collective — in order to liberate the world from bondage. Without the faith that God judges sin by taking it upon himself, every effort to speak of guilt stands in danger of being politically instrumentalized and thus of being left unresolved.

If we are to deal with the guilt of the past, we need sober and honest analysis. There must be open dialogue about injustices caused and experienced, and a willingness to experience the liberating effect of forgiveness. The church should be a place in which people can say without compulsion or fear, "We have sinned." The justifying act of God opposes all political instrumentalization of historical guilt, including individual and ecclesiastical failure.[31] Dealing with guilt in such a way within the church can help society as a whole deal with its guilt, so that earlier mistakes are not simply repeated and new injustices are averted. In this sense, Christian theology and faith can challenge interest-driven interpretations of history and offer a way forward into a common future.

2.2. *The Christian Witness to Freedom*

"Freedom" became a leading idea in Eastern and Central European society after the political changes of 1989-90. Freedom would give form to public life, the process of democratization, political and economic restructuring, and reform in the areas of education, moral formation, and culture. We must ask, however, whether freedom understood as the absence of oppression, deprivation, and injustice experienced in the past is sufficient for the future. Are there also positive characteristics to freedom as actually lived? Is there a freedom that not only leads out of the oppressive straits of the past but also protects against dependence on the new power structures of the present?

In 1992 Eberhard Jüngel drew an analogy between the European his-

---

for a new orientation in theology will be the personalization and reduction of historical guilt. Instead of confession of guilt and penitence, a search for sins and a call for retribution result. See *1972-1989 (The Boundary Question in Our Service)* (Budapest: Kálvin Kiadó, 2002), pp. 172-74.

31. "Non est tam magna peccatrix ut Christiana ecclesia." Martin Luther: *Predigt am Ostermorgen*, 9. April 1531. See WA 34/1, pp. 271-77, esp. 276.

tory of freedom and the liberating presence of God.[32] The document of the Leuenberger churches, "Das christliche Zeugnis von der Freiheit," also emphasizes this point: "In order to understand the historical experiences of limited freedom, it will be necessary to interpret them in terms of the biblical-Reformation history of freedom."[33] Liberating speech arises wherever historical experiences are interpreted in accordance with the gospel, and wherever one is able to view the world through the Holy Scriptures. Protestant theology must concern itself with social analysis, historical interpretation, and philosophical explanation in order to make world events comprehensible for the Christian faith and to clearly distinguish liberation through grace from political processes of liberation.

The message of justification is constitutive of the biblical-Reformation witness to freedom. The horizon of all Christian expressions of freedom is — to use Michael Beintker's words — the *solus Christus*.[34] *Soteriology* precedes freedom. This kind of freedom cannot be earned. It is solely Christ's act, which he entrusts to humans through faith.[35] In faith, humans recognize their captivity to sin, but also the divine act of liberation that frees them. On the cross of Christ, God has revealed his judgment of human guilt, in order to give new life to lost sinners. No human life is so trapped in sin that a new beginning is not possible. The cross enables us to speak of sin, including historical guilt and our current entanglements, in a way that does not kill but liberates.[36] Sin itself has been judged, and its weight no longer destroys the sinner.

The gospel overcomes whatever separates human beings from Christ and from each other. It neither downplays nor overlooks sin and guilt. On the contrary, it sharpens our awareness of the world's injustices and destructive powers, and strengthens our search for justice. God's justifying

---

32. Eberhard Jüngel, "Das Evangelium und die evangelischen Kirchen Europas: Referat auf der Europäischen Evangelischen Versammlung, Budapest 1992," in *EPD-Dokumentation* 17 (1992): 43-66.

33. "Das christliche Zeugnis von der Freiheit: Beratungsergebnis der Südeuropagruppe," in *Wachsende Gemeinschaft in Zeugnis und Dienst: Reformatorische Kirchen in Europa: Texte der 4. Vollversammlung der Leuenberger Kirchengemeinschaft in Wien, 3. bis 10. Mai 1994*, ed. W. Hüffmeier and C.-R. Müller (Frankfurt: O. Lembeck, 1995), pp. 133-53, esp. 141.

34. Beintker, *Rechtfertigung in der neuzeitlichen Lebenswelt*, p. 51.

35. Beintker, *Rechtfertigung in der neuzeitlichen Lebenswelt*, p. 51.

36. Beintker, *Rechtfertigung in der neuzeitlichen Lebenswelt*, p. 30.

act of liberation is not simply release from captivity. True freedom is already present where human beings no longer live under suspicion of each other. Christian freedom lies in the inner part of the human being, so that external conditions do not decide whether a human being is free or not.[37] God's liberating act reaches its goal when the liberated inner person turns to his neighbor in service and love, and demands that they grant to each other the rights of freedom that they previously refused each other.

In struggling to liberate and assist the neighbor, the Christian's internal freedom pushes outward. It becomes worldly; it becomes Christian faith for public affairs.[38] Such freedom is a matter not only of love, which is a category of personal ethics and requires personal relationship between persons, but also of responsibility. Christian freedom directed outward includes the struggle to remove structural social injustice. Christian responsibility refuses simply to accept mechanisms of oppression, or entrapment in the guilt of political or economic conditions. Because human freedom is vulnerable to misuse under the existing power relations, there will always be a need to distinguish between freedom as actually experienced and freedom as justly maintained. The Christian faith and the gospel declare that "the freedom of the children of God" (Rom. 8:23) cannot be limited. This message gives us hope and courage *to push for increased external freedom* and to encourage people *to preserve their inner freedom,* also in conditions of inhumanity.

The call for more freedom and responsibility remains insufficient as long as we do not also search for creating time and space in which people can reflect on the injustices that they have suffered, express their pain, and experience the liberating power of forgiveness. The churches have understood it as their task to open up islands of freedom in which people can deal with the burden of remembering and in which reconciliation can be practiced for the sake of a new future. In a period of globalization, society and politics are less able to create such forums for dealing with the shadows of the past. Where relation to the past stands in the service of particular political interests — and where closing or opening the files of the secret police do not serve to establish historical truth

---

37. See Martin Luther, *On the Freedom of a Christian* (1520), in *Martin Luther: Sections from his Writing with an Introduction,* ed. John Dillenberger (Garden City: Doubleday & Co., 1961), pp. 42-85.

38. Cited from Bishop Dr. Gusztáv Bölcskei, "Report to the Synod of the Churches beyond the Tisza" (Debrecen, Dec. 5, 2004).

for the sake of reconciliation — new injustices will be inevitable. Reconciliation depends on the difficult task of bringing people together who once stood on different sides or encountered each other in opposing roles. In the sheltered space of the church community, a solidarity can emerge in which victims and perpetrators alike openly express their pain and suffering and remember the past.[39] This coming to a sense of a common past is the pre-condition for a future that people shape together in freedom and mutual understanding. Through providing such forums of forgiveness, the church makes an essential contribution to the formation of a public conscience.

2.3. Reconciliation and Reparation

Calls for reconciliation sound good in both political and church statements concerning the past. They give the impression that the conflicts of the past have been resolved, that the truth has been explained, and that the country or countries in question are on the threshold of a new, just society. Reconciliation, however, is not an act that occurs once and for all but rather a process between people or groups who were previously on opposite sides — a process that does not follow any general and abstract scheme. There are great differences with respect to the conflicts that existed, the particular violations that occurred, and the willingness of individuals to be reconciled. This process has several steps: (1) the restoration of the self-respect of the individual or a community requires the discovery of truth; (2) the recovery of mutual respect depends on the establishment of justice; (3) reconciliation and forgiveness mean dealing with personal guilt and bringing about reconciliation between perpetrator and victim; and (4) this reconciliation has a *material aspect*.[40]

Frank Crüsemann shows by means of the story of Jacob and Esau

---

39. Though more the exception than the rule, such "forums of reconciliation" have appeared in many Hungarian churches. There are similar reports about home study groups in congregations of the Evangelical Churches of the former GDR, with active participation of those who played different roles in this past. See David Gill and Ulrich Schröter, *Das Ministerium für Staatssicherheit: Anatomie des Mielke-Imperiums* (Berlin: Rowohlt, 1991).

40. Hans-Richard Reuter, "Ethik und Politik der Versöhnung: Prinzipielles zu einem aktuellen Thema," in *Politik der Versöhnung*, ed. Gerhard Beestermöller and Hans-Richard Reuter (Stuttgart: Kohlhammer, 2002), pp. 15-36, esp. 36.

(Gen. 33) how this process can take place.[41] Jacob robbed Esau of God's blessing and had to flee to a foreign country. He is able to return only when he has been reconciled with his brother. That happens when he shares God's blessing with his brother — a blessing that in the Hebrew Bible is understood as having a material side: a large number of children, and wealth in land and cattle. Jacob declares himself ready to hand over these possessions to his brother, and Esau accepts Jacob's offer of reconciliation.

Reconciliation between people or legal entities has to do with justice, memory, reparation, legal agreements, and material compensation. Symbols and rituals can provide only fragmentary, anticipatory, and provisional solutions. From this perspective, the efforts of the churches in Eastern and Central Europe (particularly in Romania and Western Ukraine) to receive compensation for church property that was compulsorily nationalized are understandable. Existential needs, damages, and losses should not be ignored. Although a *restitutio ad integrum* remains God's prerogative, reconciliation does not occur without reference to people's needs. Reconciliation with another human being is also reconciliation with the image of God in him. Human beings are located in a system of coordinates with two axes: they are placed in relation both to their fellow human beings and to God. In order to avoid a theologically abstract notion of reconciliation, these two axes must be kept in relation. A one-sided concentration on relations between persons on the one side or between God and the individual on the other would distort the biblical understanding of reconciliation. It would effectively deny that God's reconciliation with human beings is the decisive ground for reconciliation among human beings.

The church should be prepared to assume a new public role in a world that has now become "borderless" but is constantly creating new borders. Excluded from speaking to social issues during the days of communism, the church today must again participate in public discourse. In order to participate competently, it must create forums and free spaces in its own life: spaces where people from all walks of life can come together to discuss their responsibility for matters of faith and ethics, and the criteria for alternative ways of life. In these islands of freedom and hope, people should

---

41. Frank Crüsemann, "Nicht 'an dir allein': Aspekte biblischen Umgangs mit Schuld und die Traditionen der Kirche," in *Verantwortung-Schuld-Vergebung: Loccumer Protokolle* 54 (1998), ed. Wolfgang Vögele (Rehburg and Loccum: Evangelische Akademie Loccum, 1999), pp. 47-48.

come to see that justice is more than a concept aligned with modernity's ideals of equality, and more than a matter of making reparations — which primarily involves questions of property. Rather, human justice always involves the "other" justice that is based in the justifying act of God.[42] This divine justice creates community with God, and community among people and peoples. This kind of justice does truly transcend boundaries — boundaries that are drawn by the guilt of the past or the injustices of the present. Because it is a justice that enables us to live in, and to strive for, true community, it holds forth great promise to the world far beyond just the boundaries of the church.

42. Michael Weinrich, "Die andere Gerechtigkeit: Zur Einführung," in *"Auf dem Pfad der Gerechtigkeit ist Leben . . .": Die "andere" Gerechtigkeit. Biblisch-theologische, systematisch-theologische und reformatorische Akzente,* ed. Michael Weinrich (Bovenden: Foedus-Verlag, 1996), pp. 2-7, esp. 5.

11 "Meaning" as a Replacement for "Justification": On the Consequences of Secularization and Pluralization

Hendrik M. Vroom

The essays in this volume concern the doctrine of the justification. In this doctrine lies the heart of Protestant theology. The question is, however, whether the justification of the sinner is still an issue in the modern, secularized, and religiously plural culture. Nobody's perfect — so why all the fuss? After all, there are much more serious problems in a world ravaged by natural disasters. Moreover, many people today no longer find meaning in their existence. Rich or poor, spiritually healthy or not — people lose the sense that their lives have direction. Often they notice the loss only later. They become depressed and burned out. They no longer experience joy in living, have no energy for taking the initiative, and seek refuge in pleasant possessions and in superficial "enjoyments," such as the hobby and travel cults of the rich nations of the world. The question of the meaning of existence can then be avoided, but underneath all the pleasure, travel, and fun, meaninglessness shows through. Some people have therefore said that the church should not stress sin and justification but, rather, should declare the Good Tidings that each life is valuable in God's eyes, that every human being has been created in the image of God. What is needed is to preach God's victory over evil.

This important question touches directly upon the mission of the church, both within the church itself and in regard to those who have lost their faith or are on the way to doing so. The question of meaning is more fundamental than that of justification, it is claimed, and because the churches do not pose this most fundamental question, they lose much ground. We cannot bypass this question — that much is certain.

We must investigate whether the question of meaning is indeed prior to that of justification, and what we mean by the word "meaning." It could be the case that one definition gives meaning priority above justification, whereas another definition leads to other conclusions. It may be that existential experiences such as meaning/meaninglessness and good/not good stand next to each other without the one being subsumed by the other. Both may be part of a more comprehensive group of experiences or two aspects of one basic experience. Still another possibility is that the question of justification is a fundamental dimension of the question of meaning.

These two questions (meaning and justification) cannot be separated from each other if we think of meaning as "successful contact with values." If it is a value to love one's neighbor as oneself, then the fact that people love their neighbors as themselves should contribute to a meaningful life. Conversely, if one is unable to love one's neighbors, then the meaning of one's own existence becomes problematic. Are people good? Let us suppose that a person succeeds for the most part in loving his neighbor as himself. He then finds himself somewhere "between" meaning and meaninglessness and "between" success and failure. Western people have difficulty separating the question, "Why am I alive?," from success and failure. Does that not lead inevitably to the question of justification?

Here the connection between "meaning" and "success" lies in "successful contact with values." Under what conditions can I say that I experience my life as meaningful because I "succeed" in realizing "my" values? Am I to be the judge of that? Do I have a capacity for self-judgment that evaluates my performance, and if the judgment is negative, lights up a red light on my internal dashboard — and thus gives me the feeling that I have not succeeded in making contact with my values? But on what grounds am I then judged? On the basis of values that I have chosen and goals that I myself have set? Or on the basis of values and norms that obtain for people in general? If I set them myself, does that guarantee their validity? If we are talking about universally human goals, how can they give *my* life direction?

In any case, the question of meaning can never concern goals that I have chosen only according to my own tastes. The experience of meaninglessness is, for many people, not in having failed to achieve their goals but rather in doubting the very validity of those goals or, more strongly, in realizing that these goals do not provide any real satisfaction. Poor people can experience life as meaningful, and rich people can experience it as meaningless. What kind of values are we talking about in connection with "meaning"? And how is "successful contact with values" to be related to "living rightly" or "not living rightly"? In these last two questions lies the heart of the problem.

In this contribution we will first look at definitions of meaning and meaninglessness and the values connected with them; will distinguish four possible ways of connecting meaning and justification; and will see which of those are valid. Then, we will analyze Paul Tillich's assertion that the experience of the loss of meaning has taken over the function that the question of justification used to perform. Subsequently, we will look at several examples of the loss of meaning and how they relate to the question of justification. Can the gospel speak to people in different ways — sometimes more in terms of the worth of the person and the meaning of life, and sometimes more in terms of forgiveness and justification? In conclusion we will ask whether every answer to the question of meaning does not also refer to the justification of sinners.

Meaning and Values

All things and circumstances worth striving for have value. Values can involve giving shape and form to something (a nice park), doing social work (providing for the needy), doing a good job, or even developing one's character. Virtue is, after all, a value. Any particular society has a great number of shared values. Many of those values have been inscribed into law: if someone is in mortal danger, we should help them; we may not steal; and we need to drive with our lights on when it is dark.

In addition to communal values there are personal values. To a certain extent these are shared values that we have made our own: someone who always drives carefully shares the value of traffic safety and makes that a priority. Every person has appropriated certain ideals for him- or herself, both in connection to a way of life (to be honest, to have friends) and as to goals (courses of study, the kind of work one does). People strive after values and (partly) choose them. We cannot realize all our ideals, and striving for one can render it impossible to realize another.[1] Life is full of choices.

---

1. See Connie Aarsbergen, *Isaiah Berlin: A Value Pluralist and Humanist View of Human Nature and the Meaning of Life* (Amsterdam and New York: Rodopi, 2006). Aarsbergen discusses the tragic element in life as well; people necessarily are confronted with conflicts of values and cannot realize them all.

Heidegger expressed that nicely in the idea that the human being is his possibilities,[2] a capacity that allows one to develop some possibilities at the price of excluding others. Every choice implies a risk, for we can never be sure that we will be able to "use" our capacities in a changing society. As long as possible, we adapt our choices to new situations, but the more we follow one track, the more limited we are in what we can and cannot achieve. We abandon some possibilities that come with our natural abilities and go in a different direction. Because such choices also depend on the influence of our larger social context, they are to a certain extent coincidental. No one can say beforehand whether other choices would not have been better.

The values that people make their own constitute a rather varied group. We can distinguish between "sorts" of values (the question here is not how to assess different values, but only to show that the connection between meaning and values is very nuanced). There are values such as the virtue of honesty that most people want to develop, and others, such as not harming others, to which they want to measure up, in addition to values that they hope to realize for themselves personally, such as having friends and acting "sensibly." And there are still other ideals that people only hope from afar to achieve, without becoming miserable if they do not. The word "sensibly" connects values and sense or meaning.[3] "Meaning" has to do with our lives as they are lived in relation to the values that we consider valid.

"Sensible" or "not sensible" is among the key emotions that guide our experience. We sometimes evaluate our behavior rationally, but we are also guided by our emotions. Some things make us cheerful, others happy; in some circumstances we are bored and in others we feel engaged. A sense of meaning is an element of such basic emotions and is therefore dependent on what happens. We cannot, after all, order ourselves to accept whatever happens to us as "sensible." Sometimes instead we must learn to value things from a different perspective.

It is helpful to compare the feeling of meaningfulness with the feeling of happiness. Paul Fries points out how widespread the idea of "the pur-

---

2. Martin Heidegger, *Sein und Zeit,* 11th ed. (Tübingen: Max Niemeyer Verlag, 1967), p. 143 (par. 31): "Dasein is in every case what it can be, and in the way in which it is its possibility" (my translation).

3. The Dutch and German words for sense and meaning are the same: *zin* (Dutch), *Sinn* (German). In Dutch, therefore, to act "sensibly" is to act "meaningfully."

suit of happiness" has become — it is, he says, one of the fundamental values in the U.S.A.[4] He is very critical of this, for one cannot simply produce a feeling of happiness. One can mow the grass, plant the bulbs, and prune the trees in order to enjoy the garden in the springtime and thus create the conditions for happiness, but one's feeling of happiness is more than just a product of one's actions. It is dependent on a wider context than just the inner courtyard of the garden and is more a disposition to see things in a positive light than the direct result of our efforts. A cheap feeling of happiness is deceptive. Moreover, there is the additional question of whether a feeling of happiness is truly an adequate criterion for a good and meaningful life. Fries argues that happiness is not all that important and certainly not in the crude versions that are fed to people through advertising. Happiness is about a delight in which one loses oneself. Sometimes people see a painting or hear a piece of music that leads them to forget themselves and, as it were, to become one with it. Sometimes people get so caught up in a task that they forget about time. Delight connects "a good feeling" with a judgment arising from one's experience that something is good and meaningful. But one can also do something meaningful that has nothing to do with a (superficial) feeling of happiness. One can believe that one must do something — even if it is unpleasant — and afterward feel satisfied, even though there is a price to pay.

That an act is meaningful has to do with how one evaluates it — whether consciously or unconsciously. Actually, evaluation is too intellectual a term, for at issue is the correspondence between someone's values and norms on the one hand and the actual situation on the other. If there is "sufficient" correspondence between our values and our lives, one can (often implicitly) experience meaningfulness. If that correspondence is missing, then one experiences a lack of "meaning" or has the impression that all one's efforts are or have been in vain. Without a "successful contact with values" the feeling of meaningfulness disappears. At this point an important distinction between happiness and meaning arises. Even under adverse circumstances, one can have the feeling of living meaningfully — a good example is the resistance fighter.

How can we define the "meaning of life" or "living meaningfully"

---

4. Paul Fries, "The Pursuit of Happiness, the Production of Evil and the New Christianity," in *Wrestling with God and Evil: Philosophical Reflections*, ed. Hendrik M. Vroom (Amsterdam and New York: Rodopi, 2007), pp. 75-90.

more closely? In his study of the relation between religious and secular ascriptions of meaning, Wessel Stoker discusses A. Burms and H. de Dijn, who say that "longing for meaning implies that we desire 'to be linked in one way or another with an external reality, with something that transcends us as individuals.'"[5] With Burms and De Dijn, Stoker can say: "that which produces in us an experience of meaning is transcendent to that experience."[6] Meaningfulness is a matter of placing our actions within a larger whole, even though Stoker does not want to see this whole as a tight unity.[7] Meaningfulness occurs if we preserve contact with important values. And we experience a lack of meaning when we are unable to achieve values that we esteem highly, or even "betray" those values.

In this regard, it is important to remember that the term "transcendent" need not refer to a (highest) being but, depending on one's worldview tradition, can be "filled in" by creation, the kingdom of God, a humane world, the acosmic brahman, Buddhist emptiness, or otherwise.

The Question of Meaning Is More Important Than the Quest for Justification

Having clarified the relation between meaning and transcendent values, we can now turn to the assertion that modern people do not ask for justification, that the confession of justification is not important or even has become obsolete, and that instead people search for the meaning of life. This view has been defended by Paul Tillich and his many followers. In his *Systematic Theology* Tillich writes that church proclamation should focus on the question of meaninglessness. The doctrine of justification should be less central than it once was.

According to Tillich, the justification of the sinner is at the core of the Christian faith. In this sense, Christian faith is radical — it goes to the root (*radix*) of human existence. The forgiveness of sins with nothing asked in return speaks to people who are trapped in the struggle "to better" themselves. Precisely through wanting to assert oneself, the individual is thrown

---

5. Wessel Stoker, *Is the Quest for Meaning the Quest for God?*, trans. Henry and Lucy Jansen (Amsterdam and Atlanta: Rodopi, 1996), p. 9.

6. Stoker, *Quest for Meaning*, p. 172.

7. Stoker, *Quest for Meaning*, pp. 80, 82.

back upon himself.[8] I would express this in the following way: by wanting to make oneself "good" and to justify oneself over and against the transcendental values that one acknowledges, one separates oneself from, and breaks connection with, the larger whole in which one stands. For that reason, truly becoming oneself requires letting go of oneself. Self-justification is a *contradictio in terminis*. It is arrogant, says Tillich, for people to think that they can conquer the evil within themselves and achieve unity with God through their own good will (p. 226).[9] Rather, they need a God who forgives them unconditionally.

Accepting this forgiveness, he writes, asks a great deal of humans, namely, the courage to believe, i.e., the courage "to surrender one's own goodness to God" (p. 226). This experience of faith — of justification by faith alone — lies at the heart of Paul's, Augustine's, and Luther's faith, even though each understands it in his own way. I will limit myself here to what Tillich says about Luther: Luther came to experience God's grace in place of God's wrath. He developed a deep and personal relationship to God that set aside the cosmic and ecclesiological contexts in which Paul and Augustine had understood faith (p. 227). Paul asked how he could be liberated from the burden of the law (self-justification). Luther cried out for a merciful God. This question is no longer posed in the modern period, Tillich claims. Doubt is now more prevalent than the (im)possibility of justifying oneself or finding grace in God's eyes. Radical doubt is uncertainty about the meaning of life. The dominant question that people now ask is not that of living rightly but that of the meaning of life (p. 227). In other words, people are no longer concerned about successful contact with values but with the very existence of values and thus their validity. How can people as "meaning-makers" derive the meaning of existence from successful contact with values that they themselves have constructed or chosen in an arbitrary way?[10]

This situation is more radical than that in which people sought for-

---

8. Paul Tillich, *Systematic Theology,* vol. 3 (Chicago: University of Chicago Press, 1963), p. 226.

9. Page numbers in the text refer to Tillich, *Systematic Theology.*

10. Paul Van Buren associates the radicalization of the trouble in which people find themselves with the radicalization of the question of God. The question is no longer whether God exists, but what the word "god" itself means, because people no longer understand the notion of a transcendent reality. See Paul Van Buren, *The Secular Meaning of the Gospel* (London: Macmillan, 1963), p. 84.

giveness and confessed that they came with empty hands, for no one can produce the meaning of life (p. 228). In this radical doubt Tillich sees a contemporary point of contact for the church's proclamation: God accepts the human person as valuable. Human beings can do nothing more than *accept* this proclamation of the meaningfulness of life.

Tillich has a good point here. Paul's traumatic experience was that even though he did more than could be required of him, he nevertheless committed radical evil: "I am Jesus, whom you persecute!" Thus, the issue of law and grace became central to his faith and his understanding of the gospel. Martin Luther also wrestled with his sin and discovered the superficiality of indulgences and self-chastisement as a way of cleansing oneself. *Sola gratia* was a joyful message because it took away fear and worry and set human beings into freedom before God. In other words, as Gerhard Ebeling writes, only as one stands before God's face does one truly see what sin is.[11] Outside of the context of a certain kind of faith, the message of forgiveness cannot be liberating.

As stated, Tillich has a point here. In a skeptical, postmodern culture in which people think that truth does not exist — just "your" truth or "my" truth — and in which values have no other basis than the will of the person who creates them, the message of *justificatio impii* will be incomprehensible. One shrugs one's shoulders and says at most: "We want to hear you again on this subject" (Acts 17:32). The question, "Am I good?," does not logically precede that of "Why am I actually alive?" It follows that the message of the gospel in some — possibly many — circumstances is that people are created by God and that their lives are meaningful to him.

Experiences of the Loss of Meaning

However, this does not imply that the question of meaning can take the place of the question of justification. There are other ways to relate meaning and justification in which one does not exclude the other. So let us have a better look at the experience of the loss of meaning.

I am not so certain that there is only one kind of experience of mean-

---

11. Gerhard Ebeling, "Theologie zwischen reformatorischem Sündenverständnis und heutiger Einstellung zum Bösen," in *Wort und Glaube III* (Tübingen: Mohr, 1975), pp. 173-204. Ebeling says that "sin is not a moral but a religious concept" (p. 191).

inglessness. Are there not many sides to human existence, each of which can lead to the loss of meaning? Whoever holds that different worldviews arise out of different foundational experiences should also look into the question of whether different kinds of negative experiences can lead to different experiences of meaninglessness.[12]

(1) One kind of experience of the loss of meaning occurs when one suddenly realizes that one is an arbitrary specimen among millions and that life is nothing but coincidences. One may have such an experience in the midst of a crowd of people: one suddenly sees that one is just like everyone else, on the way from point A to point B, determined by countless factors, entangled in a web of forces that control us, similar to the way in which the wind whips up the sand that settles down haphazardly according to the air currents: completely determined and in another sense completely contingent. Someone can suddenly be overcome by the feeling that he is like a drop in a river, a drop that can indeed believe that it leads its own life but is in fact a plaything of the many forces that drive it forward, without its contribution. This experience leads to a "naturalistic skepticism" and a loss of meaning: Who am I? What do I have that is really my own?[13]

(2) Other people have other experiences. In her comparative study of Wolfhart Pannenberg and the Zen thinker Keiji Nishitani, Christa Anbeek shows how because of merciless blows in life, people can lose heart, unable to see a future for themselves.[14] Some people go through more than can be endured. Because of earthquakes, drought, flooding, or hurricanes, hundreds of thousands can suddenly be left without shelter, or because of disease and accidents, they lose sight of the future that they had dreamed of. Who am I? I do not know — a plaything of dark fate? People lose trust in the dependability of existence.

(3) Still another experience of meaninglessness emerges from suffering constant injustice. That can be a matter of arbitrary treatment in the courts (one thinks here of Kafka's *The Process*), experiencing disloyalty, or

---

12. See Hendrik M. Vroom, *Religions and the Truth,* trans. John Rebel (Grand Rapids and Amsterdam: Eerdmans and Rodopi, 1989), pp. 321-42.

13. Precisely this experience of not-self can be "cherished" in Buddhist traditions in order to become detached from the self: "the great death."

14. Christa W. Anbeek, *Denken over de dood: de boeddhist K. Nishitani en de christen W. Pannenberg vergeleken* (Kampen: Kok, 1994), pp. 31-45.

observing that the bad often prosper but not those who look out for others. How often we hear of this in the Psalms!

Each of these experiences can lead to a loss of meaning. They are different, yet each emerges from an intense foundational experience of "determination" and non-self, of the arbitrariness of "fate" and of an immoral world. In the last two examples, what is doubted is not, strictly speaking, oneself but rather a meaningful world order in which one can live one's life meaningfully. The expression "the loss of meaning" covers different kinds of experiences.

Each of these losses of meaning is related in its own way to justification. The first case — a person who is fairly successful but suddenly experiences the hollowness of existence — is probably the best illustration of what Tillich has in mind. Here the gospel says: "You, like everyone else, are known to God, and God has given you a name." At a later stage, repentance, forgiveness, and justification by faith can emerge. If Luther's is the first kind of interconnection (one's justification enables one to find meaning in life), this scenario argues for a second: if the question of meaning is answered, the question of justification arises (though, as we will see, we can make this connection, at least from the Christian point of view, only conditionally).

In the second example, a life in great distress, the inadequacy of "the order of this world" is at issue. One has the feeling that life does not make sense and that the world falls short of reasonable standards. A *Christian* answer is that the order of this world is indeed passing away and that God will at one point be all in all (1 Cor. 7:31; 15:28).

In the third example, the justice of the world order is doubted. The pastor cannot say here: "Look at yourself; you are a sinner too." Although one must sometimes say, "No one is without sin, all have sinned," at other times one can only look at another and say, "Indeed, this is an upright person who has lived to the best of his or her ability." Whoever *always* and to everyone says, "All are sinners," does an injustice to the seriousness of injustice.

In all these examples the question of meaning has priority. That confirms that the experience of meaninglessness is a basic human experience, alongside the experience of having failed. So the proclamation of the justification of the sinner is not the only beginning point for the interpretation of the gospel.

I will give yet a fourth example. Someone works for his business, is successful, becomes rich, and does good to others but begins to feel after thirty years that his life has lost joy and has not brought him that which is truly important. This person realizes that he cannot make himself into a "good person" and that a good life does not emerge purely through one's efforts. Here where the link to the powerlessness of the law is "clear," the church can proclaim that grace is free and that God regards people as good not because of what they achieve but because of God's love, which they may now pass on to others. This experience relates more directly than the others to the proclamation of justification by faith, but here too the question of meaning is present.

It follows that Tillich and others have made an important point, but that people's situations differ from one another. One cannot simply say that the question of justification has been replaced by the question of meaning. At the same time, the proclamation of *sola gratia* is more than *iustificatio impii*. Christ conquered not only sin but also death and the power of evil — as Eastern Orthodoxy so strongly emphasizes. Life has many sides, and so does the gospel. *Sola Scriptura* also means *tota Scriptura*. Ultimately, the truth of the gospel is not a doctrine but a Person.[15] From these considerations, we can therefore conclude that the replacement view — in the past, justification, but now meaning — is too simplistic and is not true to the multifaceted human reality.

Meaning and *Iustitia Declarativa*

We must finally ask whether Christian proclamation of the meaningfulness of life replaces justification by grace or just precedes it in those cases in which it is the primary message of the church. Is the meaning of life always related to some form of justification or only sometimes? Are they related only in some religious traditions and not in others?

To start with the last question, we first have to acknowledge that not every culture thinks in terms of good and evil. Monotheistic religions make a connection between meaning and justification; other traditions do not. In cosmic religious traditions such as Stoicism and Zen, humans find meaning in being imbedded in the working of the cosmos. It is precisely the striving for a separate, personal meaning for life that hinders one from living rightly. One must learn to see oneself as part of the larger reality.

15. Karl Barth, *Kirchliche Dogmatik* I/1 (München: Chr. Kaiser Verlag, 1932), p. 285 (*Church Dogmatics* [Edinburgh: T. & T. Clark], p. 270).

Only because the whole is meaningful (or in the case of Stoicism, is considered to be meaningful), is individual life meaningful.[16] The question of the justification of the sinner does not arise. In some Buddhist traditions, such as Rinzai Zen, dualities and oppositions between beings or between thought constructions are rejected, including the opposition of good and evil.[17] Here too the question of the justification of the individual does not arise. If the meaning of life is entirely immanent, there can be miscalculations and wrong actions but no corrections other than those which people themselves bring about. If the meaning of life is entirely immanent and people even have an immanent view of "transcendence," such that they do not recognize the existence of a divinity, their concern is not for justification but for how to avoid an alienated life or a life in ignorance.

In the Brahmanic Hindu tradition, transcendence is entirely "beyond," and the divine is the hidden basis of the world. Wrong actions are primarily the breaking of this *dharma,* the order that holds the world together.[18] Through sacrifices, ritual purifications, and pure living, the order can be maintained or restored. The cycle of reincarnation is entirely a matter of the *karma* that "orders" the individual into different lives. This karma (one could say) judges what is good and wrong in one's life in order to give one the opportunity to do penance for evil and to learn from a new, reincarnated life. One can fight the loss of meaning by trusting in the supporting power and orderliness of the *dharma* and *karma,* which connect the human being with the Brahman.[19] In this worldview the key questions are: "How can I learn to act well?," and "How can I detach myself from this impure world?" Thus, *bhakti* and grace are very important in popular Hindu religion, and *sadhus* (ascetics) are held in high esteem.

The question of judgment and forgiveness emerges if we understand humans to be created to live their lives according to a moral order that governs the world. If the Creator and/or the world order decisively deter-

16. See Hendrik M. Vroom, *A Spectrum of World Views: An Introduction to Philosophy of Religion in a Pluralistic World,* trans. Morris and Alice Greidanus (Amsterdam and New York: Rodopi, 2006), pp. 134-40.

17. See Sodo Yasunaga, "Zen and the Question of Evil," in *Probing the Depths of Evil and Good,* ed. Jerald D. Gort et al. (Amsterdam and New York: Rodopi, 2007), pp. 117-34.

18. Madeleine Biardeau, *Hinduism: The Anthropology of a Civilisation* (Oxford: Oxford University Press, 1989), pp. 42-46.

19. See Vroom, *A Spectrum of World Views,* pp. 119-52. For various views of religion and evil, see pp. 179-208.

mine the meaning of our lives, the question inevitably arises as to whether we are living properly in light of this Creator's will and/or world order. Questions of sin, forgiveness, and justification become inevitable.

In dialogue with Jewish and Islamic theology, Christian theology should continue to raise the question of whether human beings in and of themselves are capable of being good and responding sufficiently to God's intentions.[20] However, we will also acknowledge that there are other views of the meaning of life in which the question of justification does not arise.

Conclusion

We have seen that loss of meaning can arise in different contexts, not all of which are directly connected to the question of forgiveness and justification. At the same time, we cannot say that for the modern person the question of justification is irrelevant. For those many people who are concerned with "developing" themselves, the question of justification arises when they discover that they are unable to realize their self-chosen life project completely on their own. Sometimes questions of meaning and of justification are intrinsically connected. But we have also seen that not every worldview concerned with the question of meaning poses the question of justification. In theistic traditions, questions of obedience/disobedience or of good/evil inevitably arise, and therefore questions of failure and sin have a place. So, too, a Christian answer to the question of meaning leads to reflections on failure, forgiveness, and justification. Moreover, only the Christian faith has an elaborate doctrine of *iustitia attributiva,* even though one can find analogies to it in other religious traditions.[21] For Christians, these analogies are evidence that there are people everywhere who know that they cannot simply make themselves good and therefore know themselves to be dependent upon grace.

This analysis of the relation between meaning and justification has particular consequences for the churches of the Reformation that stress justification by grace alone. To people who feel lost in an anonymous mass

20. One can think here of the distinction in Hindu theology between the cat and the monkey schools with respect to the view of grace: the young are either carried by the neck by the mother, or have to hold on for themselves.

21. Compare the well-known grace religions, Amida Buddhism and Hindu bhakti schools.

society, these churches can preach God's love, his knowledge of our thoughts before we are even conscious of them, and his nearness to everyone. In addition, these churches can offer a sense of community. To those who have lost a sense of living meaningfully (even though they live more or less successfully according to society's rules), the churches can preach God's intentions for their lives and help them to live responsibly. Justification by grace alone is not always the first and main point, although it sooner or later poses itself. The gospel is much more than the doctrine of justification, and *sola gratia* has many aspects that should not be reduced to just one — no matter how important the doctrine of justification is.

CONTRIBUTORS

MARTIEN E. BRINKMAN is Professor of Ecumenical Studies at the Faculty of Theology of the Free University of Amsterdam (Netherlands).

JOHN P. BURGESS is the James Henry Snowden Professor of Systematic Theology at Pittsburgh Theological Seminary (Pennsylvania, USA).

SÁNDOR FAZAKAS is Professor for Social Ethics and Rector of the Reformed Theological University in Debrecen (Hungary).

GEORGE HUNSINGER is the Hazel Thompson McCord Professor of Systematic Theology at Princeton Seminary (New Jersey, USA).

CHRISTIAAN MOSTERT is Professor of Systematic Theology at the Uniting Church Theological College, Melbourne (Australia).

DIRKIE SMIT is Professor of Systematic Theology at the Faculty of Theology at the University of Stellenbosch (South Africa).

LAURA SMIT is Associate Professor of Theology at Calvin College (Michigan, USA).

KATHERINE SONDEREGGER is Professor of Theology at Virginia Theological Seminary (Virginia, USA).

HENDRIK M. VROOM is Professor of Philosophy of Religion at the Free University of Amsterdam (Netherlands).

JOHN WEBSTER is Professor of Systematic Theology at the University of Aberdeen (Scotland).

MICHAEL WEINRICH is Professor for Systematic Theology (Ecumenics and Dogmatics) and Director of the Ecumenical Institute of the Evangelical-Theological Faculty at the Ruhr University in Bochum (Germany).

INDEX

Anselm of Canterbury: doctrine of atonement, 33, 89-94; Jenson's interpretation of, 93-94; Keenan's critique of, 142-43

Articles *(articuli)* of faith, 9

Articulus stantis et cadentis ecclesiae, 8, 43-49, 63, 86n.96, 126, 164, 231

Asceticism, 160n.33

Athanasius, 61

Atonement: in Anselm, 33, 89-94, 142-43; in Barth, 106-13; in Calvin, 94-102; and Harnack's interpretation of Latin theology, 90; in Heidelberg Catechism, 63, 103-6

Augsburg Confession (1530), 9

Babel, Tower of, 29-30

Baptism: of infants, 79-80; and kingdom of God, 182-84; as participation in Christ's death, 157-59; as shaping discipleship, 198; as understood by Council of Trent, 67. *See also* Repentance; Sacraments

Baptism, Eucharist and Ministry (1982), 174, 179

Barth, Karl: on atonement, 106-13; on Christ, 34; on the Christian life, 73-74, 118; on church and state, 208-10, 225-30; on consequences of sin, 25-26; on divine justice and mercy, 101n.27, 220-24; on election, 133-34; on God's will for fellowship, 14n.16, 29, 60; on humans as determined for fellowship, 15, 16, 18; on priority of Christology over justification, 45, 48, 185; on relation of justification and sanctification, 74-76, 86, 194-95; his view of capitalism, 217-18

Barth, Markus, 141

Belhar Confession, 120n.60

Bellah, Robert, 78

Birmelé, André, 178

Bonhoeffer, Dietrich: on cheap grace, 2, 76, 79, 82; on disciplines of life together, 84; on sanctification, 71

Busch, Eberhard: on Barth's doctrine of atonement, 106-13; on Heidelberg Catechism's doctrine of atonement, 103-4

Calvin, John: on the Christian life, 73-74; on church discipline, 83-84; on confession of sin, 69, 70n.51; on doctrine of atonement, 94-102; on God's righteousness, 54; on God as source of life, 42; on justification, 9, 63, 64, 69; on Lord's Supper, 62; on relation of justification and sanctification, 58,

264